SECRETS

OF

24

The Unauthorized
Guide to the Political &
Moral Issues Behind
TV's Most Riveting Drama

SECRETS
OF
24

Edited by
Dan Burstein & Arne J. de Keijzer

Contributing Editors
Paul Berger, David Freeman,
and Katherine Goldstein

STERLING

New York / London
www.sterlingpublishing.com

STERLING and the distinctive Sterling logo
are registered trademarks of Sterling Publishing Co., Inc.

Library of Congress Cataloging-in-Publication Data Available

2   4   6   8   10   9   7   5   3   1

Published by Sterling Publishing Co., Inc.
387 Park Avenue South, New York, NY 10016
© 2007 by Squibnocket Partners LLC
Distributed in Canada by Sterling Publishing
c/o Canadian Manda Group, 165 Dufferin Street,
Toronto, Ontario, Canada M6K 3H6

Sterling ISBN-13: 978-1-4027-5396-1
ISBN-10: 1-4027-5396-9

For information about custom editions, special sales,
premium and corporate purchases,
please contact Sterling Special Sales
Department at 800-805-5489
or specialsales@sterlingpublishing.com.

In a world of people that are second-guessing so many situations, from their own politics to the way they live their lives, this is someone who actually knows that he can make a mistake, but believes in his heart so deeply that he's correct in what he's choosing to do, that he's going to act upon that.
—**Kiefer Sutherland ("Jack Bauer")**

This is John le Carré on television. Also, terrorism has not been done, nor has there been a character like Jack Bauer, a guy who wins and loses at the same time and who is politically incorrect but taps into everyone's id.
—**Joel Surnow (co-creator of *24* and executive producer)**

In the writing room somebody will say, "Well, what's the one thing that cannot happen?" Everyone knows a TV series would never let a nuclear bomb be set off in LA. Well, then it's going to go off. We've got to do it. What can't possibly happen has been a major source of ideas for us.
—**Robert Cochran (co-creator and executive producer)**

While we don't try to represent any kind of truth, we try to present an essential truth. So when Jack Bauer tortures, it's in a compressed reality. We try to compress arguments and issues and dramatize them in obviously very unreal ways, but hope-fully in dramatic and compelling ways. And that's ultimately our master: making a compelling, adrenalized TV show.
—**Howard Gordon (executive producer and showrunner)**

Chloe is very smart and incredibly gifted at computers, but she's not so good at living in the real world. I think, like 24 viewers, she wishes that she was a little more like Jack. She admires him for his courage and for living by his own beliefs, even if they are insane sometimes.
—**Mary Lynn Rajskub ("Chloe")**

Contents

5   How Well Does *24* Reflect the Real World?   158

Dan Burstein

Introduction

Great cultural works have been generated by the experience of war—its violence, tragedy, heroism, psychology, morality, ambiguity, treachery, history, exploits, adventures, causes and effects, winners and losers, characters and character-changing drama. This has been true from ancient works, such as The *Odyssey* and *Beowulf*, to some of Shakespeare's greatest writings, to modern and postmodern classics running the gamut from *War and Peace* to *Casablanca*, the novels of John le Carré, and films such as *Apocalypse Now* and *Star Wars*.

The television show *24* premiered in our own moment of greatest anxiety, just two months after September 11, 2001. The first episode had been filmed well before those horrible events. Yet the debut plot—featuring a terrorist blowing up an airplane so she could slip into the United States to assassinate an aspiring African-American presidential candidate—as well as the overarching concept of a dramatic TV show focused on the exploits of a counterterrorism agent in a world of dire threats—created an eerie and prescient parallel to real-life events. Ever since, *24* has continued to reflect in fictional TV episodes the real-life complexities of the post-9/11 world, especially in the debates over how to respond to the terrorist threat in contemporary society. *24*'s creators, screenwriters, and actors all insist that their purpose is primarily to tell a good story and entertain their audience. Yet, in my view, the show is the most cogent, contemporaneous cultural expression of the impact of early twenty-first-century wars (the Bush administration's "war on terror," the Iraq war, etc.) on the political, psychological, and moral tenor of our times.

In *Secrets of 24*, my coeditor, Arne de Keijzer, and I seek to probe a Hollywood pop culture phenomenon through a virtual roundtable of some of the most serious thinkers about politics, terrorism, and defense policy today. By analyzing the elements that make up this quintessential cultural reflection of our times, we wanted to broaden the discussion of the powerful real-world issues that underlie the fictional *24*. What might normally be the province of think tanks and white papers is here brought to life against the backdrop of plots and characters we have seen on television's most riveting show. We hope we have succeeded in humanizing and personalizing the sometimes abstract moral and political dilemmas our society faces in the present era.

Moreover, by compiling in one volume the thoughts of various observers of *24*, we have created an extraordinary prism through which to see the cultural zeitgeist. *24* is like a collective Rorschach test. And the different things that different people see in the murky movements of Kiefer Sutherland's masterful portrayal of Jack Bauer, as he navigates the tension, suspense, and moral confusion of the show's dark alleys, tell us much about what we as a society are thinking and feeling in 2008.

When *24* first aired, Americans still shared a sense of common purpose, forged by bonds of post-9/11 unity unprecedented in more than half a century of our national experience. The stories of courage and heroism—from the World Trade Center stairwells to those who fought back against the hijackers on Flight 93—were still fresh in our minds. The collective resolve of "United We Stand" was not just strong but predominant in our culture. The invasion of Afghanistan would prove swift, thorough, and seemingly successful in overthrowing the supporters of terrorism and restoring civil society to that country devastated by the internal terror of the Taliban. In that environment, Jack Bauer was a taut television metaphor for the real-life Todd Beamers, Pat Tillmans, and hundreds of thousands of American soldiers—the new American heroes who chose to put themselves in harm's way to fight the terrorists and protect us all.

But now, seven of Jack Bauer's days—and our years—later, many believe America is losing the war in Iraq and even losing the victory previously won in Afghanistan. Our moral and political capital has been squandered since the autumn of 2001. The economic cost is measurable at over a trillion dollars. The cost in American and Iraqi lives is immense and morally incalculable. Meanwhile, Americans have been forced to accept a slow but observable erosion of privacy and civil liberties, not to mention discovering the shocking dark side represented by Abu Ghraib, Guantánamo, CIA renditions, and the bleak realities of interrogation and torture in a suicide-bomber world. In short, America's post-9/11 missions have proven very much unaccomplished. We appear to be losing the very wars where victory was once declared. So it is no surprise, then, that the America that was strong, confident, and unified in the wake of 9/11 is today weakened, confused, and divided.

Jack Bauer, too, has become bone weary, emotionally scarred, and uncertain about the future. As the six prior longest days of Jack Bauer's life have unfolded—and as we get ready for the seventh—Jack has become ever more the antihero, ever more flawed, ever more weighed down by all the evildoers he has had to torture or terminate, the loved ones he has lost, the relationships he cultivated that have collapsed, the friends and even family members he has had to kill in the line of duty, and the unending physical and emotional pain he has had to endure. Jack is a postmodern Job, who has spent so long on the front lines of action and certainty that even he—the ultimate man of action, the man with the constant moral compass pointed true north—has begun to question the things he has had to do as a counterterrorism agent and whether it's all worth it in the end.

In interviews we conducted just before the start of Season 7, we asked Joel Surnow and Robert Cochran, the cocreators of 24, if Jack Bauer was destined for heaven or hell. Surnow, a vocal conservative, opted for heaven. But Cochran was less sure, more sensitive to the moral ambiguities of Jack's decisions, declaring Jack to be in purgatory for now, with the jury still out. Indeed, we understand that Season 7 opens at some point in the future, with Jack out of power, out of favor, his excesses from the past the subject of congressional investigation.

Right-of-center impulses are clearly visible in 24. Jack Bauer is essentially a Dirty Harry for the twenty-first century, a vigilante who always seems to know who the good guys and the bad guys are, even deep within the pitch-black night of a complex conspiracy. He is prepared to do whatever it takes to promote good and thwart evil, and he has the personal, physical, and technological wherewithal to stop the evildoers just in the nick of time. Jack's signature use of torture (even torturing his own brother) to get information, his extreme breaks with procedure, and his willingness to take the law into his own hands all distinguish him from predecessors like the British secret agent James Bond. Jack is politically incorrect almost all the time—and doesn't care. It really doesn't matter what the Constitution or the law or the head of CTU says. Jack's gut is his highest authority. To many political commentators, this is a metaphor for the cavalier actions of the Bush administration in the war on terror, even a justification for those actions. So it's easy to see why people like Rush Limbaugh would preside over an all-day forum at the Heritage Foundation about the show (see Chapter 4). Or why Senator John McCain, another fan of 24, would ask for—and get—a walk-on part on the show, and why he would chat about 24 extensively with Jon Stewart on one of his *Daily Show* appearances. Or why the show would appeal to Supreme Court Justice Clarence Thomas and Homeland Security Secretary Michael Chertoff (see chapter 5). Or why Congressman Tom Tancredo (R-Colo.) would invoke Jack Bauer on national television in a major Republican presidential debate (see Chapter 4).

But if *24* is such a paean to right-wing politics, why are well-known left-of-center figures also among its biggest fans? Former President Bill Clinton called *24* one of his two favorite TV shows of all time (the other was *I Love Lucy*) and talked in detail with Tim Russert on *Meet the Press* about how to handle the "Jack Bauer moment." Barbra Streisand is said to be a fan. And Janeane Garofalo, the far left-of-center Air America talk show host, will appear as a semiregular character on the show in Season 7. No doubt part of the appeal to viewers across the political spectrum is that *24* is simply compelling television with gripping stories and finely drawn characters. Obviously, you don't have to love the mafia to have enjoyed *The Sopranos*. But it's much more than that.

For one thing, although you wouldn't always know it from the content of our national political discourse, many on the left are just as concerned about fighting terrorism and maintaining American freedom as those on the right. The critique of Bush administration policy by some left-of-center pundits isn't that it's wrong, but that it hasn't worked. *New York Times* columnist Maureen Dowd, waggishly at one level but quite seriously at another, notes the critical distinction between the Bush administration and the fictional Jack Bauer: Jack is actually competent and succeeds in his mission, whereas in real life Bush's global vigilantism has not only failed but caused severe blowback damage.

There's a lot more for those on the liberal side of the political divide to like in *24* than first meets the eye. Dennis Haysbert's portrayal of President David Palmer as a wise, articulate, strong African-American president may have been inspired by Colin Powell, but it ended up helping to clear the cultural frontier for Senator Barack Obama to become a viable candidate for the Democratic nomination for president. Season 7 promises a fictional female president of the United States just at the moment that Senator Hillary Clinton's campaign for the White House will be going full tilt. Over the last several seasons, the plots of *24* have also featured Karl Rove–like characters, insidiously encouraging the president to seek emergency powers and suspend the Constitution; corrupt businessmen who would sell their country out and collaborate with the most evil terrorists for the sake of profit; and numerous White House advisers—and even a Nixon look-alike president—committing shocking acts of treason.

In our secular, morally relativistic, individual-obsessed culture, where basic civics—let alone moral philosophy—is not taught in school anymore, it is hardly surprising that Americans are unsure about how to balance freedom and security, where to draw the line between personal rights and the rights of society, and which moral principles to uphold in the face of the messy realities of our time. If we pay close attention, *24* may be offering us some provocative food for thought. Yes, the show is fiction. Yes, it is mostly about suspenseful storytelling (and keeping ratings high). Yes, the dilemmas presented in the episodes generally lie somewhere on the reality spectrum between improbable and impossible. But *24* is also one of the few popularly accessible places where we can see these debates played out, very much in real time.

As the gears of suspense tighten, virtually every episode of *24* asks the same basic questions: What price are we willing to pay for our freedom and our security? How far are we prepared to go to protect our way of life, our loved ones, our country? Are we willing to adopt the tactics of our enemies to promote what we believe to be morally right and good? And if we feel compelled to adopt those tactics, what does that do to us—morally, ethically, psychologically, spiritually? Does living in a world of terrorist threats require us to compromise historic principles embedded in the Constitution and our rule of law? Can we deter terrorism by interring Americans of a certain faith or ethnicity? Should we join forces with one terrorist to battle against an apparently worse terrorist danger? Even though we know that torture is wrong and morally repugnant, if interrogators could have used it to get information to save civilians from a terrorist attack, and they chose not to do so, have they taken the moral high road? Or are they complicit in the loss of innocent life that ensues? If you have to break the law to defend our society and its values—including the high value we place on the rule of law—are you a Constitution-undermining vigilante or a champion of truth, justice, and the American way?

In *24*, we encounter all these questions and many more. They confront us at every turn, in every whispered conversation, and in every shocking action sequence. Heemp! Heemp! Heemp! You have to choose between your family and your country—right now! Heemp! Heemp! Heemp! You have to collaborate with terrorists to save your own life or die a tortured death—you have ten seconds to choose! Heemp! Heemp! Heemp! You have to kill a friend to save a city from a nuclear blast. You have just a split second to decide!

Extreme and improbable as these either/or dichotomies may be, the attention to detail and the creative team's brilliance in the craft of television storytelling make all these choices seem emotionally real. We suspend disbelief and plunge into the depths of the moral dilemmas that all these questions pose. What's more, almost every major danger, every major national security decision, every major plot point in the show takes place against the backdrop of nagging personal crises—a problem with a character's child, parent, spouse, lover; a professional crisis; a mental illness; a drug or alcohol problem; an estranged relationship; a compromised relationship; a dysfunctional family. In other words, *24* enhances the sense of realism because the characters facing moral decisions that affect global war and peace are simultaneously caught up in real life's thorniest quotidian problems—just as most of us are in striving to integrate our professional and personal lives on a daily basis.

For me, *24* is the first important cultural work to address the wars we have been engaged in throughout the decade after 9/11, and to do so meaningfully. It is far more complex and nuanced than its stark moral choices and fast-paced plots might suggest at first. I am sure great literature will come from our recent American experiences. But at the same time, I feel comfortable predicting that, for a variety of reasons having to do with our culture today as well as the shifting technological sands of how we tell and learn from the stories of our shared experiences, no Tolstoy will emerge to write *War and Peace* about the first decade of the new millennium. In the meantime, we have *24* and Jack Bauer.

As an unabashed fan of *24*, I am fascinated by the Jack Bauer character and how he has evolved into what I see as the mirror image of America's own political, moral, and military quagmire in Iraq and, more broadly, in the war on terror. But I am also intrigued by many other aspects of *24*. In the pages of this book, readers hear from a diverse array of world-class experts, as well as members of the cast and the creative team behind *24*, addressing a multitude of issues and ideas raised by this groundbreaking show. To launch that wide-ranging discussion, I offer my own top ten list of the ideas and issues probed in *24*, which have piqued my interest the most.

1. Time. The way the ticking clock works, along with all the techniques relating to the illusion of real time, fascinates me. Students of the classics will, of course, recognize the ancient Greek principle of "unity of time." Aristotle noted that most of the dramatic classics took place in the duration of a single day, and suggested that this was a principle of good theater. The show's ability to use the conceit of a twenty-four day, with events happening in "real time," is an impressive technique to capture and hold our interest in a world where the short attention span is the norm. So, too, is *24*'s use of other episodic, suspenseful, long-form storytelling techniques to create "appointment television," despite all the competition in our culture from new media and short-form content.

2. *High Noon*. Speaking of time, I also find the allusions to the American film classic *High Noon* particularly intriguing. Clocks are constantly displayed in that 1952 film, as Gary Cooper's rendezvous with destiny counts down to noon. *24*'s co-creators, Surnow and Cochran, have acknowledged their debt to

High Noon. Like Jack Bauer, Gary Cooper's character, Marshal Will Kane, just can't refrain from doing the right, moral thing, even as everyone else shrinks from the task and warns him of the dangers. Remembered by most modern audiences simply as a classic American Western shoot-'em-up, High Noon was actually a controversial political film when it was first released, with a not-so-subtle subtext critiquing McCarthyism and those in Hollywood who abandoned and betrayed their friends when facing the prospect of being blacklisted. High Noon and *24* thus share a political ambiguity that allows audiences to read them as either left or right—or neither, and just enjoy the characters and the action.

3. Relationships. *24* is often closest to reality when it deals with all the *other* pressures in people's lives, besides the key issues that occupy their professional lives. Episodes often reveal how dysfunctional situations—ordinary personal problems, not to mention cubicle rivalries and jealousies—can affect the workplace. This is true even at a place like CTU, devoted to protecting America from terrorist attack. Although there are a lot of romantic relationships alluded to or actually portrayed, there is almost no sex depicted in the show itself, unlike much of the rest of evening television.

4. *The Da Vinci Code*. Speaking of genre-bending suspense and action thrillers sans sex, 24 resembles, in certain key respects, *The Da Vinci Code* and other novels by Dan Brown that have been on the best-seller list during the same period as *24*. Like *24*, all four major Dan Brown novels to date take place essentially against the ticking time clock of a twenty-four-hour day. (In fact, rumor has it that Brian Grazer, the Hollywood producer who has been involved in bringing both *24* and *The Da Vinci Code* to the screen, originally tried to option Dan Brown's novel *Angels & Demons* to use as the basis for the plot of *24* in Season 3.) In each of Dan Brown's novels, a male hero must work closely with a female heroine to solve the mystery and head off some major global disaster. In each case, there are hints of sexual attraction, but no real sex scenes to speak of. The Dan Brown novels and *24* have another interesting similarity: Their fans and enthusiasts perceive them as highly realistic, yet any critic can drive large trucks through their plot holes. Despite these credulity-straining plots, readers keep turning the pages of Dan Brown novels, and viewers keep tuning in to *24*, racing to get to the next cliffhanger.

5. Betrayal. There's always a mole in CTU or the White House, and everyone, even the most trustworthy soul, is suspected of being the mole from time to time. The enemy is always among us. Here *24* plays off one of the great themes of cold war spy fiction (and fact): Who can you really trust? How can you be sure? Can you trust anyone? This not only dovetails with the classic "paranoid thriller" in American fiction, it also reflects the mood of our times, and all the conspiracies—real and imagined—going on in Washington and other corridors of power.

6. The Los Angelization of our world. Even though the show is moving to Washington, D.C. for Season 7, its six years in the warehouses and back alleys of Los Angeles have updated the *noir* genre to the postmodern age. California has been staking a claim as the geotechnological center of the global economy for a long time now and continues to assert itself as the shaper of national and global cultural trends. While critics sometimes wondered why everything on *24* seemed to happen in Los Angeles, the show is actually one of the few to exploit the new political, cultural, and demographic realities of the Golden State.

7. The face of the postmodern melting plot. Read the exotic list of actors' names on the credits and look at their faces: This is a show that looks like the America we are becoming. A Hispanic actor plays a Mideastern terrorist. An Iranian-American Jewish teenager plays another. African-Americans have had substantial parts, including not one but two presidents. No one can tell with certainty the ethnic background of Michelle Dressler or Tony Almeida. There's a place for schlumpy folks, like Edgar, and nerdy ones, like Chloe. In addition to the stock Mideast-type terrorists, the bad guys are quite a diverse lot: Mexican drug lords, British profiteers, Balkan strongmen, Russian nationalists, Chinese government agents, suave moles within the U.S. government. Both the good guys and the bad guys are interesting to look at, without being stereotypes. The female love interests are almost all beautiful in a non-traditional way—seductive without being overtly sexy, all studies in character.

8. Scenario modeling. When I was a child, and the country was led by Democratic presidents, including JFK and LBJ, we used to practice "yellow alert" drills in school, to prepare us for a nuclear attack. Today, we talk publicly about the general threats our society faces, and even color-code the level of danger. But we almost never envision what would happen if some of the worst-case scenarios took place. Every season on *24*, we get to see at least a Hollywood writer's vision of what a nerve gas attack in a shopping mall might actually look like, or what might happen if a deadly virus infused into a hotel's ventilation system, or a suitcase nuclear bomb exploded in a major city. These are imaginings, of course. Yet they give us a more visceral sense of the issues our society needs to think about than your average briefing by the Department of Homeland Security.

9. Technology. Everyone would love to have those cell phones that never die; PDAs that can instantly absorb and display any amount of complex data wirelessly; the magical ability to see through walls, or to call up all relevant data on a suspect at the touch of a keypad. Even Homeland Security chief Michael Chertoff says he would be thrilled to work with the technology shown on *24*—especially the computers, which, unlike those used by his department, never break down. Some of the technologies on the show are with us now; some are sure to come in the future (see Chapter 7). But what I find most thought-provoking in all this is not necessarily the technologies themselves, but the underlying issue of how these technologies are being deployed. American cities, following the lead of cities like London, are now actually discussing, and in some cases installing, the kind of camera systems that allow for surveillance in virtually any public place. There has already been a great debate over how to use the geolocation chips that are built into new cell phones, which can be a boon to users in emergency situations, but also allow for unwanted tracking. *24* reminds us to think seriously about these issues. Are we, as decent citizens, willing to give up our privacy for the sake of enhanced technological tools to thwart the bad guys? And how does public behavior change when we all know we're on camera?

10. The female president. Arguably, to some extent the casting of Dennis Haysbert on *24* as the first African-American president helped to pave the way for Barack Obama's 2008 U.S. presidential bid. Now, as Season 7 begins the next day in Jack Bauer's life, *24* is once again ahead of the social and political curve, casting Cherry Jones in the role of President Allison Taylor, America's first female president. She will serve in a term corresponding almost exactly to the presidential primary season in the run-up to the 2008 election. There have been other onscreen depictions of fictional female American presidents, of course. But will the performance of Cherry Jones, and the lines and plots the writers create for her (as well as those created for her first husband!) have an impact on how American voters view Hillary and Bill Clinton in the 2008 election campaign?

We invite you to join the conversation on all these issues and more at **www.SecretsOf24.com.**

A few housekeeping notes. This book contains many original contributions in the form of essays and interviews. There are also items that have been reprinted with permission from other sources; these have a credit line at the bottom of their first page and retain their original wording and style conventions. There are also specially chosen sidebars placed randomly throughout the book—quick takes on the facts, humor, and breadth of voices and ideas generated by *24*.

*"You watch 24 and you know the entire thing is ridiculous,
but you can't help yourself. You want more. We're like Pavlov's dog,
except rather than a bell, we're triggered by that digital ticking clock
and the Heemp! Heemp! Heemp! opening each segment."*
—John Kass, columnist, the *Chicago Tribune*

24: The Cultural By-Product of the War on Terrorism

Tick, tock. Chaos, shock.

It's just another day in the life of Jack Bauer, America's favorite counterterrorism agent with the violent code of honor. Six days have gone by so far; we're promised no rest on the seventh. *24* will certainly continue to reformat cable news headlines. Hyperadrenalized fiction will still be made plausible by grim realism, excruciating (but addictive) tension, and the countdown of the clock.

In the beginning, *24* didn't move the needle much on the popular culture meter. Brought to the tube within a few weeks of September 11, 2001, it evoked images of terror all too fresh in our collective mind. This was supposed to be what the producers called a "relief from the oppressive grief"? The small audience of early devotees was a passionate one, however. They blogged their enthusiasm over the Internet, show by show. Millions more would catch up when the full-season DVDs of Season 1 showed up within weeks of the last episode. By the end of Season 3, the show *Time* magazine dubbed the "weekly rationalization of the 'ticking bomb' defense of torture" had become a viral part of the culture, talked about and debated from the corridors of Washington to the editorial desks of the mainstream media. Jack Bauer had become a new and instantly recognizable cultural icon, his character another chapter in the ongoing story of the frontier thesis, the latest addition to the legions of independent, "fight for right" American heroes, and a linchpin of America's new understanding of itself in the post-9/11 era.

What makes this show so different? And what makes it so compelling?

Part of the answer lies in the original inspiration of Joel Surnow and Robert Cochran, cocreators of the show. As Surnow tells the story, stretching the normal twenty-two-episode season on television to twenty-four would allow them to create a day in "real time." When he mentioned this to his long-time collaborator, Cochran said, "I think it stinks." But the two of them got together one morning at a pancake house and, says Surnow:

> We originally thought, "Let's do a show about the day of a wedding; a romantic comedy." A couple days later . . . we said, "No, if it's going to be about twenty-four hours, it's gotta be a race against the clock. And then we needed things to have high stakes. So what has high stakes? Well, if you're the parent of a teenage kid, and your daughter is missing, you're up all night. . . . And if your job happens to be having to stop the attempted assassination of a presidential candidate that day in the city of Los Angeles at the same time, you're up for twenty-four hours. . . . It's a race against time. That's the basic concept.

What made the concept work was a complex stew of talented writing, acting, and cinematography. What ratcheted it up to such compelling television—and such a prominent place in American and even global culture—is the subject of this chapter. Critic Charles McGrath, writer-at-large for the *New York Times* and a seriously addicted fan, believes the key is Jack Bauer's character, and, in particular, the way his concern for those he loves is interwoven with his mission. Dorothy Rabinowitz, editorial writer for the *Wall Street Journal,* comments on the "full-voltage shocks" the show delivers, and its tone of realpolitik. Sarah Vowell, wry social observer and a staunch supporter of civil and human rights, surprises herself by discovering her inner torturer, rooting for Jack even as a metaphorical bust of Abe Lincoln watches over her shoulder.

We begin with a particularly influential article by Jane Mayer, veteran investigative reporter for the *New Yorker.* It is the longest and probably most substantive journalistic piece to date about *24*—and among the most controversial.

In her discussion of *24,* Mayer simultaneously attempts to probe the inner psyches of Jack Bauer as well as his creator, Joel Surnow. *24* "plays off the anxieties that have beset the country since September 11th, and it sends a political message," says Mayer.

24's creative team flatly rejects Mayer's argument that the show is consciously trying to promote the Bush administration's agenda for the war on terror. Surnow goes so far as to call the article a "rip piece."

Welcome to the controversial world of *24*. ■

Jane Mayer

Whatever It Takes:
The Politics of the Man Behind *24*

THE OFFICE DESK OF JOEL SURNOW—the co-creator and executive producer of "24," the popular counterterrorism drama on Fox—faces a wall dominated by an American flag in a glass case. A small label reveals that the flag once flew over Baghdad, after the American invasion of Iraq, in 2003. A few years ago, Surnow received it as a gift from an Army regiment stationed in Iraq; the soldiers had shared a collection of "24" DVDs, he told me, until it was destroyed by an enemy bomb. "The military loves our show," he said recently. Surnow is fifty-two, and has the gangly, coiled energy of an athlete; his hair is close-cropped, and he has a "soul patch"—a smidgen of beard beneath his lower lip. When he was young, he worked as a carpet salesman with his father. The trick to selling anything, he learned, is to carry yourself with confidence and get the customer to like you within the first five minutes. He's got it down. "People in the Administration love the series, too," he said. "It's a patriotic show. They should love it."

Surnow's production company, Real Time Entertainment, is in the San Fernando Valley, and occupies a former pencil factory: a bland, two-story industrial building on an abject strip of parking lots and fast-food restaurants. Surnow, a cigar enthusiast, has converted a room down the hall from his office into a salon with burled-wood humidors and a full bar; his friend Rush Limbaugh, the conservative talk-radio host, sometimes joins him there for a smoke. (Not long ago, Surnow threw Limbaugh a party and presented him with a custom-made "24" smoking jacket.) The ground floor of the factory has a large soundstage on which many of "24"'s interior scenes are shot, including those set at the perpetually tense Los Angeles bureau of the Counter Terrorist Unit, or C.T.U.—a fictional federal agency that pursues America's enemies with steely resourcefulness.

Each season of "24," which has been airing on Fox since 2001, depicts a single, panic-laced day in which Jack Bauer—a heroic C.T.U. agent, played by Kiefer Sutherland—must unravel and undermine a conspiracy that imperils the nation. Terrorists are poised to set off nuclear bombs or bioweapons, or in some other way annihilate entire cities. The twisting story line forces Bauer and his colleagues to make a series of grim choices that pit liberty against security.

Source: ©2007 Jane Mayer. This article first appeared in the *New Yorker* magazine, February 19 and 26, 2007, and is used by permission of the author.

Frequently, the dilemma is stark: a resistant suspect can either be accorded due process—allowing a terrorist plot to proceed—or be tortured in pursuit of a lead. Bauer invariably chooses coercion. With unnerving efficiency, suspects are beaten, suffocated, electrocuted, drugged, assaulted with knives, or more exotically abused; almost without fail, these suspects divulge critical secrets.

The show's appeal, however, lies less in its violence than in its giddily literal rendering of a classic thriller trope: the "ticking time bomb" plot. Each hour-long episode represents an hour in the life of the characters, and every minute that passes onscreen brings the United States a minute closer to doomsday. (Surnow came up with this concept, which he calls the show's "trick.") As many as half a dozen interlocking stories unfold simultaneously—frequently on a split screen—and a digital clock appears before and after every commercial break, marking each second with an ominous clang. The result is a riveting sensation of narrative velocity.

Bob Cochran, who created the show with Surnow, admitted, "Most terrorism experts will tell you that the 'ticking time bomb' situation never occurs in real life, or very rarely. But on our show it happens every week." According to Darius Rejali, a professor of political science at Reed College and the author of the forthcoming book "Torture and Democracy," the conceit of the ticking time bomb first appeared in Jean Lartéguy's 1960 novel "Les Centurions," written during the brutal French occupation of Algeria. The book's hero, after beating a female Arab dissident into submission, uncovers an imminent plot to explode bombs all over Algeria and must race against the clock to stop it. Rejali, who has examined the available records of the conflict, told me that the story has no basis in fact. In his view, the story line of "Les Centurions" provided French liberals a more palatable rationale for torture than the racist explanations supplied by others (such as the notion that the Algerians, inherently simpleminded, understood only brute force). Lartéguy's scenario exploited an insecurity shared by many liberal societies—that their enlightened legal systems had made them vulnerable to security threats.

"24," which last year [2006] won an Emmy Award for Outstanding Drama Series, packs an improbable amount of intrigue into twenty-four hours, and its outlandishness marks it clearly as a fantasy, an heir to the baroque potboilers of Tom Clancy and Vince Flynn. Nevertheless, the show obviously plays off the anxieties that have beset the country since September 11th, and it sends a political message. The series, Surnow told me, is "ripped out of the Zeitgeist of what people's fears are—their paranoia that we're going to be attacked," and it "makes people look at what we're dealing with" in terms of threats to national security. "There are not a lot of measures short of extreme measures that will get it done," he said, adding, "America wants the war on terror fought by Jack Bauer. He's a patriot."

For all its fictional liberties, "24" depicts the fight against Islamist extremism much as the Bush Administration has defined it: as an all-consuming struggle for America's survival that demands the toughest of tactics. Not long after September 11th, Vice-President Dick Cheney alluded vaguely to the fact that America must begin working through the "dark side" in countering terrorism. On "24," the dark side is on full view. Surnow, who has jokingly called himself a "right-wing nut job," shares his show's hard-line perspective. Speaking of torture, he said, "Isn't it obvious that if there was a nuke in New York City that was about to blow—or any other city in this country—that, even if you were going to go to jail, it would be the right thing to do?"

Since September 11th, depictions of torture have become much more common on American television. Before the attacks, fewer than four acts of torture appeared on prime-time television each year, according to Human Rights First, a nonprofit organization. Now there are more than a hundred, and, as David Danzig, a project director at Human Rights First, noted, "the torturers have changed. It used to be almost exclusively the villains who tortured. Today, torture is often perpetrated by the heroes." The Parents' Television Council, a nonpartisan watchdog group, has counted what it says are sixty-seven torture scenes during the first five seasons of "24"—more than one every other show. Melissa Caldwell, the council's senior director of programs, said, " '24' is the worst offender on television: the most frequent, most graphic, and the leader in the trend of showing the protagonists using torture."

The show's villains usually inflict the more gruesome tortures: their victims are hung on hooks, like carcasses in a butcher shop; poked with smoking-hot scalpels; or abraded with sanding machines. In many episodes, however, heroic American officials act as tormentors, even though torture is illegal under U.S. law. (The United Nations Convention Against Torture, which took on the force of federal law when it was ratified by the Senate in 1994, specifies that "no exceptional circumstances, whatsoever, whether a state of war or a threat of war, internal political instability or any other public emergency, may be invoked as a justification of torture.") In one episode, a fictional President commands a member of his Secret Service to torture a suspected traitor: his national-security adviser. The victim is jolted with defibrillator paddles while his feet are submerged in a tub filled with water. As the voltage is turned up, the President, who is depicted as a scrupulous leader, watches the suspect suffer on a video feed. The viewer, who knows that the adviser is guilty and harbors secrets, becomes complicit in hoping that the torture works. A few minutes before the suspect gives in, the President utters the show's credo, "Everyone breaks eventually." (Virtually the sole exception to this rule is Jack Bauer. The current season begins with Bauer being released from a Chinese prison, after two years of ceaseless torture; his back is scarred and his hands are burnt, but a Communist official who transfers Bauer to U.S. custody says that he "never broke his silence.")

C.T.U. agents have used some of the same controversial interrogation methods that the U.S. has employed on some Al Qaeda suspects. In one instance, Bauer denies painkillers to a female terrorist who is suffering from a bullet wound, just as American officials have acknowledged doing in the case of Abu Zubaydah—one of the highest-ranking Al Qaeda operatives in U.S. custody. "I need to use every advantage I've got," Bauer explains to the victim's distressed sister.

The show sometimes toys with the audience's discomfort about abusive interrogations. In Season Two, Bauer threatens to murder a terrorist's wife and children, one by one, before the prisoner's eyes. The suspect watches, on closed-circuit television, what appears to be an execution-style slaying of his son. Threatened with the murder of additional family members, the father gives up vital information— but Bauer appears to have gone too far. It turns out, though, that the killing of the child was staged. Bauer, the show implies, hasn't crossed the line after all. Yet, under U.S. and international law, a mock execution is considered psychological torture, and is illegal.

> **"W**e do want democratic process, but we also want justice. And the show allows us to have both, and that's why we love it."
> **—David Heyman, terrorism scholar, Center for Strategic and International Studies**

On one occasion, Bauer loses his nerve about inflicting torture, but the show implicitly rebukes his qualms. In the episode, Bauer attempts to break a suspected terrorist by plunging a knife in his shoulder; the victim's screams clearly disquiet him. Bauer says to an associate, unconvincingly, that he has looked into the victim's eyes and knows that "he's not going to tell us anything." The other man takes over, fiercely gouging the suspect's knee—at which point the suspect yells out details of a plot to explode a suitcase nuke in Los Angeles.

Throughout the series, secondary characters raise moral objections to abusive interrogation tactics. Yet the show never engages in a serious dialogue on the subject. Nobody argues that torture doesn't work, or that it undermines America's foreign-policy strategy. Instead, the doubters tend to be softhearted dupes. A tremulous liberal, who defends a Middle Eastern neighbor from vigilantism, is killed when the neighbor turns out to be a terrorist. When a civil-liberties-minded lawyer makes a high-toned argument to a Presidential aide against unwarranted detentions—"You continue to arrest innocent people, you're giving the terrorists exactly what they want," she says—the aide sarcastically responds, "Well! You've got the makings of a splendid law-review article here. I'll pass it on to the President."

In another episode, a human-rights lawyer from a fictional organization called Amnesty Global tells Bauer, who wants to rough up an uncharged terror suspect, that he will violate the Constitution. Bauer responds, "I don't wanna bypass the Constitution, but these are extraordinary circumstances." He appeals to the President, arguing that any interrogation permitted by the law won't be sufficiently harsh. "If we want to procure any information from this suspect, we're going to have to do it behind closed doors," he says.

"You're talking about torturing this man?" the President says.

"I'm talking about doing what's necessary to stop this warhead from being used against us," Bauer answers.

When the President wavers, Bauer temporarily quits his job so that he can avoid defying the chain of command, and breaks the suspect's fingers. The suspect still won't talk, so Bauer puts a knife to his throat; this elicits the desired information. He then knocks the suspect out with a punch, telling him, "This will help you with the pain."

Howard Gordon, who is the series' "show runner," or lead writer, told me that he concocts many of the torture scenes himself. "Honest to God, I'd call them improvisations in sadism," he said. Several copies of the C.I.A.'s 1963 KUBARK interrogation manual can be found at the "24" offices, but Gordon said that, "for the most part, our imaginations are the source. Sometimes these ideas are inspired by a scene's location or come from props—what's on the set." He explained that much of the horror is conjured by the viewer. "To see a scalpel and see it move below the frame of the screen is a lot scarier than watching the whole thing. When you get a camera moving fast, and someone screaming, it really works." In recent years, he said, "we've resorted a lot to a pharmacological sort of thing." A character named Burke—a federal employee of the C.T.U. who carries a briefcase filled with elephantine hypodermic needles—has proved indispensable. "He'll inject chemicals that cause horrible pain that can knock down your defenses—a sort of sodium pentothal plus," Gordon said. "When we're stuck, we say, 'Call Burke!'" He added, "The truth is, there's a certain amount of fatigue. It's getting hard not to repeat the same torture techniques over and over."

Gordon, who is a "moderate Democrat," said that it worries him when "critics say that we've enabled and reflected the public's appetite for torture. Nobody wants to be the handmaid to a relaxed policy that accepts torture as a legitimate means of interrogation." He went on, "But the premise of '24' is the ticking time bomb. It takes an unusual situation and turns it into the meat and potatoes of the show." He paused. "I think people can differentiate between a television show and reality."

This past November [2006], U.S. Army Brigadier General Patrick Finnegan, the dean of the United States Military Academy at West Point, flew to Southern California to meet with the creative team behind "24." Finnegan, who was accompanied by three of the most experienced military and F.B.I.

interrogators in the country, arrived on the set as the crew was filming. At first, Finnegan—wearing an immaculate Army uniform, his chest covered in ribbons and medals—aroused confusion: he was taken for an actor and was asked by someone what time his "call" was.

In fact, Finnegan and the others had come to voice their concern that the show's central political premise—that the letter of American law must be sacrificed for the country's security—was having a toxic effect. In their view, the show promoted unethical and illegal behavior and had adversely affected the training and performance of real American soldiers. "I'd like them to stop," Finnegan said of the show's producers. "They should do a show where torture backfires."

The meeting, which lasted a couple of hours, had been arranged by David Danzig, the Human Rights First official. Several top producers of "24" were present, but Surnow was conspicuously absent. Surnow explained to me, "I just can't sit in a room that long. I'm too A.D.D.—I can't sit still." He told the group that the meeting conflicted with a planned conference call with Roger Ailes, the chairman of the Fox News Channel. (Another participant in the conference call attended the meeting.) Ailes wanted to discuss a project that Surnow has been planning for months: the début, on February 18th, of "The Half Hour News Hour," a conservative satirical treatment of the week's news; Surnow sees the show as offering a counterpoint to the liberal slant of "The Daily Show with Jon Stewart."

Before the meeting, Stuart Herrington, one of the three veteran interrogators, had prepared a list of seventeen effective techniques, none of which were abusive. He and the others described various tactics, such as giving suspects a postcard to send home, thereby learning the name and address of their next of kin. After Howard Gordon, the lead writer, listened to some of Herrington's suggestions, he slammed his fist on the table and joked, "You're hired!" He also excitedly asked the West Point delegation if they knew of any effective truth serums.

At other moments, the discussion was more strained. Finnegan told the producers that "24," by suggesting that the U.S. government perpetrates myriad forms of torture, hurts the country's image internationally. Finnegan, who is a lawyer, has for a number of years taught a course on the laws of war to West Point seniors—cadets who would soon be commanders in the battlefields of Iraq and Afghanistan. He always tries, he said, to get his students to sort out not just what is legal but what is right. However, it had become increasingly hard to convince some cadets that America had to respect the rule of law and human rights, even when terrorists did not. One reason for the growing resistance, he suggested, was misperceptions spread by "24," which was exceptionally popular with his students. As he told me, "The kids see it, and say, 'If torture is wrong, what about "24"?'" He continued, "The disturbing thing is that although torture may cause Jack Bauer some angst, it is always the patriotic thing to do."

Gary Solis, a retired law professor who designed and taught the Law of War for Commanders curriculum at West Point, told me that he had similar arguments with his students. He said that, under both U.S. and international law, "Jack Bauer is a criminal. In real life, he would be prosecuted." Yet the motto of many of his students was identical to Jack Bauer's: "Whatever it takes." His students were particularly impressed by a scene in which Bauer barges into a room where a stubborn suspect is being held, shoots him in one leg, and threatens to shoot the other if he doesn't talk. In less than ten seconds, the suspect reveals that his associates plan to assassinate the Secretary of Defense. Solis told me, "I tried to impress on them that this technique would open the wrong doors, but it was like trying to stomp out an anthill."

Among the boldface names who are fans of the show: Dave Barry, Dick Cheney, Bill Clinton, Jim Cramer, Billy Crystal, Tony Danza, Trent Dilfer, Geena Davis, Bill Gates, Laura Ingraham, Stephen King, Rush Limbaugh, John McCain, Jim McMahon, Donald Rumsfeld, Seal, Barbra Streisand, Clarence Thomas, and Tina Turner.

The "24" producers told the military and law-enforcement experts that they were careful not to glamorize torture; they noted that Bauer never enjoys inflicting pain, and that it had clearly exacted a psychological toll on the character. (As Gordon put it to me, "Jack is basically damned.") Finnegan and the others disagreed, pointing out that Bauer remains coolly rational after committing barbarous acts, including the decapitation of a state's witness with a hacksaw. Joe Navarro, one of the F.B.I.'s top experts in questioning techniques, attended the meeting; he told me, "Only a psychopath can torture and be unaffected. You don't want people like that in your organization. They are untrustworthy, and tend to have grotesque other problems."

Cochran, who has a law degree, listened politely to the delegation's complaints. He told me that he supports the use of torture "in narrow circumstances" and believes that it can be justified under the Constitution. "The Doctrine of Necessity says you can occasionally break the law to prevent greater harm," he said. "I think that could supersede the Convention Against Torture." (Few legal scholars agree with this argument.) At the meeting, Cochran demanded to know what the interrogators would do if they faced the imminent threat of a nuclear blast in New York City, and had custody of a suspect who knew how to stop it. One interrogator said that he would apply physical coercion only if he received a personal directive from the President. But Navarro, who estimates that he has conducted some twelve thousand interrogations, replied that torture was not an effective response. "These are very determined people, and they won't turn just because you pull a fingernail out," he told me. And Finnegan argued that torturing fanatical Islamist terrorists is particularly pointless. "They almost welcome torture," he said. "They expect it. They want to be martyred." A ticking time bomb, he pointed out, would make a suspect only more unwilling to talk. "They know if they can simply hold out several hours, all the more glory—the ticking time bomb will go off!"

The notion that physical coercion in interrogations is unreliable, although widespread among military intelligence officers and F.B.I. agents, has been firmly rejected by the Bush Administration. Last September, President Bush defended the C.I.A.'s use of "an alternative set of procedures." In order to "save innocent lives," he said, the agency needed to be able to use "enhanced" measures to extract "vital information" from "dangerous" detainees who were aware of "terrorist plans we could not get anywhere else."

Although reports of abuses by U.S. troops in Iraq and Afghanistan and at Guantánamo Bay, Cuba, have angered much of the world, the response of Americans has been more tepid. Finnegan attributes the fact that "we are generally more comfortable and more accepting of this," in part, to the popularity of "24," which has a weekly audience of fifteen million viewers, and has reached millions more through DVD sales. The third expert at the meeting was Tony Lagouranis, a former Army interrogator in the war in Iraq. He told the show's staff that DVDs of shows such as "24" circulate widely among soldiers stationed in Iraq. Lagouranis said to me, "People watch the shows, and then walk into the interrogation booths and do the same things they've just seen." He recalled that some men he had worked with in Iraq watched a television program in which a suspect was forced to hear tortured screams from a neighboring cell; the men later tried to persuade their Iraqi translator to act the part of a torture "victim," in a similar intimidation ploy. Lagouranis intervened: such scenarios constitute psychological torture.

"In Iraq, I never saw pain produce intelligence," Lagouranis told me. "I worked with someone who used waterboarding"—an interrogation method involving the repeated near-drowning of a suspect. "I used severe hypothermia, dogs, and sleep deprivation. I saw suspects after soldiers had gone into their homes and broken their bones, or made them sit on a Humvee's hot exhaust pipes until they got third-degree burns. Nothing happened." Some people, he said, "gave confessions. But they just told us what we already knew. It never opened up a stream of new information." If anything, he said, "physical pain can strengthen the resolve to clam up."

Last December, the Intelligence Science Board, an advisory panel to the U.S. intelligence community, released a report declaring that "most observers, even those within professional circles, have unfortunately been influenced by the media's colorful (and artificial) view of interrogation as almost always involving hostility." In a clear reference to "24," the report noted:

Prime-time television increasingly offers up plot lines involving the incineration of metropolitan Los Angeles by an atomic weapon or its depopulation by an aerosol nerve toxin. The characters do not have the time to reflect upon, much less to utilize, what real professionals know to be the "science and art" of "educing information." They want results. Now. The public thinks the same way. They want, and rightly expect, precisely the kind of "protection" that only a skilled intelligence professional can provide. Unfortunately, they have no idea how such a person is supposed to act "in real life."

Lagouranis told the "24" team what the U.S. military and the F.B.I. teach real intelligence professionals: "rapport-building," the slow process of winning over informants, is the method that generally works best. There are also nonviolent ruses, he explained, and ways to take suspects by surprise. The "24" staff seemed interested in the narrative possibilities of such techniques; Lagouranis recalled, "They told us that they'd love to incorporate ruses and rapport-building." At the same time, he said, Cochran and the others from "24" worried that such approaches would "take too much time" on an hour-long television show.

The delegation of interrogators left the meeting with the feeling that the story lines on "24" would be changed little, if at all. "It shows they have a social conscience that they'd even meet with us at all," Navarro said. "They were receptive. But they have a format that works. They have won a lot of awards. Why would they want to play with a No. 1 show?" Lagouranis said of the "24" team, "They were a bit prickly. They have this money-making machine, and we were telling them it's immoral."

Afterward, Danzig and Finnegan had an on-set exchange with Kiefer Sutherland, who is reportedly paid ten million dollars a year to play Jack Bauer. Sutherland, the grandson of Tommy Douglas, a former socialist leader in Canada, has described his own political views as anti-torture, and "leaning toward the left." According to Danzig, Sutherland was "really upset, really intense" and stressed that he tries to tell people that the show "is just entertainment." But Sutherland, who claimed to be bored with playing torture scenes, admitted that he worried about the "unintended consequences of the show." Danzig proposed that Sutherland participate in a panel at West Point or appear in a training film in which he made clear that the show's torture scenes are not to be emulated. (Surnow, when asked whether he would participate in the video, responded, "No way." Gordon, however, agreed to be filmed.) Sutherland declined to answer questions for this article, but, in a recent television interview with Charlie Rose, his ambivalence about his character's methods was palpable. He condemned the abuse of U.S.-held detainees at Abu Ghraib prison, in Iraq, as "absolutely criminal," particularly for a country that tells others that "democracy and freedom" are the "way to go." He also said, "You can torture someone and they'll basically tell you exactly what you want to hear. . . . Torture is not a way of procuring information." But things operate differently, he said, on television: "24," he said, is "a fantastical show. . . . Torture is a dramatic device."

The creators of "24" deny that the show presents only a conservative viewpoint. They mention its many prominent Democratic fans—including Barbra Streisand and Bill Clinton—and the diversity of political views among its writers and producers. Indeed, the story lines sometimes have a liberal tilt. The conspiracy plot of Season Five, for example, turns on oligarchic businessmen who go to despicable lengths to protect their oil interests; the same theme anchors liberal-paranoia thrillers such as "Syriana." This season, [Season 6] a White House directive that flags all federal employees of Middle Eastern descent as potential traitors has been presented as a gross overreaction, and a White House official who favors police-state tactics has come off as scheming and ignoble. Yet David Nevins, the former Fox Television network official who, in 2000, bought the pilot on the spot after hearing a pitch from Surnow and Cochran, and who maintains an executive role in "24," is candid about the show's core message. "There's definitely a political attitude of the show, which is that extreme measures are sometimes necessary for the greater good," he says. "The show doesn't have much patience for the niceties of civil liberties or due process. It's clearly coming from somewhere. Joel's politics suffuse the whole show."

Surnow, for his part, revels in his minority status inside the left-leaning entertainment industry. "Conservatives are the new oppressed class," he joked in his office. "Isn't it bizarre that in Hollywood it's easier to come out as gay than as conservative?" His success with "24," he said, has protected him from the more righteous elements of the Hollywood establishment. "Right now, they have to be nice to me," he said. "But if the show tanks I'm sure they'll kill me." He spoke of his new conservative comedy show as an even bigger risk than "24." "I'll be front and center on the new show," he said, then joked, "I'm ruining my chances of ever working again in Hollywood."

Although he was raised in Beverly Hills—he graduated in 1972 from Beverly Hills High—Surnow said that he has always felt like an outsider. His classmates were mostly wealthy, but his father was an itinerant carpet salesman who came to California from Detroit. He cold-called potential customers, most of whom lived in Compton and Watts. Surnow was much younger than his two brothers, and he grew up virtually as an only child, living in a one-bedroom apartment in an unfashionable area south of Olympic Boulevard, where he slept on a foldout cot. If his father made a sale, he'd come home and give him the thumbs-up. But Surnow said that nine out of ten nights ended in failure. "If he made three sales a month, we could stay where we lived," he recalled. His mother, who worked as a saleswoman in a clothing store, "fought depression her whole life." Surnow, who describes his parents as "wonderful people," said, "I was a latchkey kid. . . . I raised myself." He played tennis on his high-school team but gave it up after repeatedly losing to players who could afford private lessons.

Roger Director, a television producer and longtime friend, said that he "loves" Surnow. But, he went on, "He feels looked down upon by the world, and that kind of emotional dynamic underpins a lot of things. It's kind of 'Joel against the world.' It's as if he feels, I had to fight and claw for everything I got. It's a tough world, and no one's looking out for you." As a result, Director said, "Joel's not sentimental. He has a hard-hearted thing."

Surnow's parents were F.D.R. Democrats. He recalled, "It was just assumed, especially in the Jewish community"—to which his family belonged. "But when you grow up you start to challenge your parents' assumptions. 'Am I Jewish? Am I a Democrat?'" Many of his peers at the University of California at Berkeley, where he attended college, were liberals or radicals. "They were all socialists and Marxists, but living off their family money," he recalled. "It seemed to me there was some obvious hypocrisy here. It was absurd." Although he wasn't consciously political, he said, "I felt like I wasn't like these people." In 1985, he divorced his wife, a medical student, who was Jewish, and with whom he has two daughters. (His relationships with them are strained.) Four years later, he remarried. His wife, who used to work in film development, is Catholic; they have three daughters, whom they send to Catholic schools. He likes to bring his girls to the set and rushes home for his wife's pork-chop dinners. "I got to know who I was and who I wasn't," he said. "I wasn't the perfect Jewish kid who is married, with a Jewish family." Instead, he said, "I decided I like Catholics. They're so grounded. I sort of reoriented myself."

While studying at Berkeley, Surnow worked as an usher at the Pacific Film Archive, where he saw at least five hundred movies. A fan of crime dramas such as "Mean Streets" and "The Godfather," he discovered foreign films as well. "That was my awakening," he said. In 1975, Surnow enrolled at the U.C.L.A. film school. Soon after graduation, he began writing for film; he then switched to television. He was only modestly successful, and had many "lost years," when he considered giving up and taking over his father's carpet business. His breakthrough came when he began writing for "Miami Vice," in 1984. "It just clicked—I just got it!" he recalled. "It was just like when you don't know how to speak a language and suddenly you do. I knew how to tell a story." By the end of the year, Universal, which owned the show, put Surnow in charge of his own series, "The Equalizer," about a C.I.A. agent turned vigilante. The series was a success, but, Surnow told me, "I was way too arrogant. I sort of pissed off the network." Battles for creative control have followed Surnow to "24," where, Nevins said admiringly, he continues to push for "unconventional and dangerous choices."

Surnow's tough stretches in Hollywood, he said, taught him that there were "two kinds of people" in entertainment: "those who want to be geniuses, and those who want to work." At first, he said, "I wanted to be a genius. But at a certain point I realized I just desperately wanted to work." Brian Grazer, an executive producer of "24," who has primarily produced films, said that "TV guys either get broken by the system, or they get so tough that they have no warmth at all." Surnow, he said, is "a devoted family man" and "a really close friend." But when Grazer first met Surnow, he recalled, "I nearly walked out. He was really glib and insulting. I was shocked. He's a tough guy. He's a meat-eating alpha male. He's a monster!" He observed, "Maybe Jack Bauer has some parts of him."

During three decades as a journeyman screenwriter, Surnow grew increasingly conservative. He "hated welfare," which he saw as government handouts. Liberal courts also angered him. He loved Ronald Reagan's "strength" and disdained Jimmy Carter's "belief that people would be nice to us just because we were humane. That never works." He said of Reagan, "I can hardly think of him without breaking into tears. I just felt Ronald Reagan was the father that this country needed. . . . He made me feel good that I was in his family."

Surnow said that he found the Clinton years obnoxious. "Hollywood under Clinton—it was like he was their guy," he said. "He was the yuppie, baby-boomer narcissist that all of Hollywood related to." During those years, Surnow recalled, he had countless arguments with liberal colleagues, some of whom stopped speaking to him. "My feeling is that the liberals' ideas are wrong," he said. "But they think I'm evil." Last year, he contributed two thousand dollars to the losing campaign of Pennsylvania's hard-line Republican senator Rick Santorum, because he "liked his position on immigration." His favorite bumper sticker, he said, is "Except for Ending Slavery, Fascism, Nazism & Communism, War Has Never Solved Anything."

> "**W**e always had the idea of this King Lear story, of Jack being the prodigal son, the guy who was his father's favorite but turned against his dad, and the less favorite son took over the empire. In some ways, you get to see that his family is his destiny."
>
> —*24* **executive producer Howard Gordon on the plan to give Jack Bauer "genetic responsibility for a lot of the misery by association" in Season six, when he duels with both his brother and his father**

Although he is a supporter of President Bush—he told me that "America is in its glory days"—Surnow is critical of the way the war in Iraq has been conducted. An "isolationist" with "no faith in nation-building," he thinks that "we could have been out of this thing three years ago." After deposing Saddam Hussein, he argued, America should have "just handed it to the Baathists and . . . put in some other monster who's going to keep these people in line but who's not going to be aggressive to us." In his view, America "is sort of the parent of the world, so we have to be stern but fair to people who are rebellious to us. We don't spoil them. That's not to say you abuse them, either. But you have to know who the adult in the room is."

Surnow's rightward turn was encouraged by one of his best friends, Cyrus Nowrasteh, a hard-core conservative who, in 2006, wrote and produced "The Path to 9/11," a controversial ABC miniseries that presented President Clinton as having largely ignored the threat posed by Al Qaeda. (The show was denounced as defamatory by Democrats and by members of the 9/11 Commission; their complaints led ABC to call the program a "dramatization," not a "documentary.") Surnow and Nowrasteh met in 1985, when they worked together on "The Equalizer." Nowrasteh, the son of a deposed adviser to the Shah of Iran, grew up in Madison, Wisconsin, where, like Surnow, he was alienated by the radicalism around him. He told me that he and Surnow, in addition to sharing an admiration for Reagan, found "L.A. a stultifying, stifling place because everyone thinks alike." Nowrasteh said that he and Surnow regard "24" as a kind of wish fulfillment for America. "Every American wishes we had someone out there quietly taking care of business," he said. "It's a deep, dark ugly world out there. Maybe this is what Ollie North was trying to do. It would be nice to have a secret government that can get the answers and take care of business—even kill people. Jack Bauer fulfills that fantasy."

> "If the Democrats are like the dithering 'Desperate Housewives,' the Republicans have come across like the counterterrorism agent Jack Bauer on 24: fast with a gun, loose with the law, willing to torture in the name of protecting the nation. Except Jack Bauer is competent."
>
> —Maureen Dowd,
> the New York Times

In recent years, Surnow and Nowrasteh have participated in the Liberty Film Festival, a group dedicated to promoting conservatism through mass entertainment. Surnow told me that he would like to counter the prevailing image of Senator Joseph McCarthy as a demagogue and a liar. Surnow and his friend Ann Coulter—the conservative pundit, and author of the pro-McCarthy book "Treason"—talked about creating a conservative response to George Clooney's recent film "Good Night, and Good Luck." Surnow said, "I thought it would really provoke people to do a movie that depicted Joe McCarthy as an American hero or, maybe, someone with a good cause who maybe went too far." He likened the Communist sympathizers of the nineteen-fifties to terrorists: "The State Department in the fifties was infiltrated by people who were like Al Qaeda." But, he said, he shelved the project. "The blacklist is Hollywood's orthodoxy," he said. "It's not a movie I could get done now."

A year and a half ago, Surnow and Manny Coto, a "24" writer with similar political views, talked about starting a conservative television network. "There's a gay network, a black network—there should be a conservative network," Surnow told me. But as he and Coto explored the idea they realized that "we weren't distribution guys—we were content guys." Instead, the men developed "The Half Hour News Hour," the conservative satire show. " 'The Daily Show' tips left," Surnow said. "So we thought, Let's do one that tips right." Jon Stewart's program appears on Comedy Central, an entertainment channel. But, after Surnow got Rush Limbaugh to introduce him to Roger Ailes, Fox News agreed to air two episodes. The program, which will follow the fake-news format popularized by "Saturday Night Live," will be written by conservative humorists, including Sandy Frank and Ned Rice. Surnow said of the show, "There are so many targets, from global warming to banning tag on the playground. There's a lot of low-hanging fruit."

In March 2006, Supreme Court Justice Clarence Thomas and his wife, Virginia, joined Surnow and Howard Gordon for a private dinner at Rush Limbaugh's Florida home. The gathering inspired Virginia Thomas—who works at the Heritage Foundation, a conservative think tank—to organize a panel discussion on "24." The symposium, sponsored by the foundation and held in June, was entitled " '24' and America's Image in Fighting Terrorism: Fact, Fiction, or Does It Matter?" Homeland Security Secretary Michael Chertoff, who participated in the discussion, praised the show's depiction of the war on terrorism as "trying to make the best choice with a series of bad options." He went on, "Frankly, it reflects real life." Chertoff, who is a devoted viewer of "24," subsequently began an e-mail correspondence with Gordon, and the two have since socialized in Los Angeles. "It's been very heady," Gordon said of Washington's enthusiasm for the show. Roger Director, Surnow's friend, joked that the conservative writers at "24" have become "like a Hollywood television annex to the White House. It's like an auxiliary wing."

The same day as the Heritage Foundation event, a private luncheon was held in the Wardrobe Room of the White House for Surnow and several others from the show. (The event was not publicized.) Among the attendees were Karl Rove, the deputy chief of staff; Tony Snow, the White House spokesman; Mary Cheney, the Vice-President's daughter; and Lynn Cheney, the Vice-President's wife, who, Surnow said, is "an extreme '24' fan." After the meal, Surnow recalled, he and his colleagues spent more than an hour visiting with Rove in his office. "People have this image of him as this snake-oil-dirty, secretive guy, but in his soul he's a history professor," Surnow said. He was less impressed with the Situation Room, which, unlike the sleek high-tech version at C.T.U., "looked like some old tearoom in a Victorian house."

The Heritage Foundation panel was moderated by Limbaugh. At one point, he praised the show's creators, dropped his voice to a stage whisper, and added, to the audience's applause, "And most of them are conservative." When I spoke with Limbaugh, though, he reinforced the show's public posture of neutrality. "People think that they've got a bunch of right-wing writers and producers at '24,' and they're subtly sending out a message," he said. "I don't think that's happening. They're businessmen, and they don't have an agenda." Asked about the show's treatment of torture, he responded, "Torture? It's just a television show! Get a grip."

In fact, many prominent conservatives speak of "24" as if it were real. John Yoo, the former Justice Department lawyer who helped frame the Bush Administration's "torture memo"—which, in 2002, authorized the abusive treatment of detainees—invokes the show in his book "War by Other Means." He asks, "What if, as the popular Fox television program '24' recently portrayed, a high-level terrorist leader is caught who knows the location of a nuclear weapon?" Laura Ingraham, the talk-radio host, has cited the show's popularity as proof that Americans favor brutality. "They love Jack Bauer," she noted on Fox News. "In my mind, that's as close to a national referendum that it's O.K. to use tough tactics against high-level Al Qaeda operatives as we're going to get." Surnow once appeared as a guest on Ingraham's show; she told him that, while she was undergoing chemotherapy for breast cancer, "it was soothing to see Jack Bauer torture these terrorists, and I felt better." Surnow joked, "We love to torture terrorists—it's good for you!"

> **W**hat does the future hold for Jack Bauer? And how about you? Find out every Monday. Join our *24* party, along with psychics to tell your fortune, and of course, our great selection of martinis.
> **—Newspaper advertisement for a restaurant and bar in Boston**

As a foe of political correctness, Surnow seems to be unburdened by the controversy his show has stirred. "24," he acknowledged, has been criticized as racially insensitive, because it frequently depicts Arab-Americans as terrorists. He said in response, "Our only politics are that terrorists are bad. In some circles, that's political." As he led me through the Situation Room set on the Real Time soundstage, I asked him if "24" has plans to use the waterboarding interrogation method, which has been defended by Vice-President Cheney but is considered torture by the U.S. military. Surnow laughed and said, "Yes! But only with bottled water—it's Hollywood!"

In a more sober tone, he said, "We've had all of these torture experts come by recently, and they say, 'You don't realize how many people are affected by this. Be careful.' They say torture doesn't work. But I don't believe that. I don't think it's honest to say that if someone you love was being held, and you had five minutes to save them, you wouldn't do it. Tell me, what would you do? If someone had one of my children, or my wife, I would *hope* I'd do it. There is nothing—nothing—I wouldn't do." He went on, "Young interrogators don't need our show. What the human mind can imagine is so much greater than what we show on TV. No one needs us to tell them what to do. It's not like somebody goes, 'Oh, look what they're doing, I'll do that.' Is it?" ∎

<u>Charles McGrath</u>

Confessions of a Serial Viewer:
Forget the Time, Agent Bauer. What Year Is It?

As 24 gained viewers during its first few seasons and came to have an ever-greater impact on the popular culture, opinion leaders in the worlds of politics, government, and the media began to take note, wondering out loud what this Jack Bauer phenomenon was all about.

Editor and critic Charles McGrath was one of those who came late to the phenomenon but then embraced it. McGrath, for many years one of America's leading cultural arbiters as editor of the New York Times Book Review *and still a powerful tastemaker in the world of high culture as a frequent contributor to the* New York Times, *its* Book Review *and its* Magazine, *tells us that, like all good genre entertainment, "24 offers both surprise and an even more deeply satisfying element of pre-dictability." Catching up on the prior seasons he had missed (thanks to the annual DVD compilations), McGrath succumbed to what might be called the "potato chip syndrome," an affliction affecting millions of other 24 fans: Shall we watch another episode? Well . . . maybe just one more . . .*

MY WIFE AND I WERE LATE CONVERTS to *24*, becoming hooked only a year ago, after our son gave us a boxed set of the first season on DVD. Innocently, we slipped in the first disc, listened to Kiefer Sutherland announce, "I'm federal agent Jack Bauer, and today is the longest day of my life," and then for a week we seldom left the couch, bingeing sometimes on five or six episodes at a time. "Another one?" we'd say. "Well, maybe just one."

DVD still seems the best way to watch any of the new, extended-plotline series: not just *24*, but also *Lost*, *Alias* and *The Wire*. You don't have to wait a fretful week to find out what happens next. You can watch (and pause to bathe occasionally and take nourishment) whenever you want, and by skipping the commercials you save about 15 minutes of every hour, which makes this sort of watching seem more virtuous than the other, network-controlled kind.

At the moment we're watching Season 2 of *24* on DVD, in carefully measured doses, while also trying to follow Season 5 in once-a-week real time. Keeping the two story lines straight is harder than you might think and has resulted in frequent episodes of conjugal head shaking. What are we dealing with here? My wife and I have to remind ourselves periodically. Nuclear, biological or chemical? Bombs or nerve gas? Who are the terrorists, Central

Asians or Middle Easterners? Is Jack Bauer in the bunker or in the cargo hold of an airliner? And where is Jack's annoying daughter, Kim? Is she still an au pair for the guy who beats his child, or is she with that creepy older fellow, the psychologist? And what happened to that child, anyway? She can't still be cowering in the cardboard box?

Sorting all this out ought to be easier, considering that the administrations depicted in these two seasons couldn't be more different. In Season 2 the calm and judicious David Palmer is still president—by far the best imaginary chief executive this country has ever had—while in Season 5 he's been replaced by the loathsome Charles Logan, who slinks every week to new levels of sweaty Nixonian duplicity. Just recently we learned that he actually engineered Palmer's assassination.

On the other hand there's a lot of overlap between the two administrations. The bullet-headed Mike Novick, who used to be Palmer's chief of staff, now works for Logan, and to make matters more confusing he's so much a Dick Cheney lookalike that you keep expecting him to want to call in the military when in fact he's one of the few decent people in that entire administration. The same is true of Logan's flaky, pill-popping wife, Martha, who is clearly meant to remind us of another Nixonian figure, Martha Mitchell, but is a far steadier influence than Palmer's grasping and ambitious wife, Sherry.

> "**W**e all get in the weeds sometimes, but most people kind of give each other some slack, you know? I mean, dude, seriously: chicken wings are gonna fry the same speed whether there's some guy standing behind you yelling 'Do it! DO IT NOW!' or not. "
>
> —**From the online "Journal of Literary Satire," in which a (fictional) Trent Kessler, fry cook at an Applebee's restaurant in Harrisburg, Pa., gives "feedback" on the performance of fellow employee Jack Bauer**

You can't pick up any useful clues as to where you are in the series by merely taking note of who is in charge over at C.T.U., the counter-terrorist unit to which Jack is attached, because the place is always in upheaval, with one new government flunky after another coming in and locking the unit down so the "protocols" can be changed, whatever they are. Chloe, her face scrunched up, punching codes into her laptop, is the one constant.

Meanwhile the same kinds of things keep happening from season to season. Canisters with ticking digital clocks; Jack going solo, racing around in an SUV and yelling on his cellphone; C.T.U. itself under attack. There is treachery in the White House, and sooner or later a suspect turns up who won't talk and, since the fate of the country is at stake, needs a little chemical encouragement. (With Christopher Henderson, the hard case in Season 5, it's odd that no one has noticed he's played by Peter Weller, formerly the RoboCop; he's half machine, and instead of drugs, the interrogators should be using a welding torch.)

From season to season, the shows also look and feel much alike: the same dark lighting and lingering close-ups; the same slow buildup to the cliff-hanging scene breaks, punctuated by that ominous da-dum, da-dum, da-dum. This is merely to say that, like so many TV series, even very good TV series, *24* is formulaic. There are only so many variations that the creators, Robert Cochran and Joel Surnow, can elaborate on the theme of the renegade agent who in just 24 hours—or 24 less-than-hourlong episodes—rescues his country from an overwhelming threat, and when they hit upon something that works they tend to go back to it.

But far from diminishing the show, these repetitions add an element of reassurance. It is not just superior self-control that has enabled my wife and me to ration our intake of Season 2 and even to contemplate a Monday-evening outing that might not have us home by 9. Much of the initial excitement of *24* depended on its novelty—there had never been anything quite like it on television—and once you get through that initial season, it's hard to imagine how a subsequent one could ever be as riveting.

Nor would you necessarily want it to be. Most of Season 1 was shot in the aftermath of Sept. 11; the people making the show and that first-season audience brought to the experience the kind of anxiety we were all feeling back then. If you're a first-time viewer, the early episodes of *24* scare the daylights out of you, in part because you have no idea how it's all going to turn out. (The show's creators probably didn't either.)

The subsequent seasons deal with similar material—one dire threat after another—and yet we've learned by now that although terrible things may happen (like the pointless death of President Palmer), the folks at C.T.U. will somehow avert even worse ones. Like all good genre entertainment—like mystery novels, for example, or screwball comedies—*24* offers both surprise and an even more deeply satisfying element of predictability. You know what you're going to get. In this case the show may even work as a kind of inoculation, jolting us with a little dose of manageable terrorism or nuclear threat or biological warfare as a balm to our deeper, unspoken anxieties.

The key to this process is Jack, of course, who it's becoming clearer and clearer must give up any semblance of a normal life just so we can cling to ours. He's a heroic figure but also a sad and tragic one who increasingly seems to carry with him an awareness that he's practically toxic to others with whom he might wish to be close.

Jack's dilemma is how to save those he loves while at the same time defusing the larger threat, and if he has to make a choice he invariably sides with people, not principle. He doesn't in the least mind tossing the protocols out the window. That's what makes him different from everyone else in the government—the government on TV, that is, which is in turn a projection of our very worst fears. ∎

Dorothy Rabinowitz

Full-Voltage Shocks:
The *24* Addiction

Dorothy Rabinowitz, editorial writer for the Wall Street Journal *and a Pulitzer Prize–winning journalist, is another leading opinion-shaper who came late to the 24 party. Perhaps to compensate, the editors sent her out to do a dangerous assignment that would later show up in the headline of the story: "See All Episodes, Plumb Show's Lure."*

It took her 5½ months to complete the task, watching all of the extant first five seasons. She returned an admirer, expressing impatience with those who might be squeamish about the show's realpolitik. She liked the derring-do; the no-nonsense way 24 handles the jihadist threat. Give me evil bad guys brought to swift justice, she writes. "Let someone else call the ACLU or Amnesty International."

Rabinowitz did find some "absurd elements" in the show. It disappointed her, for example, that the strong and interesting women in 24 usually morph into treacherous vipers. And she remonstrates the writers for their tendency to undermine the respect due our national leaders by letting plotlines drift toward traitors and conspiracies at the highest levels of government.

Nevertheless, for Dorothy Rabinowitz, the plots never fail to deliver "full-voltage shocks."

THE NEWS THAT FOX'S *24* led all other series in Emmy nominations could not have surprised the multitudes still captive to its hypnotic powers. For regular viewers (it's been five years since Jack Bauer and his counter-terror unit first hit the screen), the entire business of awards and nominations is very much beside the point—which is to miss no hour of the brew of triumphs and calamities that is life at CTU in Los Angeles—though Emmy talk may serve as a reminder that this hour that has its fans by the throat week after week is, after all, a show-business enterprise.

Not that it would make a difference. The willing suspension of disbelief that Kiefer Sutherland's fabulous Bauer and his impossible exploits continue to win from audiences may well have no match in television history—a fact that has more than a little to do with today's real-world history of terrorist depredations and jihadist threats, as everyone, those viewers included, knows.

It is, for huge numbers of them, the point of the show. Every time the otherwise tender-hearted hero of *24* slices a terrorist up, mashes the knee of a wounded plotter, or worse, in order to extort information about an imminent attack that could destroy the lives of Americans by the millions—that is the point. Let someone else call the ACLU or Amnesty International.

In Season 4, which boasts the sharpest writing in the series, someone does make such a call. That someone being, deliciously enough, the chief terrorist, Marwan (played flawlessly by Arnold Vosloo), whose long-nurtured plans to launch a nuclear strike on American soil are about to be realized when he learns that someone involved in the plot has been taken into custody—and that secrets will be forced from him that will undo everything. Reaching for his cellphone, Marwan crisply orders someone to "Call Amnesty Global. Tell them an innocent man is being tortured at CTU headquarters in Los Angeles."

No one needs subtitles to grasp the real-world suggestiveness of the scene in which a "Amnesty Global"—read Amnesty International—lawyer walks in with a marshal and a judge's order, stops the questioning and gets the subject released—not before delivering a mini-lecture on human rights. The only man with information that can avert the nuclear strike is being marched off to freedom—not that the insubordinate Bauer is about to allow it, as the graphic scene, in which he extracts the information in the front seat of a car, soon makes clear.

Much else about the series, including its addictive quality, can become clear in a remarkably short time. This I discovered when I set about catching up with all of the episodes—an undertaking inspired, a few months ago, by the sight of two colleagues who raced from their cubicles one day to hold forth about *24*: a series I'd seen only in bits and pieces. Here, I had to note, were two calm, serious men not given to intense talk about television offering urgent advice. "You have to see it. And keep your eyes on the screen. Don't think you can run to the kitchen for a minute. It moves too fast—you'll miss five developments."

Full-Voltage Shocks

So it happened that I watched, over the past 5½ months, every episode of *24* ever shown, abetted by the packs of DVDs that made it possible to get through a season in a few days and maybe one weekend bender. Not that one felt any wish to rush through them. Production values this impeccable, suspense more reliable, even, than in *The Sopranos*, don't come along every day. Best of all in the suspense department, and it's a rarity, nothing ever telegraphs *24*'s shocks—its unmasking of traitors and moles, its Byzantine plot turns. All arrive at full voltage.

A good thing, too, since the series is not without its absurd elements, which have to do, invariably, with relationship troubles. Seldom can we find

Bauer rushing to a helicopter or a CTU vehicle, calamity being only minutes away, without interruption via a cellphone from one or another of the extraordinarily vapid women in his life, none more irritating than daughter Kim (Elisha Cuthbert), a character who has, it's reported, inspired hopes in more than a few *24* fans that someone take her out, and soon. The strong and interesting women in the show tend to be, mainly, treacherous vipers of one kind or another, among them President David Palmer's scheming wife, Sherry (Penny Johnson Jerald)—other than, of course, the beloved, chronically dyspeptic Chloe (Mary Lynn Rajskub), a character whose name recognition is by now global.

> "**B**ut if the irrational right can claim that the news is fixed to try to alter people's minds, or that networks should be boycotted for nudity or for immorality, shouldn't those same groups be saying *24* should be taken off TV because it's naked brainwashing?"
>
> —**Keith Olbermann, host of MSNBC's *Countdown***

It is worth noting, too, that the just-completed Season Five has gone somewhat awry. This was largely the result of the writers' focus on a corrupt and treacherous new U.S. president, Charles Logan (Gregory Itzin)—a slack-jawed opportunist intended as a Nixon look-alike—and his befuddled, if vaguely principled wife, Martha (Jean Smart). She's meant to remind us—this is not subtle—of Martha Mitchell (wife of Attorney General John Mitchell), whose reported threats to expose Nixon's Watergate secrets became something of a problem for that White House.

Monsters and Thugs

As it turned out, the show's writers, who had had no problem, earlier, creating entirely believable American leaders, models of honor and decency—take that heroic specimen, President Palmer (Dennis Haysbert)—seem to have fallen on hard times in Season Five. Something, it seems—some sound aversion to the perverse, perhaps—had dried the imaginative juices, undermined their capacity to fashion credible characters out of the monsters and thugs they had conceived of, now the new leadership in the White House: among them, an American president who joins in a terror plot against his own nation, who approves the assassination of a former president, whose White House is a nest of traitors and rogue-army assassinators.

How much easier to have conceived of steadfast, unfailingly respectful Jack Bauer, a magical character Kiefer Sutherland inhabits with improbable naturalness. When the script calls on him to say "I'd give my life for you, Mr. President," we can believe him. Twentieth Century Fox doesn't need convincing—it has given Mr. Sutherland a $30 million contract for the next three years of *24*. ∎

Sarah Vowell

Down with Torture! Gimme Torture!

Sarah Vowell, one of the great dry wits of the postmodern cultural scene, is fascinated by the way in which 24 deals with the everyday contradiction between the need to protect ourselves at all costs and the need to defend the Constitution. She's also fascinated by her own reaction. Dedicated as she is to Civics 101, left-leaning as her commentaries often appear to be, concerned as she is with all kinds of cruelty in our society, a deeply ingrained human instinct somehow emerges within her on watching 24 that has her rooting for the torture-compelled revelation. Do it, Jack, do it! Don't we also inwardly cheer when Clint Eastwood's Dirty Harry drives around San Francisco and matter-of-factly and gruesomely blows away some half-dozen bad guys in the name of justice? So shouldn't we be giving Jack Bauer a medal, instead of vilifying him?

At the same time, Vowell says, the other, more "rational" part of her brain finds torture-in-the-name-of-salvation repugnant. And decidedly unconstitutional. Don't do it, Jack, don't do it! Sure, security is always a trade-off, but civil liberties are not the things we ought to be trading off, right? So shouldn't we be punishing Jack Bauer? Or perhaps we should do both—prosecute him and give him a medal.

In any case, Vowell finds her unconstitutional fantasies set off by 24 cathartic, which, she concludes, is healthy as long as we keep it compartmentalized as compelling fiction and "keep it off the TV news."

Vowell is a writer, a journalist, and a contributor to public radio's This American Life. *She is the author, most recently, of* Assassination Vacation, *a brilliant, genre-bending political travelogue about her visits to sites involved with the history of American presidential assassinations.*

WHENEVER I HEAR THE PRESIDENT mention, oh, every 12 minutes, that his greatest responsibility is "to protect the American people," the insufferable civics robot inside my head mutters: "Actually, sir, your oath, the one with the Bible and the chief justice and the Jumbotron, is to protect and defend the Constitution of the United States. For the American people are not mere flesh whose greatest hope is to keep our personal greasy molecules intact; we, sir, are a body politic—with ideals."

If the civics robot is feeling particularly nostalgic for that time in America when the word "rendition" was usually followed by the words, "of 'Louie, Louie,'" it continues to nitpick about what some of those ideals entail: Congressional oversight, due process and treating prisoners of war according to ye olde golden rule. Not only because we would hope our captive soldiers would be treated with reciprocal human decency, or because the information gleaned from torture usually turns out to be a Saddam's-in-league-with-Al-Qaeda sham, but mostly, Americans reject torture because we are not satanic monster scum.

Except, of course, the moment we pick up our TV remote controls. That's when even my inner civics robot cracks open a ginger ale, stares at Kiefer Sutherland on the beloved "24" and cheers: "Yeah, Jack Bauer! Break into that interrogation room and shoot that suspect in the leg!" There is a jarring disconnect between what I want my real-life intelligence officers to be doing versus what I want my fake TV intelligence officers to be doing. On my two favorite shows, "Alias" and "24," the protagonists Sydney Bristow (Jennifer Garner) and the aforementioned Jack Bauer bend and break the laws of the land in the name of national security with such speed and frequency, even Donald Rumsfeld himself might be outraged enough to utter a "my goodness gracious" tsk, tsk.

> Internet wisdom: Sun Tzu once wrote, "If your enemy is weaker, conquer him. If he is stronger, join him. If he is Jack Bauer, you're f---ing dead."

In "Alias," Sydney, a C.I.A. agent, will lie to senators, break into the Vatican without authorization or hitch rides on off-the-books cargo planes probably paid for by dipping into the several million dollars in questionable cash her scary, fellow-spy father keeps locked up in his storage unit somewhere in the You Can't Handle the Truth neighborhood of Los Angeles.

One thing that happens on "Alias" that I hope doesn't happen with the actual C.I.A. involves interior design. Specifically, the sleek look of Sydney's office. Her workplace is so white and chic and mod that the Web site named televisionwithoutpity.com has nicknamed it "the Apple Store." That red leather ottoman alone looks as though it was imported from Milan for at least three grand. For the record, I don't think my tax dollars should be financing fancy footstools. As a New Yorker haunted by that August 2001 intelligence memo entitled "Bin Laden Determined to Strike in U.S.," it seems like real-life intelligence analysts have put up their feet enough.

Jack Bauer is tracking down a shipment of nerve gas [in Season 6]. Trying to pry information out of a presidential aide in league with terrorists, Bauer jabs a pointy knife at the aide's face, hissing: "The first thing I'm going to do is, I'm going to take out your right eye. I'll move over and take out your left."

The others in the room, including the horrified and totally unrealistically incompetent president, all give the aide a look that says, "Dude, he's not kidding."

Sitting on my couch, under the watchful stare of no fewer than six busts of Lincoln, while wearing a sweatshirt given to volunteers at a children's tutoring center, as Bauer's knife was poised to break the man's skin, what I was thinking was: Do it. Because, if you ask me, there aren't enough detached eyeballs in prime time.

I did feel a little less guilty about the contradiction of using the same credit card to give money to Amnesty International and to buy the DVDs of "24" when I heard that Senator John McCain is such a fan of the show he will be making a cameo in tomorrow's episode. Even the man who once suffered in North Vietnamese captivity, who sponsored an anti-torture amendment, is bully for potential eye stabbings on TV. On TV being the point. Unconstitutional fantasies are normal (I hope), and on TV dramas they can be entertaining and cathartic. Let's just keep them off the TV news. ■

As I pull off the Ronald Reagan Freeway into suburban Chatsworth, on the northern rim of Los Angeles' San Fernando Valley, I belatedly realize that *24*'s production offices are to be found in the world capital of hardcore porn, as are many of its locations. It is a blank suburb appended to a series of industrial parks and huge porno warehouses, and divided by the straight, wide roads and soullessly empty streets characteristic of a planned, once brand-new city. The place exactly fits *24* cocreator Joel Surnow's description of the classic *24* location—desolate, shabby, depressing: "places that aren't Beverly Hills or the beach, places you've never been to. . . ."

—John Patterson, the *Guardian* (UK)

"Jack Bauer is a tragic character. He doesn't get away with it clean. He's got blood on his hands. In some ways, he is a necessary evil."
— Howard Gordon, executive producer, *24*

Jack Bauer, Hero for Our Times

The genius of *24* lies in the way its creators have retooled the traditional heroic myth to meet twenty-first-century standards. From time immemorial, successful hero stories have gone something like this: The hero suffers a great loss, which leads to a great quest, often with a mentor or helper. Along the way, the hero faces a set of trials that allows him (or her) to overcome evil. The hero must also escape death, often repeatedly. But, after a series of harrowing escapes, the enemy is vanquished. The exhausted hero then returns home, is welcomed back into society, finds new status, and sees his dreams of comfort and romance fulfilled. In these tales, there has to be a happy ending.

The story of Jack Bauer, however, is achingly incomplete. No successful reintegration into society for him, much less a happy ending. Indeed, Bauer is not only tired, he's disillusioned, and literally walks away at the end of the day. And we don't know whether to call Bauer a hero or a villain—because he is not just courageous, but inhumane. Is it *despite* these drawbacks that we have adopted him as our modern hero, or precisely *because of* them?

Flawed and unfulfilled, Jack Bauer is an either/or; or perhaps a neither/nor. Viewers can see him as a hero, willing to do what the rest of us aren't willing or able to do, no matter whose toes get sliced off or what the sacrifice might entail personally. As long as Jack has the guts and the grit, there is hope the terrorists and other bad guys will be foiled in their efforts to kill

Americans and destroy the country. But there is also the menacing Jack Bauer, quickly willing to dissolve every ethical and legal boundary in pursuit of higher ends. Kiefer Sutherland himself thinks Bauer's appeal lies in his embodiment of *both* hero and villain: "People respond to a guy who is trapped and succeeds on some level and yet fails on another."

The commentators and experts in this chapter come to grips with this "trapped" and ambiguous character by telling us just what makes Jack Bauer so different. One way to distinguish him, of course, is to contrast him with the heroes who have preceded him. He is not Captain America, World War II hero, socking Hitler in the jaw and selling war bonds, for example. And although there are some parallels, he is not James Bond (as Paul Berger argues here), nor Spider-Man, the rogue wall crawler who might be seen as a menace, despite his good deeds. More deeply rooted cultural contrasts and comparisons are also worthy of exploration. Jerome Copulsky, a professor of philosophy and religion at Goucher College, introduces us to the symbolic allusions he sees in Jack's experiences to the Jesus story, but then goes on to suggest some disturbing parallels between *24* and the moral philosophy underlying Nazi political theories. Deirdre Good, a highly respected New Testament scholar, deals with the theological metaphors in more detail and shows what *24* can teach us about the value of loyalty, dedication, and sacrifice. Arguably, Jack Bauer is also Jack Bauer because he's portrayed by Kiefer Sutherland, who, says *24* cocreator Joel Surnow, "was born to play [him]." Laura Jackson, biographer of famous pop culture stars like Bono, Jon Bon Jovi, and Mick Jagger, tells us why Surnow is right. We conclude the chapter with an exclusive interview with Tom Clancy, the creator of one of the most famous action/adventure heroes of the 1980s and 1990s: Jack Ryan, who also took it upon himself to take charge because America's political and security institutions were not up to the job.

John Leonard leads off the chapter with his customary verbal pyrotechnics to give us his take on Jack Bauer and the place of *24* in the culture. Leonard, a highly respected writer and commentator on culture, politics, television, books, and the media for more than forty-five years, is noted for his passionate critical enthusiasms and finely honed, acerbic wit. His erudition led the novelist Kurt Vonnegut to say, "When I start to read John Leonard, it is as though I, while simply looking for the men's room, blundered into a lecture by the smartest man who ever lived." What follows is the quintessential Leonard. Read on, as we try to get inside the head of Jack Bauer and probe this highly amped-up character-driven story. ■

John Leonard

Rush Hour

EIGHTEEN MONTHS AFTER A HEROIN-ADDICTED Jack Bauer settled the Frito Bandito hash of a bunch of petulant drug lords who sought to bioterrorize the Northern Hemisphere of the Free World, he shows up all over again at seven o'clock in the Los Angeles morning, just in time for a commuter-train wreck, a computer hack, a kidnapping by the usual ski-masked Islamic extremists, and what promises to be the first-ever "live" execution on the World Wide Web. As if Kafka himself were stuck in Groundhog Day, split-screen Jack has yet another 24 hours to save the bacon of the man he works for and the woman he loves.

The woman he loves? Yes. At least puffy-eyed Jack (Kiefer Sutherland), the night before all hell breaks loose for the fourth year in a row, seems to have had sex with alabaster Audrey (Kim Raver, last seen in uniform as an unfit mother on *Third Watch*). Never mind that Audrey isn't altogether divorced, that she is also Jack's boss's daughter, and that his boss happens to be Secretary of Defense James Heller (William Devane). What's important as Jack begins another of his long, excruciating days is that, even though he no longer works for the Counterterrorism Unit, he has a frantic personal stake in CTU's activities—and this time, praise the drug lord, that stake is not Elisha Cuthbert.

Of course he can't explain any of this to the suspicious new head of CTU, Erin Driscoll (Alberta Watson). But Jack has always been in too much of a hurry to explain anything to anybody, and if you ever saw Alberta Watson on *La Femme Nikita*, you know that she never listens anyway. I am trying to circle around the first three hours of season four, not to mention a greater number of dead bodies, without spilling any important narrative beans. I doubt that you care what I think about L.A. as the preferred target of every swarthy terrorist on Fox television, or about racial profiling, or about the relative acting chops of Kiefer Sutherland and his bearded father, Donald, who has made more bad movies seem interesting than any other male actor I can think of. As usual, Tony Plana shows up as a Third World baddie. As usual, no woman is ever to be trusted, especially if she's a professional. And as usual, these law-enforcement officials all seem to hate each other and their competing agencies more than they do actual perps, as if being on top of the

> **"A**n America that looks to Bauer rather than Batman is an altered nation indeed."
>
> —Ezra Klein, blogger and writing fellow, *The American Prospect*

Source: ©*New York* magazine, January 10, 2005. Reprinted by permission.

pecking order pissing down on the less powerful were a much bigger thrill than securing our borders and stomping on our enemies. But what really distinguishes *24* from the rest of the pack is its IV feed—not of surveillance imagery and data, but of adrenaline. Thus we have no sooner recovered from gunshot wounds, radiation sickness, and heroin withdrawal . . . from atomic bombs, plague viruses, and commercial airliners aimed at nuclear-power plants . . . from abducted daughters, murdered wives, Serbo-Croatians, and amnesia . . . than all of a sudden we are chasing bullet-headed Turks, trying to stop an Internet systems crash, and shooting a suspect in a knee to get him to talk before breakfast.

Focus on that last item. Far be it from me to suggest that Fox TV and the Bush administration have been in conscious cahoots in the past three years to desensitize the American public when it comes to interrogation techniques. But you may have noticed that what happens on *24* is also what appears to have happened at Guantánamo and Abu Ghraib. People in a hurry cut too many corners, and maybe some nerve ends. Erin orders one of her CTU operatives to encourage the flow of info with a needle. Jack, being nimble, being quick, shoots that knee. The excuse for torture on *24*, for sensory deprivation, stress positions, electrodes, and the syringe, has always been the clock—that handy digital readout to remind us that we are late, overdue, or obsolete; that unless we kill a scruple or two, we are dead meat. And this is what we seem to want to hear. ∎

Rick Moran

The Circles of Hell: Dante, Daniel Boone, Gary Cooper, and . . . Jack Bauer

An inveterate blogger on a wide range of topics, Rick Moran provides his followers in the blogosphere with some of the most interesting commentary on 24 available anywhere. Moran's plot summaries and critical reactions are especially insightful into the character of Jack Bauer and his transition from hero to antihero through the last six seasons of 24—seasons that, of course, mirror the years of America's post-9/11 experience.

In this essay, Moran expands on his thinking about Jack Bauer as a character, looking at him in the context of cultural and historical allusions ranging from Dante to Daniel Boone to Clint Eastwood. At least one of the archetypes that Moran draws on—Gary Cooper—was clearly prominent in the thinking of the show's creators early on as they developed the concept for 24. The personality of Gary Cooper's character as the lawman in the classic film High Noon, *as well as that film's suspenseful ticking of the large town clock as the film counts down to Cooper's wedding, have been referenced from time to time as part of the inspiration for the way the story unfolded in the first few seasons. Season 2 even featured an incredibly suspenseful countdown to a wedding—as Kate Warner grows suspicious about Reza, the possible terrorist her sister Marie is about to marry.*

In fact, there are many parallels between High Noon *and* 24, *not the least of which is the way audiences perceive the political issues on the minds of the creators of both works. Some see* High Noon *as a classic American Western parable about the struggle between good and evil, just as many see Jack Bauer as an action hero for the twenty-first century, fighting modern evildoers. But running through* High Noon *there is a clear critique of McCarthyism, blacklisting, and cold war cowardice that resonates with how* 24 *has, especially in recent seasons, depicted concerns about overreaching politicians who would suspend the Constitution in the name of fighting terrorism.*

Fans of 24 *who have never seen* High Noon *might want to check out this half-century-older antecedent on DVD. Consider this summary of* High Noon's *climax, based on a Wikipedia entry, and how easy it would be to substitute the characters of* 24 *into this 1952 scene from* High Noon.

In the end, Gary Cooper as Marshal Will Kane faces down Frank Miller (the chief bad guy) and three other gunmen by himself. He shoots down two of Miller's men. Amy, who is Kane's bride-to-be (played by Grace Kelly), chooses her husband's life over her pacifist Quaker religious beliefs and kills the third man by shooting him in the back. Miller then takes Amy hostage and offers to trade her for Kane. Kane agrees, coming out into the open. Amy, however, struggles with Miller, clawing his face. Kane shoots and kills Miller. In front of the townspeople who have come out of hiding, he then contemptuously throws his marshal's star in the dirt and leaves town with his wife.

Ah, if only Jack Bauer had walked away with Audrey when he could have, and thrown back his badge. But he didn't and, indeed, he couldn't have, in the context of 24. *Rick Moran helps explain why.*

JACK BAUER IS ONE OF THE MOST recognizable characters in American television today. Even people who have never seen *24* have an opinion about him. Bauer's well-known predilection for torture, violence, rebellion against authority, and a rather novel approach to civil liberties, has sparked debate far beyond the confines of the show. Serious forums involving intellectuals and constitutional experts have convened to discuss the implications of what Bauer does in order to succeed and defeat the terrorists threatening America. Articles in newsmagazines from *Newsweek* to the *New Republic* have been written about Bauer, discussing his impact on our culture and politics.

Bauer has transcended the entertainment world and become a political icon; stroked by the right and bashed by the left, *24* has become the favorite guilty pleasure of the political class in America. Even many liberals confess their addiction to the show, despite Bauer's enormously troubling use of torture and the cavalier way in which he disregards the constitutional niceties. And many conservatives, seeing Jack taking the fight directly to our enemies (along with maintaining a moral certitude that is both refreshing and emotionally satisfying), cheer their hero on as he battles evil.

- Jack Bauer has been to Mars. That's why there's no life on Mars.
- Superman wears Jack Bauer pajamas.
- How many CTU special agents does it take to change a lightbulb? Twenty. Nineteen to set up a perimeter, while Jack Bauer tortures the lightbulb into revealing the whereabouts of the socket.

—Sampling of Internet humor about *24*

We watch spellbound as he relentlessly pursues the enemies of the United States with a frightening determination and dedication that brooks no opposition from friend or foe. His disputes with the national security bureaucracy are fought with the same tenacity and brutal win-at-all-costs mind-set with which he battles the terrorists seeking to destroy us. In this respect, Bauer is a man outside the law rather than someone of the law.

Sound familiar? It should. Hollywood long has prospered making heroes of such men—although not quite in the same context. Jack might best be compared to the small-town sheriff who finds himself up against the ruthless outlaw gang as played by Gary Cooper in the classic Western, *High Noon*. Cooper's portrayal of Marshal Will Kane, who must vanquish a gang of criminals bent on revenge on the day of his wedding, had many of the same points and counterpoints found in the character of Jack Bauer. It is the solitary nature of his fight—the man willing to do his duty against terrible odds—that brings to mind Bauer's predicaments as Jack flies from the frying pan into the fire week after week, always coming out on top because, in the end, good must triumph over evil.

This lone hero motif employed in many classic Westerns is a large part of what makes the genre so attractive to us. It hearkens back to an earlier period in American history when our icons were the great hunter-heroes of the plains and the mountains. Daniel Boone was perhaps the first truly American hero, lionized in dime novels of the time as a great hunter and Indian fighter. In real life, Boone's true story was certainly dramatic enough. With a single-minded determination, he hacked a settlement out of the Kentucky wilderness while in the process losing a brother and two sons in skirmishes with the Indians.

Jack Bauer recalls this spirit of the self-reliant and courageous frontiersman. He doesn't really need the government to do what is necessary to protect us (although he relies heavily on the gee-whiz gadgetry employed by CTU in their hunt for terrorists). He improvises solutions to impossible situations, using his wits and subterfuge to escape the clutches of evil week in and week out. Americans have always admired those qualities in their heroes and Bauer is no different.

Over the years, Bauer has undergone some dramatic changes that have made his character much more interesting. From a dedicated patriot doing his duty in the first season, successive incarnations of the drama showed Jack descending down a dark, bloody path to where he seriously began to question his own motivations. His personal life also became darker, more complex, as each succeeding season saw him lose one or more of his friends in the line of duty. His wife was murdered in the first season finale. His subsequent estrangement from his daughter, his on-again, off-again love affair with Audrey Raines, daughter of the secretary of defense (a man Jack saw as something of a surrogate father), and his complex but ultimately empty relationships with other women have all served to make Jack Bauer a man apart, alone to face the demons that through the years have begun to dominate his psyche.

This transition has colored not only his relationships but his sense of duty as well. Jack grew somewhat cynical of the motivations of his superiors (reflecting perhaps the temper of the times as national unity behind President

Bush in the wake of 9/11 has given way to distrust of the president as a fact of political life). In a very real sense, Bauer has become an antihero, related more to Clint Eastwood's *Man With No Name* gunman, whose latent violent proclivities are used to protect the weak and innocent, rather than an unsullied hero who selflessly sacrifices himself for his country. No matter what you think of his methods, justified or not, the fact is that Jack Bauer has blood on his hands. No real hero would allow his personal feelings of revenge to affect his work. And yet, as the series has progressed, Bauer has cold-bloodedly executed several of his enemies while taking obvious personal satisfaction in doing so. The Jack Bauer of the first couple of seasons would not have.

Bauer has been forced by these changes in his character to confront and defeat evil as he himself becomes what he despises. In order to defeat the terrorists, Bauer descends to their designated circle of hell to confront them. From the terrorists inhabiting Dante's Seventh Circle who commit "violence against their neighbors," to the bureaucratic hypocrites, evil counselors, and falsifiers in the Eighth Circle, the tale of Jack Bauer probes deeper into archetypal mythology with each passing season. Now we are all the way down to the worst of the worst—the betrayers of their own country in the Ninth Circle where Dante saved his most gruesome descriptive of punishment— the tormented souls are condemned to gnaw on the heads of their neighbors for eternity. It is here that Bauer's own father is damned for his towering betrayal of the United States.

> "The show reflects where we are in the culture at this moment in time. Every generation has it. There's social transformation going now in the way we see the world, domestic policy, foreign policy, domestic intelligence, and foreign intelligence. All these things are becoming blurred, as are the questions that we have to face on morality. And the show does a really great job of trying to put those questions on a personal level for all of us. We're all Jack Bauer in our hearts."
>
> —David Heyman, terrorism scholar, Center for Strategic and International Studies

But unlike Dante, Jack has no guarantee that he will escape. He has been living in his own personal hell for so long that it is an open question whether he can tell the difference between the light and the darkness. For him, there is only a grayish existence, both in and out of the world. His adventures have left the stench of death upon him. Decent people shun him for it. Everyone he has known and loved over the years has either rejected him or is dead. It is Bauer's anti–Midas touch: Anyone he gets close to ends up dead.

Bauer must realize that he can never go home, that the road he must travel from here on out will be a lonely one, a road to nowhere. And the only solace he will find, the only peace available to him, perhaps the only thing that will redeem him in his own eyes, will be his own death.

The history of television is littered with the silly, the stupid, the inane, and the empty carcasses of shows that failed to do anything except kill the boredom afflicting the great mass of us when we sit in front of the box to forget what's going on in the outside world.

But when television history is written for these last, eventful years, it will note that *24* changed TV drama for good, and that Jack Bauer will go down as one of the most memorable television characters ever.

The show premiered two months after 9/11. At the time, the country was ready for a TV drama to take the American people into a world where terrorism was depicted with an intensity that mirrored the real-life experience of it on American soil and the bona fide threats to our safety and security. We forget that basic fact at our own peril. And eventually, we won't have *24* around to remind us. ∎

Jerome E. Copulsky

King of Pain:
The Political Theologies of *24*

Although 24 is clearly a product of pop culture, it has consistently attracted attention from philosophers, theologians, political scientists, and other normally high culture–oriented scholars and thinkers. Because of the issues that 24 treats, because of the way it treats them, and, ultimately, because of the ideas and reactions it stimulates in its viewers, quite a few academics have found in 24 pop culture reference points that help them explore important contemporary ideas in political theory and other academic studies.

One of the best of those academics is Jerome E. Copulsky, assistant professor of philosophy and religion at Goucher College (and a self-described "24 fanatic"). We asked Professor Copulsky to look into the soul of Jack Bauer and tell us what he found there. In the essay that follows, Copulsky takes us into a challenging cosmological world that includes the symbolic allusions he sees in 24 to Jesus and the cycle of crucifixion, resurrection, and redemption. But he also introduces us to some deeply disturbing parallels between the moral philosophy of 24 as embodied in Jack Bauer's actions, and the politically seductive but ultimately dangerous ideas of the Nazi theorist Carl Schmitt.

If you had any doubt that there's a lot more content packed into 24 than is evident in all the fast-paced action on the TV screen, take Professor Copulsky's thought-provoking tour of the intellectual messages that lie just beneath the surface of this gripping action-adventure drama.

LIKE MILLIONS OF OTHER AMERICANS, I am a *24* fanatic. For the past six years, for an hour each week, I have willingly relinquished myself to the high-adrenaline, action-packed world of Fox's hit television series. Yet I follow the exploits of the Counter Terrorist Unit with a somewhat guilty conscience.

Early on, I hit upon the show's secret: *24* is a sustained lesson in controversial German jurist and political theorist Carl Schmitt's decidedly illiberal concept of sovereignty. "Sovereign is he who decides upon the exception," Schmitt proclaimed at the beginning of his 1922 treatise *Political Theology*. To have this power is to stand outside the law, to decide upon the exception—the state of emergency—when the normal rules do not apply. "Sovereignty is the highest, legally independent, underived power."

Source: Jerome Copulsky wrote this piece for *Secrets of 24*. An earlier version of this article appeared in *Sightings*, a publication of the Martin Marty Center at the University of Chicago Divinity School.

Schmitt, who eventually joined the Nazi party, becoming a theoretician of Hitler's regime, developed his political theory against what he regarded as the fundamental weakness of modern Liberalism and the constitutional state. Schmitt believed that with its emphasis on rights and freedoms and procedures, with its penchant for endless discussions, negotiations and compromises, Liberalism resulted in a neutralization of the political and a fatal disarming of state power. Unable to make the fundamental distinction between friend and enemy, unwilling to suspend the law during an emergency, the liberal simply cannot manage an existential crisis.

It is the crisis, in fact, the time of the exception, which illuminates the meaning and the stakes of real politics. "The exception is more interesting than the rule," Schmitt wrote. "The rule proves nothing; the exception proves everything: It confirms not only the rule but also its existence, which derives only from the exception." For Schmitt, a sovereign who is not above and outside the law is no sovereign at all.

> **B**auerism: "You are gonna tell me what I want to know. It's just a question of how much you want it to hurt."
>
> —**Jack Bauer, Season 5**

This idea of sovereignty didn't emerge from nowhere. Political ideas, Schmitt argued, were derived from theological ones. If we follow Schmitt's claim that "significant concepts of the modern theory of the state are secularized theological concepts," the human sovereign is the political analogue of the omnipotent, transcendent God.

What better description could there be of counter-terrorism agent Jack Bauer, the hero of *24*? As a joke widely circulated on the internet suggested, ". . . and on the seventh day Jack Bauer said, 'I'll take it from here.'"

Devotees of *24* know that the show is all about the "exception" and that Bauer is no by-the-book agent. Rules, procedures, superiors, politicians (often indecisive or corrupt), and shadowy conspirators are simply obstacles in his single-minded effort to defuse the terrorist threat. When Bauer operates against his orders and beyond the law and conventional morals in order to interrogate a suspect—employing torture to obtain crucial information—we understand that he is merely doing what is necessary to fulfill his patriotic duty. And when bureaucrats and politicians wring their hands or quibble about Bauer's "methods," we are led to believe that they are naïve or lack the will to do what is "necessary" to stop America's deadly enemies. Let others worry themselves sick about "procedure"; Jack gets things done.

"If everyone on '24' followed Jack Bauer's instructions," went another joke, "it would be called '12.'" In the murky, fast-paced world of *24* a world where not even the American President can be trusted, it is Jack Bauer who is clearly the sovereign. He is—to use the expression made famous by our current President—the ultimate *Decider*.

But there is another aspect to the political theology of *24*, a theme which courses through the entire series: Bauer's continuing sacrifice for his vocation. Loyal and tireless, he has been betrayed by co-workers, government and family; his wife has been murdered; he is estranged from his daughter; he becomes a heroin addict; he is forsaken by his government to languish in a Chinese prison.

Another dimension was added to this theme of betrayal and sacrifice at the beginning of season 6. In the first episode, a haggard Bauer, long-haired and bearded, his back bearing the scars of his ordeal, is released by his Chinese captors to his former counter-terrorist colleagues, only to be informed that he is about to be delivered to a group of Muslim fanatics in exchange for what is believed to be critical intelligence about the location of a terrorist mastermind. Resigned to his fate, Bauer expresses satisfaction that he is going to die for a reason: "Do you know the difference between dying for nothing and dying for something? That's why I'm still alive. . . . Today, I can die for something. My way. My choice."

Like a lamb to the slaughter, Bauer is led to further torture and seemingly certain death in order to save his countrymen from further terrorist attacks. The religious symbolism is strikingly clear and unmistakable: betrayed by his colleagues, willing to sacrifice himself for the good of his countrymen, bound, bruised and tortured, Federal agent Bauer is the Christ-figure for the war on terror, the "suffering servant" of the American people.

But the show denied Bauer the enjoyment of such a redemptive death. Bound to a chair, a knife plunged into his back, Bauer's captor taunts him, "You will die for nothing." Meanwhile, his erstwhile colleagues at CTU worry that they "may have sacrificed Jack for nothing." When Bauer learns that the Americas are being duped, that his death will have no redemptive benefit, he bites the neck of one of his captors and, face covered with blood, escapes. After a brief moment of moral and existential doubt, he walks away from his Passion and heads back to work.

That Bauer is willing to sacrifice himself for his cause, that he is willing to renounce the comforts of hearth and home, reinforces our faith in his

> "**I** have fallen in love with another man. For the past five months we have been meeting in a dark room every Sunday night, while the children are tucked up in bed and my husband snores upstairs. It is crazy because I know he would love him too, but he lacks the stamina that this relationship requires. So it's just me . . . and Jack Bauer. . . . His sense of duty is unbreakable. His idea of a hot date is to bundle you into the boot of a mercenary's car and he is more interested in speed-dialing the office than sex. Yet there is a vulnerability about Jack where women are concerned. Tenderness even. He would lay down his life to get you home safely and maybe, just maybe, this time you could make him stay."
> —**Sheila McClennan,**
> *The Guardian* (UK)

authority and the righteousness of his actions. In the world of *24*, the sacrificial victim and the deciding sovereign are two sides of the same coin.

It is becoming clear that all of this is finally beginning to take its toll on Jack. At the end of season 6, his former boss pronounces him "cursed." Having just saved America, again (as well as his teenage nephew), and choosing to relinquish his wounded love, we find Bauer, in the closing moments of the season, standing before a precipice. He walks through a darkened garden, stares down at the cliffs and off into the ocean. Have we witnessed his Gethsemane?

This symbolism of sacrifice and redemptive death—and the other religious references that emerge throughout *24*—would be the stuff of high school literature classes, if not for the fact that the show has become a lens through which many think about America's current political predicament. In Jane Mayer's bracing 2007 *New Yorker* article [see Chapter 1], Joel Surnow, the co-creator and executive producer of *24* and self-described "right-wing nut job," declares that "America wants the war on terror fought by Jack Bauer. He's a patriot."

Perhaps. Perhaps we want someone like Bauer to fight the war on terror because the show is set up so that we know that he is almost always correct, because the narrative and moral arguments are stacked in his favor, because we trust his intuitions, intentions, and judgments, and because the show takes the extreme case of an imminent threat, the so-called "ticking time bomb," and makes it the norm. For an hour a week, we gladly consent to Bauer's "sovereignty," knowing that he is simply doing what is necessary to keep his nation safe. In this sense, *24* reveals itself to be within a deeply American tradition of vigilantism, one that runs through the cowboy Western, the comic book, the action hero film—a tradition which celebrates the myth of the lone man who stands outside of the system, battling evil and bureaucracy in order to protect society. Everybody wants a hero.

But how does such desire affect our moral and political judgment? In an article in the *Wall Street Journal*, Brian M. Carney celebrated the show's "realistic moral tone," its ability to expose contemporary ethical dilemmas. "You don't need to watch '24' as a kind of primer on moral philosophy," he opined, "but you should." [See Carney's full essay in Chapter 6.]

Unlike Carney, I am not so confident that watching *24* will help us think more deeply about moral problems or conduct the war on terror in a responsible manner. For one, we ought to be wary of the narratives of *24*, which tend to exhibit contempt for the very liberal democratic institutions and safeguards that Bauer and company are purportedly working to protect.

Moreover, those actually engaged in the conflict do not operate in the conditions of a Hollywood thriller but in places where the utilitarian calculus is not so clear cut, where the danger is not the imminent threat of a ticking time bomb, and where torture is unlikely to produce good intelligence.

There are concerns, too, that some American soldiers, looking to *24* as a kind of training manual, have come to regard torture as a justifiable practice, and Bauer an exemplar to be imitated. In her *New Yorker* article, Mayer reported that American military leaders have expressed misgivings about the show's significant influence on those under their command, worrying that "the show promoted unethical and illegal behavior and had adversely affected the training and performance of real American soldiers." Watching *24*, they see torture as an efficacious means of obtaining needed information. Wanting to be patriots, they may, *Imitatio Bauer,* consider themselves to be their own authorities, outside the law, ready to do what is necessary to be modern American heroes.

It's not just that *24* might sanction unethical behavior or render us civilians more accepting of what our government should do on account of "necessity." For all the dangers he encounters, for all the impossible situations his writers create for him, we have the assurance that Bauer will not be killed in the course of the season. Previous seasons have created powerful expectations: Jack will ultimately succeed in his mission, his pains will be mitigated, his methods vindicated. Bauer will always live to fight another day—so long as Fox renews *24* and Kiefer Sutherland's contract. Despite the celebrated "realism" of the show—its real-time action, its politically relevant plot points—*24* finally provides a false sense of security, morality and impunity. Far from providing us with a steely-eyed look at the war on terror, *24* is really a well-produced exercise in wish-fulfillment.

> Characters that push things over the limit are interesting characters. It's very natural to create a character like than in the world of terrorism because there are so many difficult moral, ethical and legal dilemmas, political dilemmas, that constantly arise. You want a character that's over the edge a little.
> —**Robert Cochran, co-creator, *24***

Of course, it's not necessarily a bad thing to detect the strains of political theory or to be confronted with somewhat heavy-handed religious symbolism in a popular television series. But after we spend an hour in the thrall of Jack Bauer, Schmittian sovereign and secular savior, we should be sure to remind ourselves that entertainment which exploits our fears and strokes our hopes of simple solutions will not provide the means to our salvation, political or otherwise. ■

Deirdre Good

Jack, Our Savior?

"*Are you aware of the discussions going on all over the Internet among my religious colleagues about the parallels between Jack Bauer and Jesus?*" *asked Deirdre Good when she heard we were beginning work on* Secrets of 24. *No, we replied, skeptical but intrigued. Good is a widely respected professor of the New Testament at the General Theological Seminary in New York. She is a scholar who reads religious texts in their original Greek, Coptic, Latin, Hebrew, or Aramaic and is a world-class expert on new scholarship about Mary Magdalene's role in early Christian history. She is also a highly regarded teacher, lecturer, and author, most recently of* Jesus' Family Values. *At the same time, her interest in popular culture has led to essays on the* Da Vinci Code *and Mel Gibson's* Passion of the Christ—*and to numerous contributions to our series of* Secrets *books and DVDs over the last few years.*

Deirdre Good would be the first to point out that the case for Jack Bauer as Jesus can easily be stretched far too thin. But consider this: Like the story of Jesus, 24 *conveys a way of life that places sacrifice for the greater good above the comforts of family and friends. Jesus and Jack both fight, in their own way, on behalf of the salvation of humankind. Also, the men share the struggle for personal redemption, often at great personal sacrifice. Certainly it is not hard to imagine Jack, bereft at the loss of his wife, or his closest friends at CTU, or even his traitorous father and brother, echoing Jesus' prayer to "let this cup pass from me." Then there is that scene at the beginning of Season 6 when Jack walks out of a dark, cavelike shipping container, visibly scarred from bearing the metaphorical cross of torture at the hands of the Chinese.*

24's *writers were bemused when we raised this topic with them. More likely, they are giving us another demonstration of the way good storytellers absorb the accumulated artifacts and symbols of culture and reflect them back to us, sometimes without our even being consciously aware of these allusions and archetypes. Whatever the* 24 *writers' inspiration, Deirdre Good shows us that they have given us a lot to think about in terms of loyalty to a cause, dedication to a higher purpose, and the value of sacrifice. Here, then, are Good's comments on the theological metaphors contained within* 24 *and the case for Jack as Jesus figure.*

THERE ARE STRIKING PARALLELS: A charismatic hero figure known to many who during the course of his brief, unmarried life, becomes increasingly isolated and estranged from friends, colleagues, his family of origin and his family of choice. Someone handed over to an enemy and tortured, suffering on behalf of those he serves. Two brave men who choose their cause, however reluctantly, to achieve a higher purpose.

While there are also distinctions between the two figures, the connections between Jesus and Jack, intentional or not, enable viewers of 24 to think about the type of savior we search for in today's world of global threats and global challenges. We can also ponder how terrorism challenges the values that have been passed down to us about the moral worth of human life and the universal striving for human rights.

At the beginning of his journey, Jack Bauer is admired and respected. His life is embedded in visible, real-world communities. He is connected to CTU colleagues, to friends and ex-lovers, to his family, and to the city and country to whose stability and security he devotes his professional life. In Seasons 1 and 2 we see him both as a man of power and influence with direct access to a president and as a man at home after work as a husband and father in the context of the characters' interdependent lives. Jack Bauer is striving to be a family man with a successful, if dangerous, career of preserving national security. If he, like Jesus, is a somewhat enigmatic man of few words, not given to introspection, he nevertheless seems confident and capable—someone we can admire and whose judgment we trust. To a great extent he makes independent and autonomous decisions. In some ways both men are antiauthoritarian.

However, Jack Bauer becomes increasingly isolated as the seasons of 24 progress. Life becomes darker and darker, in part because of the tasks he is given and in part because of the calamities that befall the organizations for which he works or individuals to whom he is connected. He becomes ostracized, regarded by friends and colleagues at CTU as unstable and a liability. He is excluded from access to politically powerful people (particularly after the assassination of President David Palmer). His daughter Kim expels him from her life after the murder of his wife by Jack's ex-girlfriend who, it turns out, is a CTU double agent. He moves between being an individual recipient of terror to its rationalized practitioner. It becomes harder and harder to see the distinction between terrorist and terrorized—especially at the point when Jack's father, Phillip, turns out to be a cruel and ruthless enabler of the deadliest forms of terrorism, and Jack's brother, Graem, turns out to be the Cain to his Abel.

The isolation of Jack Bauer in regard to his immediate family is at its starkest at the end of Season 6, when he is confronted with a terrible dilemma: the need to kill his father in order to save his nephew. When Jack finally stares down the barrel of the pointed gun aimed at his father, ready to finish him off, he chooses not to shoot, arguably because he knows that even his father's demise cannot restore his family. That the script of *24* calls for Jack's nephew to shoot and wound his grandfather shortly before that final moment offers cold comfort: through such an act, his nephew, standing for the next generation, is on the way to becoming the same kind of man that Jack Bauer is.

It is here that we see a clear distinction between Jack Bauer and Jesus: The Gospels portray Jesus as opposed to violence, even as he faces his own brutal death. As told in the Gospel of Mark, for example, Jesus has made a transition from action (chasing the money changers out of the temple, for example) to quiet acceptance at the time of his arrest and trial. This change is evident even in the way Mark's Gospel has been written. Jesus is the subject of all sentences at the beginning of his ministry: He calls disciples, he speaks, he teaches, he reaches out to touch, hold, and heal people. They, in turn, touch him to receive healing. But at his arrest and subsequent trial, imprisonment, torture, and condemnation, Jesus is the object of other people's actions. They grasp, seize, and hold him so that he cannot escape.

> "**W**hen men watch Tony Soprano and Jack Bauer they enter into a contract with the characters. They watch and savor the brutality but recognize how pathetic these heroes are. Guys watch TV shows such as *The Sopranos* and *24* and see all the horror, humiliations and complications of being male. Tony Soprano and Jack Bauer are not role models to emulate. They are case studies to brood upon. They are a warning. Every man knows that."
>
> —**John Doyle, *Globe and Mail* (Toronto)**

A striking similarity between Jesus and Jack Bauer can be seen in the trajectory of their respective family relations. The Gospels imply that the relationships within Jesus' family have been sacrificed to his ministry. At the outset of his ministry, God endorses Jesus as son in baptism as described in the Gospels of Matthew and Luke when God says, "This is my beloved Son in whom I am well-pleased." No higher honor could be imagined. At the same time, God's sanction of Jesus' person and message through Jesus' new identification as the Son of God effectively displaces Jesus' family of origin. Luke's Gospel encapsulates the new priorities of a teenage Jesus: To his anxious parents (who found him in the temple talking to temple leaders and religious officials after a three-day search when he went missing after a trip to Jerusalem), Jesus replies, "Don't you know I must be concerned with the things of my Father?" Jesus is answering to a higher authority than that of his parents.

Jesus identifies and calls devoted disciples who accompany him in his ministerial travels throughout Galilee, proclaiming God's realm. He draws in crowds and neutral bystanders. These two groups—supportive disciples and sympathetic crowds—substitute for and replace his original kin. We see tensions between them: "Who are my mother and my brothers?" he says to people who indicate that his family wants his attention on one occasion. "Those who do the will of God are my mother and father and brothers," Jesus declares. In these and other comments, family obligations are set aside in favor of higher concerns. But the followers in whom he has placed his hopes prove fallible. As Jesus journeys to Jerusalem in Luke and as he continues to preach in Matthew, the crowd's attitude shifts from adulation to neutrality to hostility. Jesus' inner circle of disciples fails to comprehend his ministry, particularly in the master's prediction of suffering and death. They abandon him at moments of extreme crisis in the garden of Gethsemane and after his arrest. His closest followers betray him. In isolation he faces a political trial, judgment, and shameful treatment on the way to the cross. Women followers, once close associates and disciples in ministry, offer only distant comfort.

As the plot proceeds in *24*, Jack's motivations and actions become increasingly enigmatic to the viewer, and he, too, becomes more and more isolated. A few women, however, remain steadfast allies and even sympathizers. Chloe O'Brian is perhaps Jack's closest confidant at CTU; her sympathy for him consistently overrides her questions about what he is doing. With her adept technological skills, she is often shown providing resources to Jack at great risk to herself, even when she doesn't understand his intentions and plans.

As for Jack's loyalty to a higher power, he permits the state to hand him over to the Chinese to be tortured and imprisoned in exchange for information regarding national security. And thus the state effectively declares him to be a person who does not exist. When he returns at the beginning of Season 6, stepping out of a dark, cavelike container as though from the dead, he is haggard, emaciated and mute. We do not know his state of mind. Does he remain loyal to the state that handed him over to the enemy?

Jesus, too, was handed over to the state (that is, the enemy) by followers—albeit for very different reasons. His own torture and trial resulted in crucifixion and death. Jesus' cry from the cross at the point of death could be taken as a statement of abandonment, "My God, my God, why have you forsaken me!" It stretches to the breaking point Jesus' connection with God the Father. Severed from his biological father, handed over to political enemies, deserted by family and friends, Jesus is utterly bereft at this point. Such a cry could well have been on the lips of Jack Bauer, too—were he given to externalizing the raging torments within himself. ∎

Ginia Bellafante

In *24*'s World,
Family Is the Main Casualty

*The controversies surrounding 24 generally focus on terrorism, torture,
and the spectacular violence done by, or suffered by, its characters. But,
says cultural critic Ginia Bellafante, what really should upset us is the way
the show shatters the bonds that hold people together, especially within families. Domestic horror, she writes, is as much a key part of 24's storyline as
the gloomy derring-do: Family members kill each other, stab each other,
and abuse each other day after day.*

    Ginia Bellafante is a New York Times *style reporter whose work
has ranged from an obit on the Ally McBeal TV show to a profile of
author Francine du Plessix Gray. Previously with* Time *magazine, she
famously penned a 1998 cover story under the headline "Is Feminism
Dead?" (Yes, according to her, in the sense that it has moved from revolution to spin and from calling attention to the glass ceiling to champi-
oning "adventures in cybersex").*

    *In the following commentary, written at the end of Season 6,
Bellafante turns her considerable talents to a critique of the way 24 regularly suffocates human connections. If a host of viewers and critics wonder
what the impact on our military-intelligence complex might be of sustained
exposure to scenes of torture on 24, Bellafante wonders what the impact
might be on viewers—young and old—of seeing family ties completely cor-
rupted on a regular basis.*

THE FRENETIC, LABYRINTHINE, exhausting counterterrorism drama "24" concluded its sixth year with its ratings slipping and its fans in revolt. With each
season of the series transpiring over a single day, this one, detractors lament,
has felt like 70. The producers themselves have acknowledged the challenges
of maintaining the story line's intensity and focus. Recently in his blog on
"24," the humorist Dave Barry expressed a wish for Congressional hearings
into the show's crimes against narrative cohesiveness.

    Until two weeks ago I had included myself among the dissenters, com-
plaining that digressions and strange forays into cold war nostalgia had sub-
sumed the larger plot and proclaiming, to the walls in my living room that
"24" ought to become "12"—or "8" or "6." But during Hour 21, Agent Jack
Bauer's father, Phillip (played by the gifted James Cromwell), re-emerged to

subject members of his family to renewed acts of twisted venality. And the effect was intense and chilling, a reminder that "24" has always sustained its tension by operating in two genres, not one, deploying the conventions of domestic horror in the language of an apocalyptic thriller.

Since it first appeared in 2001, "24" has successfully woven the terrors of intimate life through its narrative of an America facing potential annihilation. Parents kill children. Husbands abuse wives. Sisters try to kill sisters. Wives fire husbands—or stab them, as Martha Logan, ex-wife of Charles Logan, the former president, did earlier this year, plunging a knife into his shoulder as recompense for his treacheries, both personal and civic.

Discussions of "24" have long concentrated on its depiction of torture—elaborate to the point of parody this season—as the source of its controversy. But it is the show's treatment of family as an impossible and even dangerous illusion that truly challenges our complacency. The anxious gloom of watching "24" comes not from wondering whether the world will blow up (obviously it won't; Jack Bauer—played by Kiefer Sutherland—is protection against all that) but from knowing that the bonds that hold people together will eventually be imperiled or destroyed, perfidy and neglect so often the forces.

According to co-creator Joel Surnow, the first few episodes of 24 were heavily influenced by the movies *Three Days of the Condor*, *La Femme Nikita*, and *The Day of the Jackal*. But these episodes were "in the can" before 9/11. Afterward, and in fact for every season after the first, Surnow says the plots were influenced by "real events."

The introduction of Phillip Bauer early in the season quickly established that Jack did not inherit his rectitude from his father. Shortly after he appeared, Phillip suffocated his son Graem, forced his daughter-in-law to endanger the lives of federal agents and threatened Jack. When he reappeared, weeks later, Phillip was kidnapping his grandson, Josh, for the second time in a single day.

Parenthood, untouchably sacrosanct in so much of our culture, is on "24" a grotesquely compromised institution. During Season 4 we witnessed the show's defense secretary subject his son to torture for refusing to divulge information that might help track down a terrorist. At the same time we observed the director of the Counter Terrorist Unit labor to thwart a nuclear attack despite the deterioration of her mentally disturbed daughter in a nearby room.

That each child was portrayed as a petulant nuisance made it easier to see that the country's security imperatives had to come first. The perverse brilliance of "24" lies, at least in some part, in its capacity to elicit our sympathies for heinous miscalculations of judgment. In the end we feel less for the troubled girl than we do for her beleaguered mother, who after all has been making sound decisions every step of the way.

The most enduring relationships on "24" are not between parents and children, boyfriends and girlfriends, spouses or siblings, but between individuals and their governments and causes. And in this way the show seems committed not to the politics of the left or right, but to a kind of quasi-totalitarianism in which patriotism takes precedence over everything else and private life is eroded, undermined, demeaned. Privacy isn't even a viable concept in a world in which there is no taco stand, phone booth, laptop or S.U.V. that isn't immediately accessible to the advanced surveillance systems of the ever-vigilant Counter Terrorist Unit.

Human connection is forever suffocated. Totalitarianism, Hannah Arendt wrote, "bases itself on loneliness, on the experience of not belonging to the world at all." And above and beyond everything else, the universe of "24" is a very lonely place.

Friendship can barely be said to exist beyond the parameters of bureaucracy: the offices of the Los Angeles division of the unit and the halls of the White House. And when men and women become involved, it is not only with each other but also with the greater American purpose. Ordinary social intercourse simply doesn't exist. The idea that two people might sit down for a cup of coffee is as contrary to the show's internal logic as the idea that polar bears might someday learn to sing.

On "24" the choice to forfeit all that and respond to your country's call is never the wrong choice, no matter how regrettable the personal consequences. Five seasons ago Jack was a married man who played chess with his teenage daughter. Since then he has lost his wife (at the hands of a unit mole), his daughter (to his own emotional inattention) and various girlfriends to his unfailing devotion to eradicating the state's enemies, whatever the cost. He has killed colleagues who have impeded his pursuit of justice, lost his identity and acquired a heroin addiction combating drug lords. The price of a safe world is considerable, "24" tells us: love and the rest of it mortgaged for some other lifetime. ■

Paul Berger

Jack Bauer, Meet James Bond

*O*nce upon a time, it was called cloak and dagger, and had a certain charm. The lines of battle were clearly drawn, and the enemy generally played by the same rules as the rest of us. It was an era, at least on the surface, of moral clarity, gentlemanly derring-do, sophisticated cocktail parties, and aromatic cigars. And it lent itself to gentle spoofing—as Ian Fleming showed us so successfully with his avatar, James Bond.

A dozen years later, John le Carré wrote in a more anxious tone, and showed us a far darker side of the game. The Spy Who Came In from the Cold *opens and closes at night, in bitter cold, with a nervous agent waiting vainly for a defector at the dangerous and heartless wall dividing East from West. Bleak life histories, deformed hearts, well-practiced trade-craft, and easy betrayal would come to characterize the George Smiley novels. Still, le Carré's heroes, however flawed, retained a deep sense of commitment to a greater humanity.*

The next turn went to Jason Bourne, Robert Ludlum's man with the name not his own and a mysterious past that torments him and drives his no-holds-barred quest for answers. CIA dirty tricks, terrorist violence, and post–cold war political tumult had, by the 1980s, now trumped betrayal and quiet subversion, both in the early Ludlum novels and, a generation later, on the big screen (trimmed of the "sludge" of the books, said one critic). Bourne is propelled through a globe-spinning, head-spinning procession of violent action sequences, running to find himself, running to get back home to his family.

In 24, Jack Bauer tries to run away from himself. Away from the self that literally cut through human flesh in dark, confining enclosures in order to save the country—and himself. But Jack has no family in whom to seek solace in between his adventures, and, unlike Bond, no devil-may-care lifestyle to enjoy while awaiting the next adventure. Instead of a warm salute for his accomplishments, Jack Bauer often finds himself ostracized by colleagues and government officials alike.

Over the past five decades our heroes have thus traveled along an arc that begins with an agent demonstrating polished mastery to one who is blunt, thuggish, prone to overreaction, and misunderstood. From British elegance in black tie to a man who wears street clothes and bullet-proof vests, seeming to fit in nowhere. What does this say about the times we live in? We asked contributing editor Paul Berger, himself a Brit and a great fan of the Bond films, to search for some answers. Here is his report.

EVERY GENERATION SEEMS TO FIND the hero it needs. During the Great Depression of the 1930s, an animated Superman swooped down upon the crooked businessmen and politicians who preyed on the decent people of Metropolis. Captain America vanquished both the Nazis and the Japanese during the Second World War, even socking Hitler in the jaw. And in the post–September 11 world of America, we have an all-too-human figure, Jack Bauer, who wages an unrelenting battle against terrorism, suburb by suburb, in what was once known as the City of Angels. But there is another hero in the ranks of men to take into account. Another government agent with the initials JB who, albeit a generation ago, also did the impossible time after time to save his country and the Western world: James Bond.

Like Bauer, Bond is portrayed on film as a loner, trained to kill by a government that desperately needs him, yet keeps him and his murderous exploits at arm's length. Both men lose their wives in the line of duty: Bond on his wedding day to criminal overlord and archnemesis Ernst Blofeld (*On Her Majesty's Secret Service*) and Bauer to treasonous CTU agent Nina Myers (*24:* Season 1). Both men withstand torture, Bond for fourteen months at the hands of communist North Korea (*Die Another Day*) and Bauer for twenty months at the hands of the communist Chinese (*24:* Season 6). They both speak a number of foreign languages and they even sport similarly nondescript names.

When Bond creator Ian Fleming was asked about his secret agent's unremarkable name, he replied that he chose the plain-sounding *James Bond* to reflect a hero who was "an anonymous, blunt instrument wielded by a government department." Some would say the same of Jack Bauer.

But below the surface the similarities between these two characters end quickly.

James Bond fights in the largely black-and-white world of two superpowers waging a cold war. He defends Queen, country, and Western capitalism on a global scale, pitting himself against international crime syndicates and communist foes. His work takes him to exotic locations with exotic toys, even space (*Moonraker*) and under the sea (*The Spy Who Loved Me*). His bosses are staunch and upright, with a stiff upper lip. The enemy is wholly evil, willing to destroy entire cities and nations in their malevolence.

Jack Bauer, on the other hand, fights shadowy, amorphous terrorist groups. No dinner jackets, fine wines, exotic cars, or swank casinos for this hero—he wears Wranglers, drives whatever he can commandeer, and never checks into a fancy hotel, much less eats. Jack seems always to be operating in a soulless nightmare: the empty streets, dark warehouses, and characterless suburbs of a forlorn Los Angeles and the bleak interrogation rooms of CTU. In Jack's world, the bosses—even the president—are prone to political conspiracies, bureaucratic infighting, and treason.

Then there is the matter of torture. Though 007 is often engaged in a desperate bid to save the world from the imminent threat of SPECTRE, he is too sophisticated to resort to chemical injections, hacked-off body parts, and electrocution. Bond may take his fists to the enemy, even a woman, in order to get the information he wants, but if anyone does the torturing in Bond films it's the bad guys—because that's what bad guys do. Even in Bond's latest and perhaps darkest iteration, played by Daniel Craig in the 2006 remake of *Casino Royale,* Bond is the tortured rather than the torturer.

Bond audiences don't want to see their hero shoot a terrorist's innocent wife in the leg to force him to talk or watch 007 electrocute his girlfriend's husband with a lamp cord. These are the things that set Bond, the goodie, apart from Le Chiffre, the baddie, in the recent *Casino Royale*. But under other circumstances, the same audience that cheers on Bond may also identify even more intensely with the far more realistic, uncouth Bauer character , who is no more likely to be depicted as a suave high roller in a Monte Carlo casino than he would be charming the pants off Pussy Galore. The two men fight in ways that reflect the vastly different eras in which they were conceived. During the geopolitical maneuverings of the cold war, battles between the superpowers were fought by proxy or in the shadows. Their weapons were corrupt dictators and poison-tipped umbrellas. Therefore Bond's enemies stroll unnoticed in the real world. Moreover, their cloak-and-dagger work requires them to uphold at least on the surface, a gentlemanly code of conduct that more resembles an eighteenth-century duel than a twenty-first-century guerrilla war.

If only Jack Bauer had the luxury of such mutual respect. His adversaries are found in abandoned warehouses or as sleeper cells in suburban homes. In the era of the war on terror, terrorists threaten to execute civilians live on the twenty-four-hour news channels and successfully detonate nuclear bombs in densely populated neighborhoods. While James had weeks to wrap up a mission, Jack is racing against a constantly ticking clock, with only a matter of hours before the politician is assassinated, the gas is released, or the bomb explodes. He *has* to torture the prisoner, or even kill his own colleague, if he's to avoid the ultimate catastrophe.

In another time, this desperate hero who shoots women and tortures prisoners would have been anathema to conservatives and guardians of family values; a stark example of everything that is wrong with violence on television. But in a world where politicians insist that civil liberties and the rule of law must be bent, broken, or remade in order to prevent terror attacks, the Superman of the day must be a Jack Bauer. His exchange with a liberal attorney from "Amnesty Global" who tries to prevent Jack from "interrogating" a suspect in Season 4, is indicative of Jack's—and the nation's—moral dilemma:

MR. WEISS, THESE PEOPLE ARE NOT GOING TO STOP ATTACKING US TODAY UNTIL MIL-
LIONS AND MILLIONS OF AMERICANS ARE DEAD. NOW, I DON'T WANT TO BYPASS THE
CONSTITUTION, BUT THESE ARE EXTRAORDINARY CIRCUMSTANCES.

DAVID WEISS (THE LAWYER FOR AMNESTY GLOBAL): THE CONSTITUTION WAS BORN
OUT OF EXTRAORDINARY CIRCUMSTANCES, MR. BAUER. THIS PLAYS OUT BY THE
BOOK, NOT IN A BACK ROOM WITH A RUBBER HOSE.

JACK BAUER: I HOPE YOU CAN LIVE WITH THAT.

Jack can't. He resigns his post at CTU and engineers the release of the suspect so he can torture the prisoner as a private citizen before they even get out
of the CTU parking lot. Then he blithely rejoins his colleagues and is on his
way once again to save the day as the government's point man. In fact, every
piece of information Jack gleans, by measures fair or foul, brings him one step
closer to disarming the terrorists and saving thousands of lives. So who can
argue with his methods? The sophisticated James Bond could never have prevented these all-too-imminent attacks. He'd barely have time to order a vodka martini.

24 was in production months before the attacks of September 11 and Jack Bauer made his first television appearance just eight weeks later. As such, he was not so much a man of his time as a man ahead of his time. Before Jack was even halfway through his first action-packed day, the fantasy of abductions, assassinations, and dirty bombs had become a real threat in the minds of many of Jack's armchair fans.

But however real the threat, most heroic tales contain some small consolation for the hero, whatever trials and tribulations he faces—think every ending of every Bond film. What's surprising about Jack's popularity among his millions of fans is that this hero gets no consolation. Jack accomplishes the impossible without the glamorous cars, the cool gadgets, or the curvy women. Let's face it: It's a bleak existence for a CTU agent who is always one step away from certain death. Where are the perks? Jack's brother and father have tried to kill
him. He's lost his wife and his girlfriend. He's estranged from his daughter.
He's been tortured by the Chinese. And he's watched most of his friends die;

> "**B**rig. Gen. Patrick Finnegan, the dean of West Point, decided that he needed to do something to end the horror of Americans torturing pris-oners. So he gathered three of the top military and FBI interrogation experts and they headed for the air-port. Did they fly to Abu Ghraib? No. Guantánamo? No. One of those secret prisons where the CIA allegedly tortures terror suspects? Nope. They flew to Hollywood to meet the producers of the TV show *24*, so Finnegan could urge them to stop the actors who play American agents from pretending to torture the actors who play terrorists in the show. Really. This actually hap-pened."
>
> **—Peter Carlson,**
> **the *Washington Post***

he even had to kill one of them. And for what? He's viewed as expendable by his own government. One president has tried to kill him. And other than almost two years of detention in China, his job with CTU rarely takes him farther than the outskirts of LA or the gritty back streets of other American cities. He certainly never had the opportunity to make love to Ursula Andress aboard a boat being towed through the Caribbean on an idyllic day.

If Bond is an escapist fantasy, then Bauer is a bleak hyperreality, tapping into contemporary society's darkest fears. In this sense, Bond is a closer relative of TV shows like *The Man from U.N.C.L.E.* (which was influenced by Bond author Ian Fleming) and *Mission: Impossible,* in which each episode had a neat ending and its heroes returned to fight another day. But unlike those shows, *24* is a series of tension-filled situations that are never fully resolved until the denouement in the twenty-fourth hour. It's as though the audience has moved past the dream for the cookie-cutter secret agent and escaped into the abyss, chasing the addictive high of *24*'s action and its fast-paced existential choices.

Indeed, fans of *24* recount the experience of watching the show as being akin to an addiction. At the end of a marathon viewing, the senses have been assaulted. The audience has not only witnessed heinous crimes carried out by terrorists, they have, in effect, been complicit in Jack's immoral acts. However badly James Bond behaved—slapping women, killing unarmed villains, or carrying out political assassinations—it never came to this. And yet the audience is still with Jack, perhaps because the audience knows that however terrible his actions, the man has a soul and dwells in the same world of human failure and frailty that the rest of us do.

Although Bond is famously "licensed to kill", he always comes out the other end looking squeaky clean. The movie audience is rarely left with a feeling that the mission's events have taken their toll. With Jack, it's quite the opposite. After twenty-four hours of tension and death, viewers—like their hero—must accept the emotional and moral bankruptcy inflicted by the job. At the end of each day, it's as though another chunk of Jack's humanity has been ripped away. The camera normally bids this hero farewell without triumph; instead, he's scarred and alone. ∎

Laura Jackson

Kiefer Sutherland: Born to Play Jack Bauer

Fans, critics, and his peers agree: Kiefer Sutherland is one of the more versatile actors in the business, with an incredibly strong presence whether playing villain or hero. And perhaps the greatest tribute to his work on 24 is that one cannot imagine the show without him. "The screen hums whenever Sutherland is on it," Time *magazine has said. "As Jack Bauer, he transcends 24, creating Bauer's bitterness and nobility out of pauses and hard-eyed stares."*

Kiefer William Frederick Dempsey George Rufus Sutherland was born in England to the Canadian actor Donald Sutherland and his wife, Shirley Douglas, an actress in her own right. His grandfather, Tommy Douglas, led North America's first socialist government as premier of Saskatchewan and is revered as the man who created Canada's government-funded health care system in the 1960s.

Kiefer's first screen appearance was at seventeen, in The Bad Boy, *winning him the Genie Award as Canada's best actor. By his twenties, he had moved to New York, where he turned down a six-figure offer to appear on a soap opera; he wanted to focus on films instead. In search of work, he got in his '69 Mustang and drove to LA, where, after a stint living in his car, he began to land many forgettable roles and some that gained him attention: as the iconic vampire in* The Lost Boys, *for example, and as a sensitive outlaw in* Young Guns. *Before moving to television, Kiefer had made more than fifty films and, in the process, earned Best Actor trophies from the Golden Globes and the Screen Actors Guild, and a slew of other nominations.*

Kiefer is also famed for his colorful, often whisky-fueled social life, and a checkered love life. Two short marriages ended quickly, and a headline-grabbing engagement to the actress Julia Roberts abruptly ended in June 1991, only a few days before the scheduled wedding ceremony.

Coexisting with a tangible edge in his personality is a disarming candor, friends and colleagues say, and he is the first one to poke fun at himself. He is also generous with fans. As to how he came to be tapped for 24, *what the experience has been like, and how it has brought him an honored comeback, well, we will let Laura Jackson tell that story.*

Source: From *Kiefer Sutherland: The Biography.* Copyright © 2006 by Laura Jackson. Reprinted with permission.

"**K**IEFER SUTHERLAND WAS BORN TO PLAY JACK BAUER." So said Joel Surnow, co-creator of one of the most electrifying screen heroes ever, the star of *24*, one of the best, ground-breaking television drama series of our time. This stark statement was well understood by those who had taken a keen interest in Kiefer's career since it began 15 years earlier. The combination of his intense energy, natural ability and screen presence was always going to coil itself around a high-octane character of dynamism and maturity. Bauer was it, and with inimitable modesty Kiefer was openly grateful. "When something like *24* happens," he said, "you bow your head and say thank you."

Jack Bauer is a hero with compelling steel and hypnotic authority. "That's what is appealing about Jack," declared Kiefer, "he takes charge." Bauer also distinguishes himself by his loyalty to his country and his unlimited resourcefulness. He has a sixth, seventh, even an eighth sense, and in terms of TV entertainment he seems to have come along at the right time. Howard Gordon, one of *24*'s executive producers, said: "*24* taps into the public's fear-based wish for protectors such as Jack Bauer who will do whatever is necessary to save society from harm, but it shows a dark side too. Jack Bauer is a tragic character. He doesn't get away with it clean. He's got blood on his hands. In some ways, he is a necessary evil."

For Kiefer, the Jack Bauer role was a godsend. It came his way via a friend, director Stephen Hopkins, who urged him to read the script for the pilot, which he himself was due to helm. . . . Kiefer read the pilot for *24* on a plane on his way to Vancouver for a hockey tournament, and by the time the aircraft touched down he couldn't believe his luck. He felt in a no-lose situation. The pilot show was clever and different, with the potential to be a vastly invigorating project, but at the same time, to Kiefer's way of thinking, its unique concept stood little chance of being picked up by a major U.S. TV network. In any event, he reckoned he would be well paid to film it, and if no network ultimately weighed in, then his career would not be harmed by a dud show at this critical comeback point.

These people, the Bush Administration, manage to take their Constitutional advice from the cast of the hit show *24*, rather than from the founders of our Constitution.

—**Neal Katyal, professor at Georgetown Law, on new findings about instances of enhanced interrogation techniques in October 2007.**

The ticking countdown clock, nerve-shreddingly omnipresent, was something that initially Kiefer did not try to get his head around. Written across the front page of the script were the words: "All events happen in real time," but he ignored that and cut quickly to the dialogue; the appeal of Jack Bauer hit the spot at once. Kiefer loved the fact that here was an extremely capable hero with a Special Forces background, in charge of a nation's security, but who can't control his rebellious 16-year-old daughter. A very reactionary federal agent, everything he does has a consequence. Sometimes his impulses are right, other times they are wrong. He is fallible. On arrival at Vancouver airport Kiefer straightaway telephoned Stephen Hopkins with the words, "OK, I'm in."

In March 2001, with *24* picked up by Fox TV, Kiefer secured the challenge of becoming the show's anchor. 'When I was offered *24*, it came like a saving grace. I owe it a lot," he said. At that point Kiefer sold his huge cattle ranch in Santa Ynez and made Los Angeles his working base. He wanted his whole concentration to be on Jack Bauer, a complex character with myriad dimensions, some of which did not dovetail with his personality in real life. Kiefer consciously got very close to Jack Bauer to assume that skin. "It's funny," he said, "because I'm strongly opposed to the death penalty and I don't believe in 'acceptable losses.' It's complicated for me to play this character. Yet one of the big draws was, here is a guy who is ordinary in a lot of ways but due to his profession he's placed in extraordinary situations that he has to make right with action and with thought."

The plight Bauer finds himself in when his dedication to his demanding job conflicts with his responsibilities as a husband and a father was a factor that Kiefer deeply identified with. "It's an aspect of Jack I really feel connected to," he maintained, and he firmly believed it was a personal dilemma that would resonate with many viewers. "By the end, Jack realizes how important family is to him but isn't completely forgiven for all he's done. That sounds like life to me," he said. The breathless pace of the show also appealed to Kiefer's energetic nature.

Filming began around spring and would spread over the next ten solid months. As the new kid on the block, *24* was not shot in a Beverly Hills studio lot. Instead, the set was built in less glamorous surroundings in the LA suburb of Woodland Hills, in the San Fernando Valley. CTU's offices were constructed inside a disused warehouse in a nondescript business park that appeared to have no address. A chain-link fence and two layers of security ringed the set, mainly to ensure airtight secrecy for the gripping drama's edge of your seat plotlines.

The schedule was grueling—12 hours a day, five days a week. For Kiefer, weekends entailed preparation work, sitting for interviews and doing photo shoots. "Towards the end, we were into hard nights, 5:00 p.m. until 5:00 a.m.," he said. They would get through around eight script pages a day. As Kiefer pointed out, working on a season of *24* is the equivalent of making 12 movies back-to-back.

From the beginning, Kiefer had a certain degree of input into *24*, but at times his views were overruled. Such was the fascination with Jack Bauer that the show's devoted fans started debating the tiniest detail of his behavior. Kiefer himself began querying things like: when does Bauer get to grab something to eat? He is careering from one crisis to another from midnight without food, drink, sleep—anything. When Kiefer suggested a moment in the show when Jack buys a hot dog from a burger van, the writers downed him—they believed viewers would think that was funny. According to Kiefer, he and the powers that be got into an argument over this eating issue. A compromise was found when, more than half way through, having rescued his family, the exhausted federal agent gets to bolt a tray of food while waiting at CTU to be debriefed on his renegade behavior over the past few hours.

Meticulous attention had to be paid to every aspect of Kiefer's appearance. Although *24* took 10 months to film . . . the action supposedly happens in a single 24-hour period, which meant that facially and bodily Kiefer has to stay exactly the same throughout. He also had the most action sequences to undertake, so fitness was an issue. Since signing on the dotted line to become Jack Bauer, Kiefer had not taken part in rodeo riding. Between his passion for rodeo, skiing and ice hockey, he had in the past broken his collarbone, a knee, an elbow, both wrists, one ankle and all his fingers. . . . He continued to smoke, which made all the running about he had to do on screen more than a little arduous. On camera it never looked as if he struggled at all, though, and the cameramen were amazed that a man who lit up as often as Kiefer could sprint to order like he did. As Jack Bauer, Kiefer had somehow to maintain an almost manic energy level throughout all 24 episodes. Not surprisingly, after a long shoot, he went home tired to his LA apartment. After walking [his pet dog] Molly, the pair would then crash in front of the television for a while. Kiefer often fell sound asleep, while Molly, curled up at his feet, would happily chew on a bone. With such a demanding workload Kiefer lived alone, had no special lady in his life and scant time to socialize. At one point the only people he met outside *24*'s cast and crew were shift workers breakfasting at Denny's at dawn.

24 was destined to be the hottest show on TV, and Kiefer felt the fact that director Stephen Hopkins had not worked on a television series before played a massive part in helping to create that success. "Although things are changing, particularly in network television, there are creative limitations, but Stephen was unaware of them so he rode right over them," said Kiefer.

Kiefer had never before had the opportunity to work on something unremittingly for so many consecutive months, and *24* threw up the chance for cast and crew to become well acquainted. Kiefer and Carlos Bernard [who played CTU agent Tony Almeida and would accrue his own fan base] hit it off from the first days of filming [on Season 1]. . . . Dennis Haysbert, with whom Kiefer would have a close onscreen interaction as would-be president and federal agent [until Haysbert, much to his bitter disappointment, was "assassinated" at the end of Season 4], has also recalled happy times. He described working with Kiefer as being akin to working with his best friend, calling Kiefer a genuinely good guy. . . . Elisha Cuthbert, who took on the role of

Bauer's headstrong daughter, Kim, knew all about how Kiefer had been a Hollywood golden boy when he'd been about her age, which made her a little unsure of what the actor playing her father would be like. "When we met, he made it very easy," she recalled. "He was really down to earth."

The other corner of the Bauer family triangle was Jack's wife, Teri, played by Leslie Hope, whose respect for and friendship with her screen husband is very apparent. . . . During filming, Leslie declared: "I may be having the best time of my life. . . . Kiefer is gracious and generous, has the patience of a saint, is a good listener and his butt looks awesome in his Wranglers!"

Georgetown University Law School is offering a class in spring 2008 called "the Law of 24," to be taught by Lt. General Walter Sharp, staff director for the Joint Chiefs of Staff. The course will cover "a very wide range of U.S. domestic and international legal issues" raised by the show.

Kiefer's intensity was the other striking factor for those around him. . . . To the cameramen, Kiefer's actorly precision was manna from heaven. It made acting out even the toughest, fastest fight sequences go smoothly, because once Kiefer and the director of photography had worked out the physicality in a scene, no matter how many takes it took to complete, Kiefer never varied from the plan. From a cinematographer's point of view, that is a rare quality in an actor.

Long before the show's debut in November 2001, the director, producers and writers felt fully vindicated in their choice of Kiefer Sutherland as Jack Bauer. Robert Cochran enthused: "Kiefer brings a dark side with him, and it's a tremendous sense of three-dimensionality, layers and complexity." Executive producer Howard Gordon declared: "Kiefer elevates everyone else's game. He insists on a certain level of commitment. The urgency that he creates informs the entire show and the quality of acting among the ensemble. He is the single best actor I've ever had the privilege of working with."

By now, Kiefer had bought a home in Toronto quite close to where his mother lives; mainly he stayed at his LA apartment, where he enjoyed chilling out in a variety of ways. His prized guitar collection had risen to 37 instruments, and he enjoyed quietly strumming away. He had also acquired a taste for cooking. "I'm not a very complicated chef," he admits, "but I find it incredibly relaxing."

When he wasn't running lines of dialogue through his mind as he sifted flour through his nimble fingers into a baking bowl, he loved as ever spending time with his daughter Sarah. They played chess and liked reading together. "Something I enjoyed was reading *To Kill a Mockingbird* aloud with Sarah and talking about what it meant to be in the South at that time." Kiefer recently declared proudly: "She's pretty clever and not half as rebellious as I was at her age. I'm very impressed."

Despite being careful off set not to endanger life and limb, Kiefer's exuberance once led after all to an accident on set when he shattered a kneecap pulling off a stunt. "Fortunately when it happened we had three weeks left to shoot before the Christmas break and there were a lot of car scenes," he said. "Still, we had to scramble and figure out all the scenes where I'd be prone, which weren't all that many." It was an accident that threw up extra challenges for the writers and left Kiefer hobbling around with a walking cane for a while.

Some time back, producers Joel Surnow and Robert Cochran had indicated that they knew how the show's convoluted plot would end, but when the cast got their final scripts, there was a shock in store. Robert Cochran said, "24 never gave out a 'don't worry be happy' vibe. After all the stuff that happened, if everyone had ridden off into the sunset it would have felt false." Kiefer conceded, "We knew something was going to have to give. We knew there was no way everyone was going to walk out of this fine." What no one expected was Teri Bauer would end up being shot dead. When Kiefer discovered his screen wife's fate, at first he was vehemently against the decision to kill her off, and indeed many of the show's vociferous fans would not much like it either, but Kiefer's objections were overruled without appeal. It showed Kiefer that in 24's pecking order, he then ranked roughly fourth.

Once he could take his emotional reaction out of the equation, however, he could see that he had been wrong to oppose the decision to ice Teri Bauer. Cochran called the shock true to 24, and Kiefer now believes Teri's death was the first marker to both cast and audience that no character was safe, including his own. 24 without Jack Bauer is unthinkable, yet Kiefer made a valid point when he said that if the audience is so sure that no matter what peril he is in, he will win through, it would harm the dramatic tension, perhaps fatally. People care about Jack Bauer and it matters what happens to him.

By the time filming finally finished, it had been some ride for Kiefer. He had turned 35 in December 2001, and was a calmer person. Now when he was tired, he would consciously slow down rather than think himself invincible and so end up burning out. He had a sense of perspective when it came to work, that felt better balanced, and he was not being emotionally drained by having to cope with a turbulent love life. Asked if he had regrets about having two failed marriages behind him, Kiefer replied: "How

"While we don't try to represent any kind of real truth—obviously 24 hours in the format makes it impossible—we try to, I think, present an essential truth, or an essential problem. So when Jack Bauer tortures, it's in a compressed reality. . . We try to compress these arguments and these issues and dramatize them in obviously very unreal ways, but hopefully in dramatic and compelling ways. And that's really ultimately our master . . . making a compelling, 'adrenalized' TV show."
—**Howard Gordon, executive producer of 24**

can I? I have a beautiful daughter and many happy memories."

Throughout 24 Jack Bauer has the U.S. President's ear, and people some-times wonder if, considering his Douglas family background, Kiefer would in real life be tempted into politics. . . . He has strong political views but—entering that particular minefield? He answered: "With my past? Are you kidding?"

On 9 September 2001, Fox TV officially announced that 24 would make its debut on 30 October. Two days later, the terrorist atrocity of 11 September numbed the whole world, and plans to launch 24 on the announced date changed. . . . Like billions of people, Kiefer was devastated by the scale of the appalling acts of terrorism. . . . He felt useless, he said, insignificant in the scheme of things . . . [which] made him a little tetchy when in the following weeks people came to him, excited at the prospect of 24 starting [the debut date was now 6 November]. . . . Kiefer's first inner response was to be appalled or even angry at the facile outlook, until it dawned on him that he was being too harsh. People *needed* normality, escapism, some relief from the oppressive grief and the suffocating air of tragedy and fear.

Once the critics and fans reacted so positively to the show Kiefer Sutherland was again the name on everyone's lips, but he said of his career at that point: "I've been up and down the ladder so many times, it's a relief I didn't hit the ground." He had said a decade earlier that the really good work for an actor does not start until he is in his thirties. Shirley Douglas said of her son: "Kiefer's whole life is now concentrated on 24. Those bags under his eyes are not just for the character! He's always short on sleep, but he's extremely happy and that's all that matters." Kiefer's father may have once had a distinct aversion to television, but Donald too had kept abreast of the huge changes in this medium. He said: "I have no objective viewpoint of Kiefer's career. 24 just takes your breath away."

24 was a solid gold hit, and success the second time around was certainly very sweet for Kiefer. Yet he remained genuinely modest. "On a career level, I have to say that this has been the most important year for me. I thank 24 all the way home and all the way back to work every day," he said. His stunning, critically acclaimed portrayal of Jack Bauer catapulted Kiefer back into Hollywood's A-list. He was now also affectionately labeled Tinsel town's latest comeback king. This bright spotlight brought a deluge of attention from all quarters, which steadily increased the number of unusual situations Kiefer had to cope with. On a ski lift once, a real life CIA operative jokingly tackled him for being an impossibly capable federal agent. Apparently, the CIA operative's mother thought that Jack Bauer was so much more efficient than her son.

Recognition came Kiefer's way when he received an Emmy nomination for Outstanding Lead Actor in a TV Drama Series, and a Golden Globe Best Actor in a TV Drama nomination. He then . . . picked off the Golden Satellite Award for Best Performance by an Actor in a Series—Drama.

Then on 20 January 2002, at the Golden Globe Awards ceremony in Los Angeles, he won the coveted Golden Globe, beating back stiff competition from Simon Baker in *The Guardian*, James Gandolfini for *The Sopranos*, and Martin Sheen for *The West Wing*. On the glitzy evening, before an international television audience, Kiefer was overwhelmed as he clutched his Best Actor trophy. He later said, "My mind went totally blank and my body went numb. It was a very surreal moment. It was a great night. I admit, I felt really cocky for about twenty-four hours and then I had to go back to work." ∎

From Jack Ryan to Jack Bauer: Thoughts from the Master of the Political Thriller

24 *is the greatest television potboiler of our time. So who better to ana-lyze the themes behind 24 than one of America's greatest thriller writers, Tom Clancy?* The Hunt for Red October, *Clancy's first novel—about a Soviet submarine captain who defects to the United States, along with the Russian nuclear sub he's commanding—was propelled onto best-seller lists in 1984 when President Ronald Reagan described the book as "unput-down-able." Since then, Clancy's hero Jack Ryan has battled foes as varied as Irish terrorists and Colombian drug cartels. Fifteen years before Jack Bauer witnessed Muslim terrorists detonate a thermo nuclear device at the Super Bowl, Ryan was battling Islamic extremists who detonate a nuclear bomb at the Super Bowl in Colorado.*

Clancy is not just an expert in the field of fiction. He is an expert on military history too, who takes pride that his novels are largely based on real life weaponry and technology. If a missile shoots down an airplane in a Clancy novel, you can be sure it would do so in real life, too. (If 24's attention to detail stretched that far, Jack Bauer probably wouldn't last more than a couple of hours.) Clancy's encyclopedic knowledge of warfare extends to detailed books on submarines, aircraft carriers, fighter wings, and U.S. Special Forces, as well as examinations of military campaigns cowritten with generals Frederick M. Franks and Anthony Zinni.

We spoke to the mega-best-selling writer at his Camp Kaufmann estate, overlooking Chesapeake Bay in Maryland, where an American World War II tank stands guard a few hundred feet from his front door. Here, in his trademark no-nonsense style, Clancy explains how the world order has changed since the cold war days of Jack Ryan, why torture is never an option when dealing with the enemy, and what Clancy thinks about the mind and motivations of the world's most wanted terrorist, Osama bin Laden.

Your thriller stories were set against the backdrop of the cold war, while *24* is set against the backdrop of the current war on terror. What do you think is the main difference between these two world orders?

Nation-states made it easier to know the enemy's worth. They had flags and borders and armed forces you could practice against. But terrorism is amorphous. It's hard to identify the bad guys.

What about the nature of fear today? Season 6 of *24* showed how the U.S. government might someday react to a terror attack by rounding up Muslim Americans. Do you think people are more afraid now than they were during the cold war?

Look, twenty years ago there was this country called the Soviet Union. It had more than fifteen thousand nuclear weapons, sitting on top of ballistic launchers, aimed at the United States. They're not there anymore. So the world is definitely a safer place than it was. It's just that the current enemy is harder to classify.

What about the public perception of fear?

I don't think the American people are all that worried. The average truck driver works all day, he goes to Safeway, he buys his food, and he takes it home to his wife. He sleeps soundly in bed every night. He's got more immediate things to worry about than nuclear war. Reality is something you have to deal with every day. And, for the most part, reality is working, getting paid, and using the money to support your family.

You speak to people in the military and intelligence communities. Do you feel we are doing enough to address the terrorist threat?

The name of the game is to identify the threat, to localize the threat, and to destroy the threat. Now could we do that better? Hell, yes. We could do it a lot better. We need to build up the clandestine arm of the CIA. We need to increase the number of field spooks who go and talk to people and find out what's going on. The CIA is a fact-finding organization, a bit like a news service. Spooks do the same thing as reporters. But they are a little bit smarter than your average reporter: You don't have to pass an intelligence exam to join a newspaper.

The military is the one part of the federal government that actually works reasonably well. They have their own methods of gathering information and they are pretty good at it. But mainly they respond to threats that other people identify.

A moment ago, you mentioned the difficulty of identifying who the enemy is. Can you elaborate a little bit on your thinking about the "stateless terrorist."
Actually, I am writing about it right now. There are few problems in all of human history that could not be solved with a forty-five-caliber bullet. But you have to find out who these people are and where they are before you can target them. So the name of the game is to get that information. That's why we have the CIA, the NSA, the DIA, and a whole bunch of other government agencies, whose job it is to go out there and locate threats. But it's hard to identify these people because we don't know where they live and we don't fully understand their motivations. The threat now is certainly different than any threat we faced before. But the world has changed and we have to change with it.

What do you think of Jack Bauer's method of gathering information by torturing people?
It's a gross violation of the Constitution. And the Constitution is the supreme law of the land. You violate the Constitution at your own great peril. Alan Dershowitz, up at Harvard, once said that in Israel they are allowed to torture people, so why shouldn't we? He said a judge would need to sign off. Can you imagine a judge sitting down and saying, "Okay, you can break his finger bones but you can't cut off his balls"? I don't think so.

The fundamental problem with torture is that it doesn't work. Somebody will tell you anything to make the pain stop, whether it's true or not. And so, in the practical world, torture is ineffective—as well as being evil and sinful and wrong.

If Jack Bauer's actions are evil, why is he such a popular hero?
Public taste is public taste. I'm not an arbiter of public taste. I operate in that marketplace and people like my books and buy them. They like the way I tell stories, but aside from that I don't make the rules of society.

The Bourne movies are gritty. The latest Bond film is darker than usual. Do you think hero films have become bleaker?
Not really. Look at Hollywood detective stories. There is always this guy who is outside the law. He's got all kinds of personal problems but he overcomes those problems and solves the mystery.

The problem with this Hollywood scenario is that reality is not like that. If your hero has all these problems, how can he be effective? I had open-heart surgery last September, which was quite an adventure. As I was lying there on the table, looking at everybody getting ready to gas me and knock me out, I was thinking, "I want the surgeon to feel like it's a great day." You don't want somebody with lots of personal problems with his hands on your heart, do you?

In Season 6 of *24*, a disgruntled former Soviet general sneaks five suitcase nuclear bombs to Muslim extremists, who use them in attacks on Los Angeles and to threaten other U.S. cities. Do I detect a similarity to a certain Tom Clancy story line in *The Sum of All Fears*?

No, I was a little bit more realistic than that. In my case it was an Israeli weapon that got lost in 1973. Is the *24* story line possible theoretically? Yes. But is it likely? No. The Russians probably have such weapons, but for reasons I can't disclose here, I don't worry about them one little bit—not at all.

Does anything keep Tom Clancy awake at night?

Biological warfare, maybe. I researched that for my 1996 novel *Executive Orders*. I went to experts on infectious diseases up at Johns Hopkins Hospital and the first thing they told me was that biological weapons are not effective on the battlefield but psychologically they are very scary.

So biological weapons worry you because they spread fear?

They can get people excited, yes. But Americans don't panic that easily. Even September 11, which was a terrible tragedy, didn't make the whole country panic. The media likes to tart these things up. But the average guy out there isn't worrying about dying tomorrow from something like this. And if anything does happen, after the initial shock the American people will quickly settle down and deal with the problem. We are good at that.

In *The Sum of All Fears* it turns out that the bomb that is detonated in a U.S. city was made in America. In other words, a deterrent became a weapon used against its creators. What do you think of the nuclear deterrent today?

Nuclear weapons are a tool of the state and states use their tools. They are nice things to have if you have to deal with people like North Korea. Their leader, Kim Jong-il, is a madman. His greatest ambition in life is to be a movie producer; he personally made a Korean version of *Godzilla* with a guy in a rubber suit stomping on a miniature city in a movie set. But mad or not, Kim must know that thirty minutes after the president picks up the phone, Pyongyang is a smoking parking lot. Knocked flat. One submarine could do that with one missile. We have twenty or so such submarines with twenty-four missiles each. That's what deterrence is all about—keeping madmen like Kim Jong-il in their box.

But, as you mentioned earlier, it's harder to keep terrorists in their box if we don't know who they are or where they are. Where should we begin?

The most important thing is to look at the world through the terrorist's eyes so that you can predict what he's thinking and what he's going to do.

But we know so much about Osama bin Laden, and yet we still haven't managed to locate him.

Look at a map. Al Qaeda are in really awful terrain. Sir Edmund Hillary climbed Mount Everest because it was the tallest rock in the Himalayas. He didn't climb every rock because that would have been too hard. We are dealing with people who don't want to be found and who are reasonably clever at not being found. The smart guy doesn't sleep two nights in a row at the same house.

Do we know al Qaeda well enough to defeat them?

It depends what you mean by *defeat*. Denying them their objective is a victory in the military context. If we deny them what they want, then we win and they lose.

You seem to have thought a lot about al Qaeda. Will they make an appearance in your next novel?

Of course.

You are renowned for doing an enormous amount of research and having a strong element of truth in your stories.

One of the reasons that the people I write about like me, and why the military is good to me, is that I portray them the way they really are. They are fairly smart people. They are well motivated. And they play by the rules.

Your Soviet characters also seem very realistic, yet you've never been to Russia. How did you get inside the Russian psyche without ever traveling there?

You try to look at the world through the eyes of your adversary so you can predict how he thinks and how he is going to act. It's easy to do conceptually, but you have to make the effort to do it. In the case of the Russians, everything was politics. So you just immerse yourself in their political thinking and just look at the world through their eyes and you can do it.

Since you are currently immersing yourself in the modern-day Islamic terrorist, can you describe, in a nutshell, who he is?

I think Osama bin Laden pretends to be a religious figure, but actually he's a political figure who uses religion as his entrée into the world. There are a billion Muslims in the world and he wants to be the guy they all turn to for opinions and guidance. He wants to be the world's head Muslim. Is he really a religious Muslim? He pretends to be but I rather suspect he's not. Islam is a religion. Like all religions, it calls to the better angels in human nature. It tries to make the world a better place. It doesn't say, "Let's go out and kill some unbelievers." It says, "Let's all worship God and do what God tells us and the world will be a better place." He has perverted what is a noble and honorable religion. ■

On the Set of *24*

Throughout *Secrets of 24*, a variety of experts comment on this iconic pop culture TV show—terrorism and national security professionals, political pundits, cultural commentators, moral philosophers, theologians, op-ed writers. In this chapter, the actors themselves—as well as the creators and writers of the show—speak about the characters and stories that give *24* its distinctive edge.

The compelling, some would say addictive, nature of *24* stems in large part from the show's unusual mix of characters. From their exotic names to their idiosyncratic personalities, this ensemble of characters looks like the postmodern American melting pot, and their supercharged interactions—propelled by the inexorable tyranny of time—get deeply under our skin.

Take the distinguished African-American actor Dennis Haysbert, who played President David Palmer in the early seasons of the show. As the rock-solid nucleus in Jack Bauer's peripatetic orbit, Haysbert talks here about his concerns when he learned that his character was going to be assassinated on the show. James Morrison, who played the unflappable CTU director, Bill Buchanan—always cool, even when disaster loomed—shares some of his personal feelings about where America and the world are headed. Kal Penn, the gifted young actor who played the terrorist Ahmed, talks about television, *24*, and racial profiling. Shohreh Aghdashloo, whose brilliant portrayal of a terrorist sleeper cell wife and mother has become a case study in morality and terrorism, reminds us that the soul of Islam is not what the jihadists sometimes lead us to believe.

So attuned to the character and the times, so pitch-perfect in his portrayal, Kiefer Sutherland, as Jack Bauer, has become synonymous with *24*. Indeed, it is nearly impossible to imagine the show with any actor other than Kiefer Sutherland in the lead role. Fighting his own real-life demons, Sutherland was arrested for a DUI violation just as he was preparing to begin filming Jack Bauer's trial scene at the opening of Season 7. Here we collect some of the best of Kiefer Sutherland's comments on the character of Jack Bauer and his experiences portraying this complicated, postmodern, American hero.

Carlos Bernard (as Tony Almeida) and Mary Lynn Rajskub (as Chloe O'Brian) are partners, running buddies, and dramatic foils for the Jack Bauer character. Each one has a cult following. They are so integral to the show that Tony Almeida has been brought back from what appeared to be his certain death at the end of Season 5 to re-emerge again in Season 7. Here "Tony" and "Chloe" give readers special insights from exclusive interviews we conducted with Bernard and Rajskub just before the start of Season 7.

We begin this chapter with excerpts from lengthy discussions we held on the set of *24*, in Chatsworth, California, with the key members of the creative team: Joel Surnow and Robert Cochran, cocreators of *24*, whose vision infuses the soul of the show; Howard Gordon, the current executive producer and show runner; and writers Evan Katz and Manny Coto. These are the people who think up the impossible dilemmas, weave the complex plotlines, imagine the scenes you've never seen before, and breathe dramatic life into each of the characters, making us care about what happens to Jack, Tony, Chloe, President Palmer, and all the rest.

Over and over again, the creative team told us that they have no specific political or ideological agenda. True, Joel Surnow has made no secret of his conservative views. But he is fundamentally a master storyteller and entertainer, as is his partner Robert Cochran. Together they worked for years on the cult hit *La Femme Nikita*, which has interesting resonances in *24*. The publicists of *24* take pains to point out that only two of fourteen members of the current writing/producing team are conservatives; the rest consider themselves one or another shade of liberal or moderate. No matter what their political leanings, the whole team is committed to telling stories through *24* that address how the characters respond to some of the most pressing political, moral, and philosophical issues of our day. In the discussions that follow, they delve into the heart of *24* and reveal the dynamics behind this show's mass appeal. ■

There Is Nothing Like It on TV

Joel Surnow, gracious even amid the frantic first days of shooting Season 7, clearly had some serious thoughts on his mind as he talked frankly with us about what makes 24 so qualitatively different from almost everything else on television. He also relished engaging in the show-as-politics discussion, telling us that the famous—or infamous—profile of him written by Jane Mayer for the New Yorker *(see Chapter 1) was a "rip piece," and wondered out loud about whether the series may have run the course of its television life.*

Surnow's creative instincts and his extraordinary ability to translate them into compelling television led him from episodes of shows like Miami Vice *and* The Equalizer *to the creation (with Robert Cochran) of the award-winning series* La Femme Nikita *(1997–2001), in many ways an inspiration for* 24. *He has garnered eight Emmy nominations and two wins for his work on* 24, *including the 2006 Outstanding Drama award.*

Great acting, good stories, and great writing obviously distinguish *24*. But, beyond that, people say *24* has changed television forever. Why?

No other show in the history of television has been a suspense thriller. There are dramas—talking head dramas or police action shows—but this is suspense. This is John le Carré on TV. Also, terrorism has not been done, nor has there been a character like Jack Bauer, a guy who wins and loses at the same time and who is politically incorrect but taps into everyone's id. Then, too, there's the lack of a happy Hollywood ending. That's what gives *24* a different spin from what has been on television before.

You might add that the show seems to be ahead of the culture, as was the case when you cast Dennis Haysbert as the nation's first Black president in Season 1.

True, but that was a creative decision, a way to raise the stakes, and not one based on political correctness. We were writing the first season in the aftermath of Rodney King [the black LA motorist beaten by white police officers whose subsequent acquittal in 1991 sparked a terrible riot on the streets of LA]. It was also a time when people started talking about Colin Powell as a potential presidential candidate. So there was this confluence, and the time seemed right for our storytelling purposes to use this context to make the stakes higher.

You and your fellow producers often remind fans and detractors alike that the show has no political agenda. It's simply entertainment—albeit amped-up entertainment. Nevertheless, the issues raised by the stories are politically charged.

I don't think there's a political angle to it when I say that all of us who were outraged by 9/11 feel to some degree that we are in a war, and that the rules of engagement are a little different than in conventional wars. The show doesn't originate from that idea, but as we get into the stories and our characters find themselves in these urgent situations, we don't default to some politically correct idea that doesn't make sense in the context of the story. If there is a nuclear bomb going to go off in a city and a guy can tell you where it is, I don't know how you don't do what we do. If you extrapolate that into a political argument, you can say that's a false premise, and I would agree with you. I also agree that you should pay the price if you do violate human rights. But there's the letter of the law, and then there's the reality of the street, as any cop can tell you. You may have to do something illegal, but you do it anyway, because that's just the rule of the jungle. We're just showing a really hard-core guerrilla war that's being fought on the streets of America, and you do what it takes to save innocent life. This is neither a left nor a right approach.

Even if you don't build the show on a political premise, *24* is certainly championed by conservatives.

What conservatives like about it, from I have been told, is that it depicts radical Islam as a threat in an unashamed, unapologetic, and unfalsified way. The left seems to take issue with America, the right seems to take issue with radical Islam, if I were to break it down really simply. The show does not blame America first. It says, "These are the enemies"—plain and simple. And that's what conservatives like about the show—and they can't see it anywhere else in Hollywood.

So then aren't people right to connect your publicly stated conservatism with *24*'s point of view? Just as Jane Mayer famously—or infamously—did in her profile of you in the *New Yorker*?

That hogwash? It was ridiculous. I think it was just a rip piece based on her personal agenda. She came in to do an article about what it's like to be a conservative in Hollywood, but the result was a teaser headline on the cover that said, "Torture on *24*." But shame on me. I should have known better. I had my ego stoked: They were going to do an article about me in the *New Yorker* and that's a big deal. But the piece was agendized, poorly written, and full of innuendo. She was trying to connect the dots: Joel Surnow is a friend of Rush Limbaugh; there is torture on *24;* so they must be in the arms of the Bush White House. But as is so often the case when there is a fluff piece about how things are done behind the scenes, they are wrong. I have no clue about what's really going on at the White House and she had no clue as to what really goes on here.

Some viewers read a certain theological dimension into the show—Jack Bauer as a Jesus figure, for example, suffering on our behalf. But Jack does terrible things. So is he going to go to heaven or hell?
JB as JC? [chuckling]. I think heaven for sure, isn't he? Jack's moral certainty—is that evil? He is fundamentally good, with a very clear sense of right and wrong—and wrong must be punished. He does everything out of a love of goodness and freedom and saving innocents.

Season 6 suffered an unusual amount of criticism from its fans, and the ratings dropped a bit. Was it that people were getting inured to the violence and the counterintuitive plot twists? Or that we are now generally less fearful than we were post-9/11? Or that, in these days of the short attention span, people tend to lose interest more quickly?
People say we have shorter attention spans, but look at *Harry Potter.* People sit down and read hundreds of pages at a time. Now that's commitment. It shows people still want a good story.

As for the other points, I think there's just a natural erosion of any show. Were people less interested in *ER* after six seasons because they overcame their fear of being sick? After six years of the show, we only went down 7 percent in real numbers and we were opposite *Heroes,* the biggest hit of the year. I just think that there are some people—and I'm among them—who reach a certain saturation point with any show after seeing it X number of years. But we buck the conventional wisdom that viewers watch only eight or nine shows a season, even when it comes to a hit series like *ER.* Our show has viewer commitment and we are acquiring people who watch all *24* episodes—*and* buy the DVDs.

Still, there is probably some saturation, and in some ways the show is probably done. I thought *The Sopranos* went two years beyond its time; I didn't really know what Tony Soprano was about anymore. Our life has gone on for 144 episodes. How many more people can Jack Bauer beat up, and how many more doors can he knock down, and how many more times can he save the world? Yet that is the show and the business of doing television requires that you keep going.

But the window of story possibilities gets narrower and narrower with the passage of time. When you have done everything, where do you go without repeating yourself? So in Season 6 there was probably some repetition setting in for the first time.

Are you optimistic that you can overcome those hurdles for the new season?

I don't know. Season 7 has been the hardest season we've had to create, because we want to try and find a new space and a new way to tell the story. So we've changed it in a big way. We got rid of CTU, and the story now takes place in Washington, D.C. It's a new look, a new president, a new cast, and new everything. Will that do it? Or will that be just window dressing? Let's see. ■

A Creator's View:
How *24* Became *24*

Creating the characters and story lines that drive television's most adrenalized show is a continual—and immense—challenge. It takes a team, of course, but it all has to flow out of a single, highly focused, tightly controlled vision. For Robert Cochran, cocreator of 24, it has everything to do with developing and maintaining the highest level of suspense possible. In this virtual master class in screenwriting, Cochran takes us directly into this process, telling us about how he and his collaborators create the character-driven stories, ratchet up the tension, and then watch what happens. It's a strict yet highly improvisational process, in which hour-by-hour plot decisions often depend on how a character develops and what an actor does with the part.

The story of how Robert Cochran and his longtime writing partner Joel Surnow came up with the concept over pancakes one morning has now become legend (see our introduction to Chapter 1). Less well known, perhaps, is how 24 was influenced by their earlier collaboration on the TV cult series La Femme Nikita, *referenced by Cochran here. In* Nikita, *the heroine carries out ruthless antiterrorist work on behalf of a secret government agency, all the while struggling to keep her moral integrity. It, too, had a complex plot structure more commonly associated with quality spy fiction than standard television drama.* 24 *is in a creative space all its own, of course, and here is why.*

Once you and Joel Surnow worked out the basic premise of the show—that characters would have to stay up for twenty-four hours to deal with parallel crises in their personal and professional lives—what came next?

Creating a pilot episode that would take the elements we knew we had to have to tell a coherent story while leaving a little bit of an open end so that we could sell a second episode—even though we didn't really have too much of an idea what the next episodes would be at the time. Our challenge was basically to come up with that scene that makes people want more, one episode at a time. We weren't trying to revolutionize television—I wasn't, anyway—we were just trying to get the story right and leave enough threads so that we could come up with another episode and then another one. As it turned out, it's been 144 so far.

Can you give us an example of a scene that "made people want more" even though, at the time, you didn't know what "more" was going to be?

An example that people often find amusing or hard to believe or both: In the pilot, there was a phone call to Senator Palmer. He answers the phone and he says, "What? If you print that, I'll end your career. That's outrageous." And he slams the phone down. His wife comes up to him and says, "What was that about?" He says, "I don't want to talk about it," and walks out of the room.

Well, we didn't have any idea what that phone call was about. We just thought that's a cool thing to have happen. We all will want to know, so we'll have to think of something some day. But right now, we don't have to think of it. Eventually, of course, we did pay it off.

Speaking of President Palmer, how did you come up with the idea of an assassination attempt?

As we were planning the pilot, we had movies like *In the Line of Fire* and *The Day of the Jackal* in mind—movies with assassinations. But in those movies the target wasn't actually present. We wanted to ratchet up the tension by having the viewers identify with the character. The more you want him to survive, the more tension there is.

So a character who was either the president or running for president came to mind. We made him African-American, I think, because as horrible as it would be for a presidential candidate to be assassinated, if he was an African-American it would be even more horrible, particularly if the assassination were done in LA. Again, we were trying to raise the stakes as high as we could for the sake of the tension and the suspense.

In addition to being very well cast, in the person of Dennis Haysbert, David Palmer really struck people as presidential.

Yes, they wished they could vote for him.

How did you create that in the character?

You want to be rooting for the hero, which means the person Jack Bauer is trying to save has got to be worth saving. That suggested a character who was noble by the standard of politics. He's not perfect. That phone call indicates he has skeletons in his closet, but he's a good man. You want to feel he'd be a good president; otherwise, some of the air goes out of the balloon about saving him.

President Palmer's wife, Sherry, played by Penny Johnson Jerald, quickly became quite a popular secondary character. Did you know that she'd turn out to be as evil as she did?

No, absolutely not. We didn't even know if she'd be a major player in the show. In the pilot, she was just a presidential wife, but not a Lady Macbeth. The kind of stories we like to tell usually do have an element of the perverse in them, and she started playing that stuff so beautifully that we just gave her more and more to do. Pretty soon, she took off as a character and it was great for the show and fun to write. She did a great job and we loved writing that stuff with all of Sherry's scheming and intrigues.

Then there was Palmer's successor, Charles Logan, a president whose abject cowardice and incompetent decision making in Season 4 were revealed as a cover for his treason in Season 5.

It goes back to the point of creating the best story—one that is riveting, that grabs you. If that means Jack Bauer has to torture somebody under certain circumstances, then we'll do that. If it means the president is bad, we'll do that, too. We didn't know Logan would turn out to be the mastermind behind everything, but Gregory Itzin, the actor who plays Logan, did such a great job as a weasel that we wanted to write to that.

You and the creative team develop wonderful characters, some of whom become very popular with the audience. Yet you still have the guts to kill them off. How do you make the decision to do that?

The show is about suspense and tension. Historically, a lot of television has been what I would call pseudo-tension. People are in danger, they're in jeopardy, and you go, "Oh, gosh, I wonder how they're going to get out of it this time?" It's fine. But we're trying to do something a little edgier. We don't want people going, "I wonder how they're going to . . ." We want people going, "Oh, my God!"

To get that reaction, you have to spill some blood. The signature moment for us, as well as for the audience, was when Teri, Jack Bauer's pregnant wife, was shot dead at the end of the first season. If the people you kill don't mean anything to the audience, it has no impact. Therefore, you kill people the audience cares about. First of all, that jolts them and lets them know anything is possible. And, secondly, it keeps that suspense as high as you can ratchet it.

So anything could happen?

It's more than that. In the writing room, somebody will say, "Well, what's the one thing that *cannot* happen?" Everyone knows a TV series would never let a nuclear bomb be set off in LA. Well, then it's going to go off. We've got to do it. What can't possibly happen has been a major source of ideas for us.

Which brings us to the controversy about how closely *24* relates to reality. Everyone knows it's just a show but why, then, is it also perceived as being so realistic?

When George Tenet left the CIA, he wrote a book and started lecturing. At one of his talks, I'm told, someone said, "Well, Mr. Tenet, it's all fascinating and everything. But what's it *really* like to work at the CIA?" And he said, "Watch *24*." Secretary of Homeland Security Michael Chertoff is also a fan of the show, and *he* has called the show "very realistic."

Now this is interesting because, on the face of it, the show is *not* realistic. I mean, the technology and stuff we make up. And the pace of things is absurd. More stuff happens in an hour than could happen in a lifetime. So what's real about the show? The answer is that it's realistic psychologically and emotionally. We collectively have the sense that another 9/11 could happen at any moment; that if you make the wrong call about a driver's license, or about a person coming through the metal detector, that might lead to another plane crashing into a building.

The sense of tension created by having responsibility for possible dire consequences, and having to make impossible choices as a result, is a reality for the people doing security-related work. And that, to me, is what we're trying to do as storytellers. I don't care whether you can reposition a satellite in eight minutes. What I do care about is the emotional and psychological struggles and dilemmas that all these people must go through, with Jack Bauer leading the charge. If we get that right, then it will seem real to people.

So torture on the show happens because it grabs viewers emotionally?

My personal feeling is that there are very narrow, yet definable, circumstances when torture is justified morally. It may well be that those circumstances rarely occur in the real world, which is great. I hope they don't. People who work in the national security area have assured us that those circumstances simply don't come up in the way we depict them on the show. And I'm truly glad.

But that doesn't take away the possibility. If you can save thousands of innocent lives by inflicting pain on a person who's responsible for the jeopardy, and you *don't* do it, then you're saying, "My conscience is too pure to inflict pain on this person, but it's not too pure to allow these thousands of people to die." Now, that's a conscience I can't wrap my mind around.

We will ask you the same question we asked Joel Surnow: How far can Jack Bauer go in fighting evil without becoming evil himself? Will he end up in heaven? Or in hell?

If you watch the show, you know he's paying a price both in terms of what happens to him and in terms of how he feels, because he's not 100 percent certain all the time that he's doing the right thing. So Jack is living in purgatory. Whether he ends up going to heaven or hell isn't clear yet.

But you have put your finger on the right question, and we asked it of ourselves when we did *La Femme Nikita*, and we ask it of ourselves now: How far can you go fighting evil without becoming evil? Without becoming the thing you're fighting?

What's the answer?

I don't know. I don't think there is an answer. The show is highly situational, and constantly in a gray area. I think if we *had* found the answer, there would be no show. ■

A Fictional Version of Issues You Read about on the Op-Ed Page

Three Members of 24's Creative Team Discuss the Stories They Tell and How They Tell Them

*E*ach episode of 24 is the product of multiple creative ideas and inputs from a large team of writers, directors, and producers. While the first episodes of Season 7 were being filmed, we sat down with three key members of the creative team to discuss where the show has been and where it's going: Howard Gordon, the Princeton-educated showrunner of 24, who has been with the show since its inception; Manny Coto, a Cuban-American writer best known in the television community before his arrival at 24 in 2005 for his work as show runner on Star Trek (Coto is described as the "other" conservative on the creative team, besides Joel Surnow); and Evan Katz, a writer/producer who has been with the show since Season 2. What follows are excerpts from a lengthy conversation with these three.

You guys are the key people who create the hour-by-hour, moment-by-moment stories that make 24 tick. In your view, what is 24 all about, at its core?

Howard Gordon: Essentially 24 is the story of Jack Bauer. It's the journey of a guy who is flawed but essentially heroic in a very complicated and lonely world. Jack is a guy whose work life and home life collided to catastrophic effect, but he is trying to knit them back together. Every season has marked a step in the evolution of this guy's life. The contract we have with our audience was formed when Jack lost everything, including his wife, tragically at the end of the first season. After that, anything could happen.

The ideas and the characters on the canvas of a season of 24 are pretty mythic. We certainly explore power and the price of power. Both Jack and David Palmer are powerful men. Palmer is a leader; Jack is a soldier or a policeman. And, in some ways, they occupy points on the same axis. Their families have paid very steep prices for their acquisition of power or for their heroic pursuits.

These themes are a bit Shakespearean. People are always trying to do things for the right reasons in their own minds and yet they become impossibly tangled up and twisted. Shakespeare dealt with kings and princes. We deal with presidents, generals, and foot soldiers.

Manny Coto: There is one grand theme that runs through the series: What price is it proper to pay—morally, culturally, and spiritually or philosophically? Where is the line that we cross into immorality in the defense of our country when faced with evil? Where is the moral boundary? These questions have a lot to do with the torture debate, of course. They are also questions that have been asked since the end of World War II, when the United States dropped two nuclear bombs on civilian populations. Those actions are still being debated now, and that's the kind of debate that the show engages in actively.

Evan Katz: One of the key internal engines of our show is we present a series of impossible dilemmas. For instance, with a lot of shows on TV the engine is, "Who done it?" But instead of asking "Who done it?" we ask, "What would you do? How far would you go? What would you do if you had to kill three hundred people in a mall in order to save twenty thousand?" We are very much about these ridiculously impossible dilemmas. That, in fact, is why we get to torture. It's not as if we decided we are going to be the "torture show." It was a natural outgrowth of putting Jack in seemingly impossible positions and asking the question: How far would you go?

Some critics have called 24 a promotional tool for the Bush administration's war on terror. Yet it brings up critical issues relating to constitutionality in a time of crisis, human rights, civil rights, privacy, and so on. Rush Limbaugh loves it, but so do Bill Clinton and Barbra Streisand. How does the political stuff play out in the writers' room?

Evan Katz: The writers span a wide political spectrum. Joel Surnow, is a very vocal conservative. On one level, you could look at the show as a reflection of that. But on the other hand, the show depicts a mainstream conservative nightmare. For example, corporations run by evil, white men are always the villains.

Howard Gordon: I don't think the show was perceived as right wing until Joel went public with that *New Yorker* article [Gordon is referring to the Jane Mayer piece reprinted in Chapter 1]. No one ever accused us of being a mouthpiece for the Bush administration until Joel's politics became public; the only politics we had was the politics of a good story. From the beginning, this show could have been accused of having unabashedly left-leaning ideas, like a black president.

Manny Coto: The bad guys always turn out to be white guys after oil. So you can make the argument that this is a supremely left-wing show. A plot may start off looking like Muslim terrorists are doing all the evil acts, but then we find out that behind the Muslims are the white guys. The only thing that's right wing about the show is that you have a guy who's willing to defend his country against bad people. If that's right wing, there's a bigger discussion that we need to have over all this. Season 5 featured a corrupt president launching a war for oil. It could have been written by Michael Moore.

Howard Gordon: I think what we do is really point out the complexity of the situation. Hopefully, we ask compelling enough questions, but there never really is a right answer. I think we have been a little bit ahead of the curve of the national debate, or at least we have presented a fictional version of many things that you read about in op-ed pieces every day.

Evan Katz: We had a wicked debate last year, remember? Would the president fire a nuke at a supposed enemy country? I think that the question of how to retaliate after the suitcase nuclear bomb is a good reflection of the way the show works. You had a weak president who didn't want to do anything, and then you had a guy who seemed at first rabid, powerful, wanting to nuke a country that wasn't officially involved in the attack. We had really spirited debates, not about whether it was the right thing to do, because it was rhetorical, but what would we do? If that character did that, would the audience hate him?

Talk to us a little more about the Jack Bauer character. What makes him the defining superhero of the early twenty-first century?

Howard Gordon: Jack is about trust. And Kiefer really picked up on this and plays this part naturally. When Jack says something and gives his word to somebody, those bonds become sacred, inviolable. One of the things critical to understanding Jack is that he isn't just fighting terrorists. He's also fighting the bureaucracy, which is alternately incompetent or corrupt. Jack's goal is always to stop innocent loss of life and to do the right thing. It can be debated how he gets that done, but he gets it done, often in spite of a corrupt or ineffective bureaucracy.

Evan Katz: Jack is an interesting character because he never really does anything in the interest of self-preservation. He doesn't fear sacrificing himself. This is very different than James Bond, for example, where personal sacrifice is never a real question.

Manny Coto: Every year Jack seems to edge a little bit more toward the dark side, and he becomes more prone to do bad things—like in Season 5, when he shoots the wife of one of the guys he is trying to get information from.

Howard Gordon: One thing Kiefer was specific about, and we feel the same way, is that Jack is a self-loathing, burdened guy in a very heavy place. This character has been kicked in the teeth, in the chest, and in the head so many times. And you can't get any lower than last year [Season 6]. Consequently, for Season 7, we made a very conscious attempt to start him out actually having gone through the darkness and stepping out the other side to a place of peace. He is resigned and self-loathing, but he is also OK. He has a line in the first episode, something like, "I can sleep at night. It took a while to get there, but I can sleep." And that's where he is. He doesn't owe anybody any apologies. He's not carrying that heaviness anymore. Because it was really becoming very onerous for Keifer to play, and frankly to watch, too.

Evan Katz: At the beginning of every year we talk about being true to what Jack has been through psychologically and where all that should have placed him. We are not one of those shows where the character doesn't change. We were really boxed in last year [Season 6] because really, Jack was dead in many different ways. Last year we purposely did not do a cliffhanger that put him in an even worse situation, because we wanted to clean the slate.

Manny Coto: We wanted to give him leukemia.

Howard Gordon: We actually contemplated that. People may have compared Jack to Jesus, but he is much more like Job. He has a family, and then he loses them one by one. He has this redemptive moment with Audrey, he hangs up his spurs and his guns and he says I'm going to put on a suit. But he is always drawn back in. He loses Audrey in tragic fashion. By last year, Jack had been stripped bare. He was praying for his own death. He was drawn back in, following a nuclear blast. And then the distaste of having to kill Curtis added to this list of terrible things. He would say, "I can't do this anymore," but he had to do it.

Then we went into some of Jack's past and discovered the parts of his destiny that were defined by his tragic past. We find out he had this first love, who he lost to his brother. His brother is jealous of him. Those are mythic elements. We always thought King Lear was going to be the story. Let the father be this guy who Jack disappointed, a guy whose father wanted him to have a certain destiny that Jack didn't share, and a brother who is the lesser man but who took up the father's mantle, even though he never quite won the father's respect. That was a story we always had in our back pocket and never found a place to tell it until last year, when we finally got the chance.

You know, we start every year saying, how much more can we really do with this? Every character in any drama needs to want something. And the challenge is that Jack Bauer has now lost everything. And if a character has lost everything, there is really nothing driving him any more. So we have to start giving him something back, arming Jack with something to want again, giving him reasons to be human. That's what we are doing this year. We start with Jack being called to testify before a Senate committee. In a sense he's fighting for his legacy. ■

Kiefer Sutherland on Jack Bauer

*K*iefer Sutherland, the actor, and Jack Bauer, the character he plays on
24, are indelibly intertwined in the public mind. Sutherland was "born to
play Jack Bauer," as the show's cocreator Joel Surnow has said. Here we
present some of Kiefer Sutherland's most provocative thoughts about himself and about Jack Bauer, drawn from the handful of major interviews he
has given over the last few years, including sitdowns with Larry King,
Charlie Rose, Rolling Stone, and others. A profile of Sutherland, from a
recently published biography, can be found in Chapter 2.

On when he had his first inkling that he wanted to become an actor:
One year the theater department in my high school put on *Anything Goes,* and
me and the guys in the class went to go laugh at it. But it was really good. I was
amazed. Then, when I saw my mother in a production of *Who's Afraid of Virginia
Woolf?,* I realized I wanted to act. Somewhere between the first and second acts,
someone I had known as my mother became somebody else. That had a very
profound effect.

On leaving school at seventeen to strike out on his own:
My parents weren't exactly pleased with my decision to act, but I think my
mother was so sure I was going to spend a large part of my life in prison that
she was relieved.

**On his checkered success during the 1980s and 1990s and his "second
chance" with *24*:**
I've been up and down the ladder so many times, it's a relief I didn't hit the
ground. Now, on any given night, more people watch *24* than have watched
any single film I have ever made.

**On his lifelong love of playing the guitar and the pleasure of owning his
own studio, Iron Works Music, which actively promotes young musicians:**
I've been in a bunch of bands and that's what I wanted to do earlier in my life,
but I just wasn't good enough. So now I collect guitars. And even now, when
all the professional musicians leave my studio, late at night, that's when I go
in with one light on, and get lost playing for hours, because I love it.

   If you were to give me the choice of who to be for a day, John Lennon or
James Dean, I'd rather be John Lennon, easy. Without hesitation. James Dean
needed a crew of ninety people and a script to make a film. And John Lennon
only needed a guitar to make a song. And the song could get written in a day,
and recorded in a day, and the film would take you fifty days. And between the

Beatles or the Rolling Stones? For me, the Beatles. For the craftsmanship and the impact they made on music. . . . I could drive across the country and listen to *The White Album* the entire way.

On his checkered love life:
I'm really a hopeless romantic at heart. Or maybe I'm just hopeless!

On what made him decide to undertake the role of Jack Bauer:
The first time I read the very first script, I remember at the very top it said all events take place in real time and I was like yeah, yeah, yeah. But my real attraction to the piece was that I thought the character of Jack Bauer was beautifully rounded.

This was a very highly trained, very dedicated man, who had flaws. This was a man who was in charge of the safety of millions of people, and he couldn't keep his own fifteen-year-old daughter at home and she wouldn't listen to what he was saying. This was someone who would always carry a level of failure with him, in his ability not only to do his job but to protect his family and be the kind of person that he wanted to be.

When I was offered *24*, it came like a saving grace. I owe it a lot. When something like *24* happens, you bow your head and say thank you.

On what, for him, the show is all about:
I think at the heart of it, the show really isn't about terrorism. The show is about the interaction of these people. In Season 1, for example, it wasn't as much about the assassination threat as it was about the relationship that developed between Jack Bauer and the incumbent President Palmer, and the relationship between me and my wife and me and my daughter. . . . Terrorism was the scenario that was created to create a heightened sense of reality.

On *24* and real-world politics:
I can tell you one thing. We had the first African-American president on television [in Season 1], and now Barack Obama is a serious candidate. That wouldn't have happened eight years ago. Television is an incredibly powerful medium, and it can be the first step in showing people what is possible. [In Season 7, the show, although set in 2015, will feature a female president.]

Yes, there are bad guys, including people who are working within the United States government who are doing things that are not on the up and up, and that are doing things that are not sanctioned by Congress, and the writers have delved into that. And that is a very risky area to go into in this country. The writers are seemingly fearless in their ability to take on what they believe to be real issues.

On what it is about Jack Bauer that makes him so popular:
Nothing's for free. He loses. He can save the president and he can save his daughter, but he loses his wife. He can be incredibly proficient and have the

responsibilities of the world on his shoulders, but he can't handle a sixteen-year-old girl. And I think people can really relate to that. He also doesn't deal with all of the situations he faces in a politically correct way. In a world of people who are second-guessing so many situations, from their own politics to the way they live their lives, this is someone who actually knows that he can make a mistake, but believes in his heart so deeply that he's correct in what he's choosing to do, that he's going to act upon that.

On Jack Bauer's ambivalence about what he does:
I think he absolutely has a problem with a lot of the things that he does. One of my favorite things in all of the seasons was a scene that he had in the pickup truck where he just starts to cry . . . at the end of one of those days, and the weight of what he not only was responsible for, but the way with which he carries some of the things out, absolutely has to bother him.

On making the kind of choices Jack Bauer is asked to make:
He makes a choice—like shooting a man in the leg—because there is very little time with which to figure out and solve a situation. Do I morally agree with handling a prisoner like that? Absolutely not. It's in the context of this show. But at some point down the line, Jack is going to have a problem with what he did as well, and I love that about that character. He makes choices based on instinct, he makes them based on previous experience. But in the very quiet moments, where he has to live with himself, he will ask himself, Do you think God will forgive me for what I've done? And his answer to himself is no.

On why the character of Chloe is so loyal to Jack Bauer:
Because she thinks he's right. She has a very strong perception, just as Jack does, of what is morally correct and what is not, and what is tolerable and what is not, even though they articulate it in very different ways. And they have, I think, a very healthy contempt for authority. They go about usurping authority in two very different ways. But they need each other.

On torture in reality and torture as portrayed on 24:
For me on a personal level, I think torture is wrong. Someone was explaining to me why they thought Abu Ghraib was a justification [for the notion] that if you're going to fight terrorism, this is how you have to do it. And I think that's wrong. I think you have to absolutely go and show people that there is a better way and you're going to teach them about democracy; you have to follow that all the way down the line. That's my personal view.

On those who have criticized the show harshly:
I've read and seen a lot of silly stuff. If you don't like it, don't watch it. It's a television show. Yes, I believe in the Constitution of the United States. I believe in due process. I do not believe in torture. In the context of our show, these are unbelievably extreme events that within matters of hours the entire place will

be gone. It's a fantasy about that, and those are the devices that we use in the fantasy. Again, for anyone who's got a problem with it, there's five hundred channels on the telly. Use one of the others.

On how he finds new aspects of Jack's character every year:

A small example is the whole reintroduction of Audrey as a character and myself as a character who is alive. Every scene that I had with her, I wanted three beats or three lines to really play how much he loved her and how much he wanted to be with her, and the fourth beat would always be, "I can't. The second this is over, I have to disappear." And then the next beat, the new measure would be, "I love her, I love her, I love her, I can't. I love her." I know it sounds really simplistic, but it's not an easy thing to keep that meter in your head. Or maybe it is for others. It's not for me. It takes me a minute to get into that groove, but I remember when it worked, [director] Jon Cassar turned around and went, "What was that?" It was just a complexity of playing two things at the same time. . . . This has taught me to kind of try and find a blend of both.

On the inner tensions of acting on *24*:

There's a point that I get to where I just go, "F--- it." It's selfish and self-absorbed and it's a dangerous thing, thinking that if you work really hard, you should be able to reward yourself by going out and getting s---faced. I should be able to wake up in the morning without going, "Oh, no! Where's my boot?" Or "Where am I?" Or "One of your friends didn't happen to bring my car home, did they?" It's not a very clever way to live, and I don't want to live like that. But it's the kind of trade you have to make.

On the possibility of *24*, the movie:

The show is big enough in itself: but *24*, the movie? Bring it on! ■

Geek Chic: The Awkward Allure of Chloe O'Brian

*B*efore she joined the cast of 24, Mary Lynn Rajskub was best known as a comedienne and actress in movies like Punch Drunk Love—*an unlikely choice as a main character on a tension-filled TV thriller. But Rajskub's quirky Chloe O'Brian quickly became popular with fans. Since her first appearance in Season 3, Chloe has evolved into one of Jack's most reliable and dedicated collaborators. But her appeal is based on much more than a partnership with Jack. Chloe's idiosyncratic facial expressions provide off-beat comic relief between terror attacks and torture. Her touching scenes with coworkers, like ex-husband Morris and fellow techie Edgar, have given us some of the show's most moving moments. And she has simultaneously become a pinup for male viewers (Rush Limbaugh once planted a very public kiss on her) and an assertive role model for female fans. We spoke to Rajskub in the offices of 24 at the start of Season 7.*

How did you make the transition from comedy to this sober TV show?
Being part of such a serious show was something I never imagined. I'd played quirky before but not aggressive-quirky.

When I originally got the call for *24*, I had just had a really bad audition for *CSI*, and I was feeling down. I hadn't watched the show and I thought to myself, "I'm not doing it." But my agent said, "They really want to see you. You should go in."

But when I watched some tapes of the show, I thought it was cool. Then I talked to my mom. She had been watching it since Season 1 and she said, "You have to go on it."

My mom is a total Nielsen viewer: totally Midwest, totally middle/working class. She loves her TV. But she's also very discerning. And she got *24* right away and had watched it from the very beginning.

So I went in. The part wasn't written yet, so all my character—Chloe—was given to say was just "Yes, Jack" and "No, Jack." And I thought, "I'm not going to do this." But I met Joel Surnow in the hallway afterward, and he said, "I know there's not a part written there. But you're great. I want to write a part for you." It was like a total dream come true for an actor.

How did you manage to maintain a comedic quality in such a serious show?

After a few episodes I thought I was going to be fired because I was too weird. So I started trying to fit in a bit more. And Joel came up to me and said, "What are you doing?" And I said, "I've got to fit into the tone of the show." And he said, "Don't do that. You stick out, but that's why we like it."

***24* is an action thriller, but it's also a workplace drama with Chloe as one of the central players. How did you come up with that socially awkward character that people recognize and identify with?**

Really, it's my own social awkwardness. I could never work in an office. The closest I ever came to communicating with other people was waiting tables. And the interface between me having to render a service and communicate with other people is a little awkward. Plus I'm really bad at organizing. I get stressed out just writing files and putting them in folders. The simplest task is completely overwhelming to me. So to play somebody who's really good at that and also in the middle of all this office politics is very cool. The difficult part is playing within the constant level of intensity that always surrounds CTU.

What about Chloe's relationship with Jack? Can you explain why she's so dedicated to him?

Chloe is very smart and incredibly gifted at computers, but she's not so good at living in the real world. I think, like *24* viewers, she wishes that she was a little more like Jack. She admires him for his courage and for living by his own beliefs, even if they're insane sometimes.

How do you feel being cast in a show that is perceived as political?

I like to think of the show as fantasy and I'm glad that people, for the most part, don't take it seriously. When I was in Europe, there was one guy who was really worked up. He kept saying, "So you think Jack's a hero? Is that what a hero's like to you? Why doesn't he just reason things out?" And I said, "Because if he reasons things out there's no show. What are you, some kind of Zen master?"

Generally, I try to avoid news and politics. So there's a part of me that doesn't really care. Then there's another part of me that feels like an idiot and thinks I should start having opinions. And another part of me is just excited to be on a show that's so well regarded and that is pushing people's buttons. I think that's the mark of a good show—that people care about it and want to talk about it.

So the fact that it's perceived as a right-wing show doesn't enter into the equation at all?

I definitely feel disconnected from that aspect of it. I'll come on the set and they'll say, "We got a call or letter from West Point, saying to tone down the torture." And I'm like, "People are getting torture ideas? No way."

What about Kiefer? What do you think he brings to the show?

Well, as soon as he's on the set, your pulse quickens—Kiefer's here. I suppose there's a little bit of the celebrity thing and the fact that the boss is here. But there's also a feeling that Jack Bauer has arrived. Even though it's just Kiefer, he brings that aura with him. He is so committed and so intense about it. He talks really fast. He sets the pace. And that all feeds into the energy of the show.

So how does Chloe evolve from here?

I have no idea. After I'm done talking with you, I'm going to go right upstairs and ask them that same question. Every day when I wake up, I wonder what's going to happen to Chloe. Why won't somebody tell me? ■

Resurrecting Tony:
A Chat with Jack's Best Friend

Carlos Bernard, who plays Tony Almeida, is one of the few actors to have been with 24 from the beginning. Untimely deaths are a hazard of appearing in 24. Even so, it came as a shock when Tony was stabbed with a lethal dose of chemicals in Season 5, robbing Jack of one of the few people in whom he could confide.

It's impossible to say whether Tony's apparent death was a factor in 24's subsequent slip in the ratings. But there's no doubt that Tony was important enough for the writers to bring him back for Season 7.

Bernard is an accomplished TV and stage actor, performing in plays by Chekhov, Shakespeare, and other classical and modern playwrights. We talked to Carlos Bernard on 24's set, between shooting scenes for Season 7, and asked him about the important role Tony plays in Jack's fictional life.

What do you think are the key elements that have made Tony so popular with fans?

Obviously, there's been a real evolution of the character through the seven years. But I think one constant has been the contrast with Jack Bauer. Jack is steadfast in the decisions that he makes. He never looks back and doesn't let his actions affect him until the end. But Tony lets the personal issues surrounding his decisions affect him. Because of that, he's not always as good at his job as Jack can be.

Tony isn't an average guy. But he's more of an average guy than Jack is. And I think that's probably why the audience likes him. They can relate to him. Maybe they wish they could be a lot more like Jack, but really they are a lot more like Tony.

You mean Tony is more human?

Not exactly. I mean Tony thinks through the implications before he acts. He considers the consequences for the people involved. Whereas Jack acts without being troubled by the consequences because he knows what he is doing is for the greater good. It only comes back to haunt Jack later on.

And yet, even though these two guys have a completely different approach, they manage to remain friends. How do you feel about your character as a friend of this unusual superhero?

Jack and Tony are working in a world where trust is earned the hard way. And part of the reason they trust each other is because they clash so often. Think of schoolyard fights, for example. More often than not, you end up being really good friends with that person afterwards because there's something that happens when you lay yourself on the line like that. It's the same with Jack and Tony. In basic terms, Tony is one of the few people who will tell Jack to f- - - off. So I think they earn their trust through being straight with each other and disagreeing. I think they are not unlike two brothers who always knock heads but who are there for each other.

It's interesting that you mention trust, because *24* often implies that people in authority are the ones you should trust the least.
Exactly. In the first season Tony was a by-the-book kind of guy. But as the season progressed he quickly learned that's no way to get the job done or to stay alive. He learned that from Jack. And later on, he went even further and broke all the rules himself.

The idea of people in authority using their power for personal gain is a timeless theme. As an actor who has played such roles on stage, do you see such themes reflected in *24*?
All great storytelling reverts to classic roots. And *24* often draws stories straight out of Greek tragedy. You have these people who devote themselves to their country, only to have it thrown back in their face by their government. Hypocrisy—and governments using their soldiers as pawns—goes back to man's earliest story lines.

You've been a victim of the writers' penchant for killing off characters the audience admires. When you died onscreen, did you know you were coming back in Season 7?
Well, we knew it was left open for a reason.

Considering everything you've said about Jack and Tony's relationship, is it possible you were brought back because of your character's ability to act both as a friend and as a moderating influence on Jack Bauer?
I don't know. But I do know that it's the characters—and the relationships between those characters—that make the story relevant. I think that the show runs a risk of losing those relationships when characters die.

As someone who has developed a character for so long, do you find yourself saying to the writers, "Look, this character wouldn't say that or wouldn't do that"?

From Day 1. I even helped choose the character's name. When I joined the show, the character was named Andrew Geller. He was just some upwardly mobile, ladder-climbing, office guy. And I said, why are you sending me this script? Do I look like an Andrew Geller? When Joel Surnow decided to cast me in the role, he said, "Well, we can't call you Andrew Geller." So, literally fifteen minutes before we were shooting the first scene of the pilot we were bouncing names around until we came up with Tony Almeida.

I have also written scenes that the writers have used. And as far as futzing with dialogue, it's always a collaborative effort. The writers are really smart. And they are smart enough to know that any help they can get is great. Part of what makes it so much fun working here is that there is a lot of give and take, and bouncing ideas around.

Do you have any insights into why and how the show works so well? There were questions at first about how long the 24-hour time clock format could be sustained, yet here we are at Season 7.

To be honest, I really don't know. I don't even watch the show; reading the scripts is my watching the show. And when we are working on a season, all I have in my mind is the scene I am working on that day. As far as how it works all together—I have no idea. You can rehearse a comedy in a theater for two months and you don't know how it is going to work until you get out onstage in front of the audience. All I know is it just keeps working.

What kind of influence do you think 24 has had on society, particularly politics and the debate surrounding torture and the war on terror?

Like any good piece of literature or theater, I think the show makes people think. I think it's the job of the media—books, TV, film—to discuss the hot issues of the day and to get people talking about them. But I don't think 24 gives an answer. And I don't think it should give an answer. First and foremost it's entertainment. Otherwise, it's meaningless.

I Choose All of My Roles
with a Pair of Tweezers

*S*hohreh Aghdashloo is an award-winning actress featured in the fourth season of 24 as the character Dina Araz, who is a mother, wife, and member of a terrorist sleeper cell family recently awakened for action in the terrorist bombing mission that is the dramatic basis for Season 4. Although Aghdashloo appeared only in twelve of the twenty-four hours of Season 4, the perfect emotional pitch of her acting (which the New York Times called "painfully realistic") and the intense drama of the moral choices she faces in the story have combined to make hers among the most memorable of the 144 hours that have aired to date.

Born and raised in Tehran, Iran, Aghdashloo began acting at the age of twenty and was, at one point, a prominent Iranian film star. She fled Iran for England in 1978 due to the turmoil of the revolution that would eventually overthrow the pro-Western dictatorial monarch Shah Mohammed Reza Pahlavi and turn Iran into a Muslim theocracy. Aghdashloo studied international relations in hopes of becoming a journalist. But eventually she returned to acting and moved to the United States, where she founded a theater company with her husband, Houshang Touzie. She has since played a wide range of film and TV roles, from Elizabeth in The Nativity Story, a 2006 historical drama about the birth of Jesus, to Nadi in House of Sand and Fog, a contemporary tale about an Iranian family, for which she was nominated for an Academy Award in 2004.

In the 24 plotline, the Araz family first appears to be a typical Los Angeles suburban household. The audience soon learns, however, that all three members of the family are deeply involved with the morning's bombings and that additional attacks are planned for later in the day. While their religion, ethnicity, and nationality are never explicitly stated, the show plays on the viewer's post-9/11 assumptions and biases to imply that the Araz family are Islamic jihadists from somewhere in the Middle East. It is a curious bit of Rorschach trickery: Almost everyone who watches these episodes draws the conclusion that the Araz family is Iranian, or Palestinian, or otherwise Middle Eastern, yet when one watches the episodes closely, there is actually nothing specific said about their ethnic or religious background.

Dina's husband, Navi Araz (powerfully played by a Hispanic actor, Nestor Sarrano), comes across as a stern and controlling patriarch, espe-

cially angered when he realizes their teenage son Behrooz (Jonathan Ahdout—who in real life is from an Iranian Jewish family living in California) has not ended his relationship with his American girlfriend Debbie (Leighton Meester), as he was told to do.

Finding out that Debbie followed Behrooz on a secret delivery, Navi is furious and demands that his son kill her because she knows too much. Instead, Behrooz tries to help Debbie escape. Then Dina steps in. Angry at her son's weakness for not being a true soldier on behalf of their unexplained cause, Dina kills Debbie on his behalf by serving the girl poisoned juice.

The plot gets further tangled—as it always does on 24—when the viewer learns that Dina killed Debbie preemptively because she was afraid of her husband's reaction to their son's disobedience. But Navi does not believe Dina's story and, behind his wife's back, sends Behrooz out with another member of their terrorist cell to be executed for his failures. Behrooz realizes what is happening and runs away, and once Dina learns that Navi arranged to have their son killed, she flees with Behrooz from Navi's violence and control. The plotline reaches a climax as Jack Bauer must save Behrooz from his father in exchange for Dina's giving Jack the critical information he needs about the impending terrorist attacks.

The dramatic story involving the Araz family generated much lively discussion and controversy among viewers, the media, and even within academia. The Araz family's implied ties to Islam and the "terrorist-next-door" plot was so believably performed that it prompted Fox, at the urging of Muslim groups, to televise a public service announcement featuring Kiefer Sutherland and explaining that American Muslims are patriots and good American citizens and shouldn't be stereotyped as terrorists or viewed with suspicion.

In this interview, Aghdashloo discusses her professional journey from Tehran to Hollywood, her search for meaningful roles, her thoughts on stereotypes about submissive Muslim women, and her confidence that 24's viewers are able to distinguish between fiction and reality.

As someone who has been very active in the Iranian-American arts community, you've pointed out that many roles in movies and television stereotype Middle Easterners and you have refused to take them. What drew you to the part of a terrorist on 24?

I first came to America in the 1980s, and while living in Los Angeles, I started looking for acting jobs in Hollywood. The only parts I was being considered for had two lines, like "Ya Allah [Oh God], my baby is dying." This was nothing more than tokenism and certainly did not explore my cultural identity. In another instance I auditioned for a small part and was sent home because I was too beautiful to play a downtrodden Middle Eastern woman. That was how things were back then. That was why I decided to form a theater company with my husband, Houshang Touzie, a great actor/playwright/director, whose popular plays not only helped the theater company survive, but also turned it to the most successful Farsi-speaking theater company outside of Iran. The theater company, nearly twenty years later, still tours around the USA, Canada, Australia, and Europe.

The role of Dina Araz on *24* came years later. Here the character not only had a soul, but was also a rounded person; she was a devoted mother and a dutiful wife as well as being an accessory to terrorism. I chose to play Dina Araz because I am an actor who prefers sophisticated and challenging roles; I also knew I could do a good job. When I first read the script I was fascinated by this woman's ability and courage. My decision was derived from an artistic origin rather than a political origin.

You have said in many interviews that Islam is not a religion that promotes terrorism, but you have also drawn criticism for saying that 99 percent of terrorists are Muslims. Would you like to elaborate?

What I said was, "Not all Muslims are terrorists but unfortunately most of the reported acts of terrorism in the current global climate appear to be from the Muslim communities." In the same way, a few decades ago they were Irish, and before that South American, and so on. I say this because the Islam that I was born into in a previous Iran [under Shah Mohammed Reza Pahlavi] absolutely forbade suicide under any circumstances. So much so that if people committed suicide they were not allowed to be buried in the same cemetery as the others and their relatives had to bury them in a cemetery for suicide cases only.

The script of *24* portrays the Araz family's dedication to a terrorist cause but doesn't explain their motivation and background. Do you think the writers perhaps want to let the viewers assume they are Muslim extremists?

The family's origin and religion, in fact, were never revealed throughout the season. The audience was expected to connect the dots and draw their own conclusions about Dina and Navi's motives. This was part of creating the tension and confusion that characterizes the mood of *24*.

I'm glad that *24* didn't define Dina as a Muslim because, as I said, terrorists have always been around and they have not always fought in the name of Allah. In my humble opinion, I believe that the mission of terrorists is nothing more than to destroy and terrorize those who value freedom and appreciate democracy. These are the people who are incapable of negotiation and seeing another point of view and can never change their minds.

Many people stereotype Muslim women as being submissive and dominated by men, but Dina clearly breaks this mold. Yet at the beginning of Season 4, there are overtones that the Araz family is traditionally patriarchal. What are your thoughts on this and do you think it provides any social commentary?

You are right that there is a general belief that Muslim women are submissive. But, coming from a Muslim society, I have to tell you a little secret: Muslim women are pretty strong and have an enormous influence on their men through pillow talk and other feminine tricks that they learn from their mothers, sisters, and aunts. They allow their men to believe that they are in charge of everything, when actually they are not.

But with regard to the character, Dina lives in America, a modern society. She is allowed to make choices that she believes are right even under the pressure both from her husband and her cause. She is a very independent woman! If we are to assume that she is Muslim, I would want viewers to appreciate that not all Muslim women are the same and our society is full of many kinds of women, just as in any other society.

Since *24* is so popular, many people think it has an influence on actual public opinion and events. Are you concerned about the blurring of lines between fiction and reality?

Here's how I see it: The character Dina kills her son's girlfriend by putting poison in her juice and then shoots her. My own teenage daughter, Tara Jane, and her friends who are also *24* fans, love my cooking and often drink juice at my house. To date, no one has feared that I may do to them what Dina did to Debbie. As far as I'm aware, no Muslim family has killed their son's girlfriend so I would say *24* is indeed a great work of fiction created by the wonderful writers of the show. This leads me to believe that the *24* audience is pretty smart and can clearly distinguish the line between fiction and reality.

You play the role of Elizabeth—whom the gospel of Luke portrays as a relative of the Virgin Mary pregnant by John the Baptist—in the 2006 film, *The Nativity Story*. The film is the story

of the birth of Jesus and had its world premiere at the Vatican. Obviously, this is a very different woman from Dina on *24*. What was your experience playing a historical figure in a film with a Christian point of view? What drew you to this role?

I wanted to play a saint to wash my sins for the lethal tasks I carried out in *24*!

But on a serious note, portraying a pious woman with a good heart devoted to humanity was indeed a great experience. Elizabeth reminded me of my own grandmother who used to take me to the slum areas of Tehran with food and confectionary to distribute among the poor. That is essentially why I wanted to play the part. As an actress, the part and the story are always more important to me than any other element involved. In fact, my approach was more cultural and historical than religious. I researched the role by looking for references to Elizabeth in the New Testament, getting to know her good deeds and her good thoughts, and combined these with my grandmother's physicality. That is how I developed her portrayal.

It has been reported that you wanted to become a journalist when you were younger in order to pursue your interest in social justice. Have your political beliefs and activism informed your decisions to take certain roles?

Having studied politics at a university in the UK and obtaining a BA in international relations, I naturally would look at roles that are offered to me from this point of view. Somehow over the years the work I have been offered and my thinking has met in the middle. So, yes, you could say my interest in social justice has informed my choices. Believe me, I choose all of my roles with a pair of tweezers! ■

Ahmed Speaks: Actor Kal Penn Talks About Racial Profiling and *24*

*A*ctor Kal Penn, *who plays Ahmed Amar, a son in a Muslim family living in a comfortable LA suburb, was born as Kalpen Suresh Modi and raised in Montclair, New Jersey. His recent projects have propelled him beyond his earlier comedic roles, such as Kumar in the cult flick* Harold & Kumar Go to White Castle. *In addition to his role on* 24, *Penn has received critical praise as a dramatic actor in Mira Nair's* The Namesake, *a film about an Indian family trying to adapt to living in America. Penn is also following his strong intellectual interests by teaching classes on race, media, and representation in the Asian American Studies Program at the University of Pennsylvania.*

The plotline of the Season 6 episodes involving the Amar family is that Ahmed's father is accused of terrorism and detained. The Wallaces, Ahmed's sympathetic and protective neighbors, are convinced that the boy has nothing to do with any crimes and take him in. This turns out to be a huge mistake. In a dramatic plot twist, Ahmed is revealed as the terrorist in the family, not his father. Not without some second thoughts, Ahmed turns on the Wallace family, forcing the father to unknowingly deliver a nuclear device, which will explode later in the day—an explosion that Jack Bauer has been desperately trying to head off.

So why would a smart young actor, concerned with media representation of minorities, play the part of the much-stereotyped Muslim terrorist? Penn gave a high-profile interview to New York *magazine about his part in* 24, *in which he was quoted as saying, "I have a huge political problem with the role. It was essentially accepting a form of racial profiling. I think it's repulsive." In our interview, we give Penn a chance to more fully respond to why he took the job, if he thinks the character promotes stereotypes, and what exactly he finds repulsive about Ahmed.*

Tell us a little about what went into your decision to accept the role of Ahmed on *24*.

Contrary to popular perception, my first concern was, "How am I going to overcome such a wonderful acting challenge?" Every single word the character utters, every action, every particular emotion is so foreign to who I am as a person that I welcomed the opportunity to portray him.

Why did you decide to accept a role that you described in *New York* magazine as "a form of racial profiling"?
I think my words were taken a bit out of context in that article, and I also probably should have taken the time to elaborate a little more on that particular issue, so I appreciate the chance to clarify my thoughts. I approached my role on *24* as an incredible acting challenge, first and foremost. But I don't live in a bubble, and I am aware that roles and images do not exist in a vacuum, so I acknowledge that a plethora of social and artistic interpretations of this role are possible—one such interpretation being that of racial profiling.

So do you think the part of Ahmed perpetuates stereotypes?
When groups of people are depicted in a singular way repeatedly over time, I understand that stereotypes can be created and perpetuated. But I don't agree that there is one single interpretation of my role, which reads: "Do not trust your American neighbors if they happen to be brown, or Muslim. They are terrorists." Such a reading of the character is not only morally repulsive, more importantly, it's overly simplistic.

How did you create such a complex and believable character for the show?
I did a significant amount of research into what's been happening in the UK: British-born citizens engaging in acts of violence against their fellow citizens in the name of their particular reading of religion. That's what I based Ahmed on. I looked at patterns in the UK, created a backstory within Ahmed's life, and then discussed this with the directors and writers. As an actor, I think you have to ground your character in reality.

When it comes to terrorism, do you think shows like *24* promote or reflect an "us versus them" mentality?
Based on the definitions of statehood and terrorism (and conventional warfare), terrorists are very much the "other." I mean this strictly in the sense of what terrorism means, and the ways in which terrorists operate outside of accepted norms for conflict resolution. I don't think that terrorists are always constructed as "foreign" or "other" on *24*, but even if they were, I don't think that's too far off from the reality of what's happening. Even domestically, folks like Richard Reid and Timothy McVeigh are very much viewed as "them," not "us."

As one of the best-known Indian-American actors, do you think there is undue pressure on you to be a role model and spokesperson?
Let me ask *you* a question: Why am I described as an "Indian-American" actor? Why does an ethnic signifier precede my professional title? People within and outside of various ethnic and racial communities are deeply passionate on all sides of identity politics. I personally try to disengage from those discussions as much as possible. I find them generally boring because they detract from the ability to play compelling characters. ■

CTU Director Bill Buchanan
Speaks Out

*If Jack Bauer is the ultimate man of instinctive action on 24, his some-
time CTU Director Bill Buchanan is the ultimate man of coolheaded,
thoughtful, cerebral reaction. In the midst of the chaos, violence, and
political and moral madness that is 24, Bill Buchanan appears to be
inspired by the Rudyard Kipling poem "If":*

> If you can keep your head when all about you
> Are losing theirs and blaming it on you . . .
> If you can trust yourself when all men doubt you,
> But make allowance for their doubting too. . . .

*For consummate actor James Morrison, the part of Bill Buchanan
comes naturally. In addition to a long career on stage, in TV, and in
film, Morrison brings a variety of other life experiences to the role.
Perhaps his early training as a circus wire walker or his many years
mastering hatha yoga have contributed to his ability to appear as such a
calming, well-balanced character in the show.*

*As played by Morrison, the Bill Buchanan character exudes dignity,
integrity, and moral conviction. Eminently grounded, he is perhaps the
only person who has ever been able to exert any positive control over
Jack Bauer.*

*A poet, a playwright, and a filmmaker, Morrison is also outspoken
on political and social issues. In the interview that follows, he shared with
us the same kind of frank, common sense, logical thoughts about 24 that
we have come to expect from Bill Buchanan.*

Is 24 "just entertainment" or is it contributing to discussion of important issues?

I'm of the opinion that while the show is not "just entertainment"—it's far too grim and humorless for that—it's hard for me
to take it seriously as social commentary. Sure, it addresses current events and concerns, sometimes artfully, and it explores
important issues, such as big lies and threats. As a thinking
person, I appreciate that. But regardless of genre, those are just
the required elements of good drama.

As for the discussion it may stimulate about the state of the
world or our country's political climate: It still only qualifies as

good drama. I suppose it's a compliment, though a bizarre one, to the artists involved, but when politicians, critics, or policy makers use the show as an example of how we should or should not be operating on a national security level, it only discredits them and reveals the superficiality of their beliefs and their agenda. It's absurd to have to state this, but terrorism and torture existed before *24* came along—in real life and as dramatic devices—and the writers of the show have been very clever and opportunistic in reflecting and exploiting the country's collective consciousness since 9/11.

But I believe very strongly that unless what you do promotes peace, mutual understanding, equal opportunity for all, and in some way helps leave the world a better place for our children, not ideologically but environmentally, it's arrogant to assume that any contribution you're making is significant on any level. As good as *24* may or may not be, I'm not convinced the world at large is necessarily a better place because it's been on the air. The show has the opportunity to make positive contributions. They are doing that now in the form of working to make the production of *24* itself carbon neutral, for instance. The show and its makers are not frivolous or irresponsible, and ultimately their hearts are in the right place—unlike those who hold *24* up as an example of realistic behavior or desirable policy, and even those who consider it "propaganda."

What do you think of the "torture" debate and *24*? Is the show making a subtle argument that torture works? Is it credible to think that soldiers in the field have become more aggressive in interrogation techniques because they have seen it work on *24*?
It's all about context. Torture, in this context, is a dramatic device. Torture in another context is real and wrong. Did *The Deer Hunter* suggest that Russian roulette "worked"? In the context of the movie, perhaps. In another context, probably not. The writers and creators of *24* are dramatists, not polemicists. They're storytellers, not propagandists. Regardless of what anybody says to support their own narrow agenda or attack the show, it's ridiculous to assert that the storylines of *24* are agitprop. I think the only reason this has become an issue at all is because the network that airs the show is Fox and Fox has a propaganda channel masquerading as a news channel. My guess is that, to those with an understanding of, and respect for, objective and fact-based journalism, this makes everything Fox does that might be considered the least bit political completely suspect. While television dramatists are just as subjec-

tive as any other artists, they cannot let their politics or personal opinions outweigh the dictates of the story they're telling and expect to succeed. And it's patently absurd to assume that everyone in the network's employ has the same politics and agenda as their "news" channel.

What is the show telling us about racial profiling? What is your reaction to the role of Nadia and her experiences in the story, as well as in past seasons to the Dina Araz character and to the way the Chinese characters have been depicted?

I don't believe the show is telling us anything except what every other successful television show is telling us: a compelling story. If you have a mind-set that is hungry for fear, even if you sit in isolation it will still be fed without help from anyone, including a TV show. As the Zen master said, "A fish doesn't look for water. A bird doesn't look for the sky." The storylines are, as they say, ripped from the headlines just as is the case with the plot lines of other shows. (Look at all the shows that deal with homicide.) Personally, I'd like to see *24* do a story about fundamentalist Christian terrorists but they aren't nearly as deadly as the current crop of Muslim terrorists. They are every bit as ignorant and insane, but not nearly as deadly. And since *24* is drama, not comedy, they'd do well to stick with the deadliest crop of insane religious zealots and leave the merely foolish ones to the satirists.

What's it like on the set itself? Are people as serious and intense as the show suggests? Given your life in theater, do you think the sense of being "in character" is particularly strong on *24*?

Remaining "in character" can be detrimental to morale on a show like this. We're human beings first; actors second. The best know this and are ultimately the most human in their work between "action" and "cut" and between shots. It's pretend, remember, just an illusion. Like Stanislavski said, "Love the art in yourself, not yourself in the art." I'm pretty sure he was talking to those who take themselves and what they do far too seriously for the good of all involved.

What did you think of Dennis Haysbert as president? What about the parallels to Barack Obama? How do you think a woman president will impact the show in Season 7?

Palmer as president works for me because I can see him being elected. His campaign for the presidency and winning the popular vote is feasible and logical because he's a man of integrity. He's charismatic, intelligent, and honorable. Not that those attributes are required to be elected president, by any stretch, but wouldn't it be nice if they were again someday? That being said, I'm constantly astounded that the ideas put forth on *24* are considered a bell-wether for anything. The great thing about fantasy television is that they don't have to explain how something could have happened. There is no accountability—and that's acceptable in a fantasy world. What is not acceptable is when politicians, our so-called leaders, have no accountability.

Those with half a brain don't need a television show to tell them that it's time to wrest control of the country away from angry, underachieving white men with little regard for the Constitution who consider themselves above the law and put corporate welfare before the people's needs. It's time for a woman or a person of color or a non-Christian to hold the office of president because we are a country founded and built upon the principles of possibility, progress, and, above all, freedom from oppression, and not just because a TV show suggests it's attainable.

Does your experience as a yoga master impact your ability to project the calm, centered character of Bill Buchanan?
The main thing I've learned from my yoga and meditation practice is what it is to be calm and steady under duress. Or rather, how uncomfortable and unnatural it feels when I'm not. That applies to my work as an actor regardless of the nature of the character I'm playing.

What do you think of Jack Bauer's six-year journey from macho superhero to conflicted, existential antihero?
I think what you're seeing is a natural evolutionary process. We change and grow and deepen as we practice something. There is a maturation process going on here—by the writers as they've been able to examine their task and goals more deeply, by the actors who've had a chance to settle into and develop their roles, and, most notably for obvious reasons, Kiefer as Jack. ∎

Stephen Applebaum

Dennis Haysbert on President Palmer: "They Killed Me for the Sake of the Ratings"

Dennis Haysbert, the actor who played President David Palmer in the early years of 24, still casts a towering shadow over the show, even though his character was assassinated several seasons ago.

Haysbert exudes the qualities many Americans would love to see in a president—courageous leadership, the ability to make tough decisions, a strong moral compass, intellect, charisma, and genuine gravitas. A 6-foot-4-inch, middle-aged African-American in real life, Haysbert's fictional backstory as President Palmer makes him an NCAA All-American basketball star while at Georgetown, a U.S. senator from Maryland, and then, ultimately, the first African-American president of the United States. And he has clearly won the hearts and minds of Americans as their favorite fictional president. In a 2006 opinion poll he bested even Martin Sheen, the popular President Jed Bartlet of West Wing fame.

Haysbert's role on 24 is thought by some political and cultural commentators to have helped create the space, if not the inspiration, for Barack Obama's 2008 U.S. presidential bid. But the David Palmer character actually shares more historically with Bobby Kennedy: In the very first episode of 24, we meet David Palmer campaigning for the presidency in the California primary and facing an assassination plot that Jack Bauer is assigned to foil. Bobby Kennedy, of course, was actually assassinated on the night he won the California presidential primary in 1968. In substance, David Palmer is a president who seems much more like Bill Clinton than any other real-life president. And in a long-running subplot, President Palmer must deal with the subterfuges and machinations of his powerful wife Sherry, whose evil schemes go far beyond even the vast right-wing conspiracy's worst imaginings about Hillary Clinton.

Large numbers of Americans disillusioned by the George W. Bush presidency have longed in retrospect for Bill Clinton's approach to leadership. Similarly, 24 fans wish David Palmer could come back to life, having had to endure the decidedly Nixonian evils of President Charles Logan (whose physical resemblance to Nixon is played up by every camera angle), not to mention the comparatively weak leadership of President

Source: © 2007 Independent News and Media Limited. Used by permission.

Wayne Palmer, David Palmer's less capable, less inspiring brother.

The life—and death—of President Palmer has a certain spillover effect outside the realm of TV entertainment. To this day, actor Dennis Haysbert remains unhappy with the creative decision by the writers and producers to assassinate his character. He explains why in the excerpted interview that follows, which originally appeared in The Independent, *a UK-based newspaper.*

"I'M A LITTLE JET-LAGGED, warns Dennis Haysbert, dropping his trim 6ft 4in frame into a chintz armchair in a London hotel. "If I doze off, just yell at me."

The 52-year-old has made a career out of playing characters whom you are convinced would never fall asleep on the job. In America, he is the face of Allstate insurance and the voice of the Military Channel. He is the actor the producers of *24* went to when they wanted a president with a strong moral backbone, and is currently playing the reliable-under-pressure field commander of a counter-terrorist team in David Mamet's hit series *The Unit*. And when the film-maker Bille August needed someone to play Nelson Mandela, in an adaptation of James Gregory's book *Goodbye Bafana: Nelson Mandela, My Prisoner, My Friend*, he contacted Haysbert.

Haysbert's most famous and popular role to date is still President David Palmer. So admired was Palmer, he says, that some commentators in America have written that one of the reasons why Barack Obama now has a chance of being elected to the White House is "because there was a good fictionalized President on television, whom everybody loved in every walk of life."

Filming President Palmer's assassination at the beginning of the fifth season was a deeply unpleasant experience for Haysbert—he wanted the producers to change their mind about killing off the character. But he was not being driven by ego or money, he says. "We have a legacy of killing off our leaders," says Haysbert. "Malcolm X, Dr Martin Luther King, JFK, RFK. . . Why do that to a fictional character that everybody loved, just for ratings?"

When he refused to go back and shoot the scene, one of his best friends from the show, Howard Gordon, was sent to convince him. Was he contractually obliged to return? "No, no, no," Haysbert says. "They had to come to me and I had to say yes." He lets out a long sigh.

When did he start regretting his decision? "I was regretting it while I was doing it," he says. "If I had to do it over again, I wouldn't do it. But then again I don't know what it would have done for *The Unit*, which is also a Fox studio show, if I hadn't gone back. So who knows?"

Since Haysbert's departure, *24* has found itself increasingly under fire over its violence. Kiefer Sutherland's Jack Bauer now uses torture almost as a matter of course to extract information. Haysbert has heard that Ann Coulter—the conservative pundit—and the talk radio host Rush Limbaugh have visited the set, while Vice-President Dick Cheney and the former Defense Secretary Donald Rumsfeld are said to be fans of the series. "Once it got to the torture, I think the show really defeated its own purpose," says Haysbert, "and it has been skewed malignantly in another direction. It's really, really sad that it happened."

The show's Republican-voting creator, Joel Surnow, recently said that *24* "makes people look at what we're dealing with" in terms of security threats. "There are not a lot of measures short of extreme measures that will get it done; America wants the war on terror fought by Jack Bauer. He's a patriot."

But Haysbert says the show is not reflecting the world we live in: "It's exploiting it."

Such has been the concern that, last November, Army Brigadier General Patrick Finnegan, the dean of the United States Military Academy at West Point, and three of the most experienced FBI and military interrogators in America visited the *24* producers and writers to warn them that many cadets now regard torture as a legitimate practice because of what they have seen on the show.

"When you start citing a show," says Haysbert, "when cadets from West Point are starting to say, 'Well, *24* does it, Jack Bauer does it, why can't we?' you've got to say something." ■

"The writers of 24 grasp that when it comes to terrorism we are desperate for answers. Almost maliciously, they dangle something plausible in front of us. Then they yank it away at the last minute and replace it with something utterly outrageous, leaving us with nothing to believe in but the darkness itself."

—Matt Feeney, cultural critic, *Slate.com*

24 and the Politics of Culture

24 is politics and culture joined at the hip. Television fusing uncertain times with unpleasant moral choices. Monday night services for both the conservative faithful and the liberal skeptics.

The use of Jack Bauer to score political debating points should not surprise us. What sometimes surprises is who argues what. There are notable exceptions on both sides of the debate, but political conservatives, who otherwise might be expected to deplore this gory prime-time fare, denounce the way *24* trashes the rule of law, or question why a rogue government agent is lionized have instead found their inner hawk. "You say that nuclear devices have gone off in the United States, more are planned, and we're wondering about whether waterboarding would be a bad thing to do?" asked Rep. Tom Tancredo (R-Colo.) on a TV debate. "I'm looking for Jack Bauer at that time!"

Political liberals who might be expected to champion unfettered freedom of expression and tolerate moral relativism are in revolt against the show's penchant for brutal torture. Some even muse about the need for censorship. Democratic senator Jay Rockefeller (D-W.Va.) has all but threatened it: If broadcasters won't police violence, he says, "the Federal Government must step up."

24 is also part of the debate about political correctness. Perhaps the best example lies in the way the American Muslim community has reacted to the show's negative portrayal—at least inferentially—of Arabs and Muslims as terrorists. "The program's repeated association of acts of terrorism with Islam will only serve to increase anti-Muslim prejudice in our society," said a statement issued by the Council on American-Islamic Relations during Season 6. Not all Muslim groups are troubled. *24* is "quite fair" and an "opportunity for American Muslims to fight the real enemy, Islamism," says M. Zuhdi Jasser, chairman of the American Islamic Forum for Democracy and a former U.S. Navy officer. Sensitive to its image, Fox Television issued a statement saying that, in effect, *24* was an equal opportunity offender. Invoking the wide range of villains that inhabit the show, Fox said that "no ethnic group has been singled out for persecution or blame."

This chapter casts light on how *24* figures in the sharp political/cultural debates of our times. It opens with a column by Maureen Dowd, the Washington-based *New York Times* columnist and verbal agent provocateur. Dowd makes the point that the reality of the Bush administration's war on terror is but a poor shadow of the fictional one waged by CTU. Brown University professor Tricia Rose, an in-demand commentator on today's culture and the media, tells us that the outside-the-law actions of Jack Bauer echo a far darker side of American history: vigilantism. Frank Rich's op-ed columns for the *New York Times* regularly castigate the Bush administration for what he has called the "politics of fear." One might thus expect him to be critical of the show. But his view of *24* is highly nuanced. And talk about the unexpected: Even though the Chinese government is portrayed as villainous and its agents especially brutal, young viewers in China, usually hypersensitive about slights to their country, seem to like the program, according to a report written for us by Shanghai residents Jing Guan and Ben Liaw. They quote one viewer who told them he liked the show because it "reflects the spirit of individual heroism"—a character trait not exactly prized by China's leaders.

Next, we present a roundup of the latest political news being made by *24*. Colin Freeze, national security correspondent for the *Globe and Mail* of Toronto, quotes U.S. Supreme Court Justice Antonin Scalia as telling a prestigious international judicial panel that it would not be practical to criminally charge a real-life Jack Bauer for his rogue actions. "Is any jury going to convict Jack Bauer?" the justice asked rhetorically. "I don't think so." Rosa Brooks and Clarence Page, veteran newspaper columnists, give us two perspectives on how *24* influenced the politicking of the Republican presidential candidates in the run-up to the 2008 election campaign.

The chapter concludes with what has become a touchstone in the cultural/political wars about *24:* the Heritage Foundation conference featuring Rush Limbaugh and an A-list of Washington's real-world terrorism experts alongside the creative team behind the show. Their topic: what's real and what's fiction on *24*. Tune in for the answers. ∎

Maureen Dowd

We Need Chloe!

YOU'D THINK MICHAEL CHERTOFF would have something more important to do.

The hapless homeland security chief could snatch more money away from American locales most likely to be hit by Al Qaeda. Or let another wonderful city fall into a watery abyss. Or go on TV and help cable news hype the saga of the Miami gang of terrorist wannabes who look like they couldn't find the local Sears, let alone the Sears Tower.

These guys were so lame they asked an informant for boots, radios, binoculars, uniforms and cash, believing he was Al Qaeda—and that jihadists need uniforms.

Instead, the cadaverous Chertoff was gallivanting on stage yesterday morning with some fictional counterterrorism experts from "24." The producers, writer and three actors from the Fox show appeared at an event sponsored by the Heritage Foundation, at the Ronald Reagan Building and International Trade Center.

Drawing on his old scripts, Mr. Reagan was a master at mixing fiction and fact, but he was a piker compared with the Bush crowd.

The audience included Clarence Thomas and his wife, Ginny, who held a dinner at the Supreme Court Thursday for the Tinseltown terror brigade. Rush Limbaugh, who said that Dick Cheney and Rummy were huge fans of "24," was master of ceremonies for the panel, titled, " '24' and America's Image in Fighting Terrorism: Fact, Fiction or Does It Matter?" It doesn't in this administration.

Better to have a panel in praise of Jack Bauer than admit we have no real Jack Bauers to find Osama and his murderous acolytes. Better to pretend that rounding up a bunch of Florida losers whose plan was more "aspirational than operational," as one F.B.I. official put it, is a great blow in the war on terror than to really turn our intelligence agencies and Homeland Security into the relentless, resourceful and fearsome organizations they are in fiction—and should be, given the billions spent on them.

Lulled by our spy thrillers and Tom Clancy novels, we used to take for granted that our intelligence agencies were just as capable as heroes on the screen. Jack Ryan, either the Harrison Ford, the Alec Baldwin or even the Ben Affleck version, could have gotten Osama single-handedly in the two hours allotted.

Even though they still haven't captured the fiend behind 9/11, W. and Dick Cheney still blend fact and fiction by using 9/11 to justify their wrong-headed venture in Iraq.

As the vice president told CNN's John King this week, when he was asked about his claim that "we would be greeted as liberators" in Iraq: "It does not make any sense for people to think that somehow we can retreat behind our oceans, leave the Middle East, walk away from Iraq, and we'll be safe and secure here at home. 9/11 put the lie to that."

In a macabre metric of improvement, Dr. Death also noted that things were looking up. "There are a lot more Iraqis becoming casualties in this conflict at present because they are now in the fight," he said cheerily.

Some of W.'s closest allies have begun privately calling Vice "an absolute disaster," but when will W. realize how twisted his logic is?

In the new book "The One Percent Doctrine," Ron Suskind writes that C.I.A. officials referred to Mr. Cheney as "Edgar," as in Edgar Bergen and Charlie McCarthy, and that W. had to ask his domineering second to pull back a little at meetings and not offer him advice in crowded rooms so they could continue to pretend that Mr. Cheney was not the puppet-master.

> **"24** dispenses with the politically correct evasions that pervade prime time episodic television. . . . It identifies the terrorist enemy without flinching and lets the good guys fight to win—without apologies."
>
> —**Christian Toto,**
> the *Washington Times*

On the homeland security set, Mr. Chertoff, flanked by the actors who play the beautiful technogeek Chloe and President Logan, seemed a little fuzzy about whether the fancy technology on "24" exists.

He noted, "One thing you don't see on '24' is when the computer's crashing and having to get the I.T. people to come in to reboot and get the computer working again." Given that the F.B.I. is struggling to get a computer system that can simultaneously search for "flight" and "schools," his answer was not all that funny.

Asked about the slashing of anti-terrorism money given to New York, he replied that "we've put a lot of extra money into northern New Jersey." (Wow, I feel better already.)

Mr. Limbaugh slyly suggested the producers give Jack Murtha a cameo as K.G.B. chief. He praised "24" for giving torture a good name.

This past season, the show began exploring what happens when a Nixonian president becomes so obsessed with national security that he starts undermining the country's laws.

That's the kind of fiction you hate to see become fact. ∎

Tricia Rose

24 and the American Tradition of Vigilantism

*A*s *we have seen, 24's intensely topical story line and complex characters lend themselves to a wide variety of interpretations and insights. One of the most provocative is offered here by Tricia Rose, an avid fan, a frequent commentator on American pop culture, and a professor at Brown University specializing in twentieth-century African-American culture and politics. Professor Rose believes the plot of 24 is not just dark and violent generally, but evokes the long and infamous American tradition of vigilantism specifically: action, usually violent, taken by self-appointed heroes who deal with those whom the law can't, or won't, touch.*

Jack Bauer and many other fictional characters may act in the name of the "greater good". But, she says, in the real world those who don the hero's mantle tend not to act so nobly. Especially when it comes to dealing with the "outsiders within"—perceived interlopers who don't belong because they don't look and act like us. Then the impulse toward vigilantism can quickly escalate from frightening rhetoric to threatening actions and, finally, to deadly force. Never more so, says Professor Rose, than "in the context of ethnic and racial enslavement, colonization and discrimination." The most obvious example being, of course, the Ku Klux Klan, with its nearly 150 years of racist lets-take-it-into-our-own-hands-because-the-law-or-the-government-won't-help-us vigilantism.

Jack Bauer's antiauthoritarian streak and rogue actions therefore reflect a potentially dangerous tendency in society, according to Professor Rose. But there is a deeper worry, she says: What latent influences are we responding to when, along with millions and millions of other fans, we eagerly watch vigilantism as entertainment?

THERE ARE MANY PLEASURES ASSOCIATED WITH the high-adrenaline television show 24. Its "ticking time bomb" strategy extends the climax point hour by hour throughout a season, making what would otherwise be one mundane day flowing into another, an ongoing, tension-fueled state of consciousness. In this heightened state, much is forgiven, overlooked, and understood as a by-product of crisis management. Under these conditions survival is paramount. This attenuated state of adrenaline relies on split-second, pivotal decision making and sets the course of the next hour and beyond, perhaps determining the future of the world.

In this context, the role of the individual hero is paramount. There is no time for bureaucratic review, consideration, processing, public debate, or collective decision making. Larger principles of fairness, justice, and equality, beyond those embodied by the hero, seem cumbersome. The general public is inert—indeed, invisible—on *24*; "we" are going on with daily life even while a nuclear threat hovers overhead and the government (itself saved by a renegade Bauer) works to keep us free. Part of the pleasure of *24* is in this sense of immediacy and the power of action in the face of imminent threats. And, of course, it doesn't hurt that Jack is always right.

There are countless examples of the power and allure of individual heroism in *24*. Jack Bauer has been given (fictional) license to act as an official representative of the government as well as being informally authorized to act as a renegade soldier/agent who makes "illegal" individual decisions—often violent ones—to get at the "truth."

On *24*, renegade, swift, violent action saves the day time after time. The show and its belief in the power of individual action against the odds is seductive and exciting. We all want to imagine that, despite our seeming powerlessness, we can have a meaningful impact on the world and the people around us; that our actions will have a clear and positive effect. Who doesn't want to save people and be hailed as a hero for doing so? Bauer helps us tap into that desire.

Beyond this more general longing for individual efficacy is the desire to squelch the feelings of alienation the brilliant American essayist and novelist James Baldwin described as the "brutal anonymity of American life." Anonymity in our modern world heightens and distorts our drive to matter and to be an important, even indispensable, part of our society. We long for this not just because action feels good, but because, without it, we feel invisible.

The alienated person cum individual hero who seeks recognition from the broader society for doing something right while others stand by is part of a deep tradition in American culture. This is not necessarily a bad thing. We need to feel powerful and able to contribute to the larger social world in productive ways. And yet, we need to be quite cautious about this kind of heroic vision, tweaked by alienation—especially because it has been consistently wedded to a complete disregard for the very law and order "our hero" appears to be defending. Moreover, it has also depended on, or at least fueled, hatred and violence toward others in the name of community protection.

Many Americans believe that these times—more than ever—require this kind of individual heroic action and the kind of "instinctual" extralegal behavior that defines Bauer's character. Since 9/11, especially, Americans have expressed fears of vulnerability to random, individualized acts of terrorism. The absence of an identifiable enemy army in the traditional sense promotes our belief that this is a new moment, one in which we are facing a unique kind of internal invisible threat to "our way of life," and, more ominously, one that will come from people who have "infiltrated" our society.

This seems to be an unprecedented situation for us as a society and, in some crucial ways, it is. As many commentators remind us, we can't go back to our previous way of life. This unfamiliar era, some contend, requires a different approach to self-defense. James Carafano, a terrorism expert at the Heritage Foundation, put it this way: "If you are waiting for someone in Washington to do something before we start saving lives, we are all gonna die."

But ultimately we are not, and cannot, be Jack Bauer. Any renegade citizen action is highly unlikely to yield lifesaving information or prevent anything at all. So what happens when we act independently and outside the law? What buried, unacknowledged, and inchoate ideas about Muslims, Arabs, and other nonwhites shape our perceptions and interventions when "those people" are seen as proxies for terror? How many innocent people are mistreated, injured, or perhaps killed? What does this "we-have-to-save-ourselves" mentality do to a sense of cooperative multiracial and multiethnic living? How does this idea of citizens charged with the role of saving "our" society contribute to a hostile state of mind against a blurry, nonwhite "them," especially in the context of a history complicated by ethnic and racial enslavement, colonization, and discrimination?

Despite this uncharted situation in which the United States finds itself, this kind of hyper, fear-based, renegade logic of violence in the interest of "saving our society" is not new: It has always worked to support vigilantism and self-styled, citizen-based militias. A heightened fear of an internal threat that requires regular citizens to take the law into their own hands has a long and powerful history in our nation.

Jack Bauer's outlaw heroism relies on an acceptance of vigilantism. What we must consider is how much Bauer's actions—and our collective comfort with them—speak to a cultural embrace of the logic of vigilantism in American society.

There is a long, well-documented history of vigilantism in America and much of it was viewed as heroic and performed in the service of society at large, especially at times when legal agencies were thought to be inadequate to deal with the perceived threats. While vigilantism is usually a group activity, our popular culture has channeled the spirit of "'vigilantist'" thinking into the individual lone hero who "must" operate beyond the law to achieve his (righteous) goals. Actor Clint Eastwood's "Dirty Harry" character is one of our most celebrated and well known of such heroes.

This use of private violence, which supposedly takes place in the interests of the greater society, often targets the less powerful, the disliked, even the despised members of society—immigrants, the poor, African-Americans, and other nonwhites or non-Christians. These "outsiders within" are considered a particular threat to white, middle-class society. These supposed interlopers are often perceived as less worthy of full legal protection, their guilt presumed, and normal levels of punishment too lenient for them. They have to be kept in check not only to protect "us," but also to reinforce values and strengthen "our community." Once we have an amorphous "them," all associated individuals are tainted and judged by their membership in the stigmatized group. This is a powerful anchor for discrimination.

American vigilantism was a particularly favored response after the Civil War to newly freed African-Americans in the form of lynch mobs and the terrorism carried out by the Ku Klux Klan. The culture of white supremacy that was unquestioned under slavery was threatened by emancipation, and many Caucasian communities feared that African-Americans would be granted equal rights. The KKK, founded in 1866 (one year after the end of the Civil War), was essentially a community-sponsored vigilante group, which primarily worked to keep white Protestant American society "safe" from the "threat" of African-Americans. But the Klan also targeted other despised groups who were perceived as dangerous: Jews, Catholics, and other nonwhites. The KKK and other vigilante groups operated under the assumption that the government and the legal system were not sufficient protection against this peril from within.

Beginning in earnest during Reconstruction but extending all the way to the present, vigilante groups lynched thousands of black Americans; many operated with tacit police and judicial approval and sometimes with their active participation. African-Americans were regularly arrested on flimsy or unsubstantiated charges and were then dragged out of police custody to be tortured, mutilated, and hanged without any pretense of due process.

The overall support of the larger community for the culture of vigilantism is critical to sustaining groups like the KKK and the violence for which they are known. Thousands of regular citizens supported public torture and murder in towns all across America, and hundreds and sometimes thousands showed up from near and far to join in the "festivities." Lynching and the culture of vigilantism that supported it became, in fact, mass entertainment. Indeed, the reinvigoration of the Klan in 1915 was spurred by the newfound power of the media through the film *Birth of a Nation*.

I am not suggesting that Jack Bauer's character is defined entirely by his frequent use of torture and the perverse logic of vigilantism that underlies it. Both *24* and its hero are more complex than that, and offer many kinds of enjoyment independent of this one. But there is a problematic strand of pleasure associated with vigilantism in the show as well as our cultural propensity to validate such action. The constant use of torture to "save" the American "way of life" in *24* cannot be easily dismissed as mere "entertainment." To say that vigilantist heroism is "just entertainment" misses the point—because it denies the extraordinary American history of vigilantism as entertainment. ∎

Judith Warner

Jonesing for More *24*

The fact that Judith Warner is fascinated by 24—possibly even addicted to it—is an important clue to the show's popularity among surprising demographic segments. Warner writes the Domestic Disturbances *column for the* New York Times *and is also a regular online commentator on the* Times *website. She is the author of* Perfect Madness: Motherhood in the Age of Anxiety, *a thought-provoking book about the challenges of motherhood in the twenty-first century.*

Judith Warner is not the target audience for typical action/adventure TV shows. But at one point a couple of years ago, she and her husband, like many other couples, discovered they had developed a virtual addiction to 24. *"We stopped answering the phone," Warner writes. "We stopped going out. We lived, breathed, loved* 24.*"*

Warner's not-so-guilty pleasure in 24 *crops up with increasing frequency in her commentaries and the online responses to them. In 2007, just after Fox had announced that Season 7 of* 24 *would feature Cherry Jones as a female president of the United States, Warner again penned an Op-ed piece commenting on the curious parallels between fictional* 24 *and real American politics.*

Many cultural commentators have written about the addictive qualities of 24 *but no one with more delicious precision than Warner. What follows is a good example of her unique cultural and social analysis.*

MONDAY NIGHT, IN THE NEXT-TO-LAST MINUTES of "24" [in Season 5], as Jack Bauer locked lips with Audrey Raines in anticipation of some much-needed R&R, I found myself thinking, If that man were prone to migraines, after the day he's had, he'd be in for a real doozy tomorrow.

In the end, of course, my worry was unfounded. Jack was whisked off to what looks like a lifetime of torture by the Chinese ("He'll never get to go to the bathroom now," my husband, Max, said), and it was I who ended up feeling the blood vessel-expanding crash of withdrawal from this hyper-adrenalized [fifth] season of "24."

I wasn't alone.

For as I discovered the next morning, reading through some of the hundreds of thousands of posts on Fox's "24" message board, a whole lot of people were jonesing, 12 hours out, in the worst possible way. "As soon as I saw Jack on that ship and knew then I had almost a year to wait, I started getting the shakes!" one wrote. "My vision became tunneled. The drink I had in my hand fell to the floor. My only thought was reruns please. I need a fix already. I got the '24' withdrawal bad."

Another advised: "If you watch 3.636 hours from season one, once a week, you will be able to see all the episodes before we start up again."

I was thrilled to have discovered this Shangri-La of like-minded and similarly foul-tempered souls ("You don't like my CAPS? TOO BAD" was the kind of thing they wrote each other), but I peeled myself away. I resisted the urge to watch a "24" stylist discuss the problem of hair "continuity." Instead, I whipped off an e-mail to Dr. William Stixrud, a D.C.-area neuropsychologist whose very interesting lecture—on television, video games and the brain—I had attended a few months earlier.

In his talk, Dr. Stixrud had described how TV super-stimulates the brain by continually setting off its "orienting response"—a primitive neurobiological process that keeps people alert. This orienting response is hard-wired; it's a survival thing, and, with a quickly changing screen, it kicks on again and again—kind of like my dog, who barks every time a truck goes by, or someone parks a car down the street, or a squirrel breathes, or someone opens a mailbox in Kansas.

The experience of having your orienting response incessantly stimulated is draining. When it ends, you are exhausted, but also left with the memory of how much better you felt when it was happening.

Dr. Stixrud talked about dopamine, attention and addiction and noted that watching TV violence puts people into a hyper-activated "fight or flight mode" because the "primitive" regions of our brains can't distinguish TV violence from a real threat.

Now I asked him by e-mail, "Given all the violence, the jump cuts, the surprises and the multi-screen, multi-socket, emotional roller-coaster ride of each action-packed episode, could '24' itself actually be addictive?" ("If you want to give me a quote saying that this is a ridiculous line of inquiry, that's fine," I signed off.)

"It's a reasonable thing to assume," he responded. "Anything that's intensely stimulating has an addictive quality."

Copy that.

This spring, Max and I watched "24" every single night of the week—sometimes two, three episodes a night. Not just the entire fifth season, which aired on Monday nights, but, each Tuesday through Sunday, seasons one and two as well. You see, we'd come to "24" late, sometime in February, and we needed to make up for lost time. We'd also quickly developed one of the weird, intense, short-term fixations (Donald Rumsfeld, the pop star Robbie Williams, Scrabble, Chipotle, grad school), to which our marriage has long been prone.

We had not been huge Kiefer Sutherland fans, though in the early 1990's we had, rather remarkably, seen both "Flatliners" and "Flashback." But we couldn't get enough of Jack Bauer—his wondrous, heart-licking voice, never dreamier than in the DVD interstices of season one, when he virtually moans, "This is the longest day of my life"—and his satellite phone and his biceps and his highly vulnerable invulnerability.

We stopped answering the phone. We stopped going out. We lived, breathed, loved "24." I developed a thing for poor, dying George Mason. (So grumpy! And yet so good!) Max became fixated on blonde Kim Bauer's dark eyebrows. ("What's wrong with them?" "What's wrong with her?")

"I'm 10 minutes out!" he took to shouting into his cell phone, as he rounded the corner of Connecticut Avenue on his way home from work.

"Keep this line open!" I'd scream. Our children, muttering words like "stupid" and "weird," kept right on chewing their pasta. But they took it all in.

Monday was a real humdinger of a night: Two episodes! Right at bedtime! We planned our operation many days in advance. We read aloud single paragraphs. We raced through the lullabies. We said good-night. We went downstairs.

Then Emilie had a toe itch. And Julia needed a Band-Aid.

"MEDIC!" Max shouted. I flew for the Scooby-Doo box. He jumped the banister.

"It's starting!" he yelled. "WHAT IS YOUR LOCATION?"

"Candy?" I heard Emilie whisper, as Julia's bedroom door clicked quietly shut behind them. "Don't worry, Emmie," came the response. "Julia has it all under control."

"Enjoy your show, Mommy," Julia called from her room. "And have a great evening!"

I felt a pang. What would my children do now that, absent Jack Bauer, they'd be submitted to the full force of the Mommy-and-Daddy Show, beaming straight at them, live, all day and all night?

"I REPEAT," came from downstairs. "WHAT IS YOUR LOCATION?"

Open a socket. It's time to rent season three. ∎

of Republican 2008 candidates joining right in. What does that say about the contemporary political and cultural zeitgeist? Could we really elect a president running on a pro-torture platform?

As 9/11 has receded, so, to some extent, has 24's ratings, and so has the effectiveness of tough-guy theatrics from politicians of either party. Nearly six years after 9/11, the Jack Bauer posturings of Republicans seem to be something of a sideshow and not necessarily determinative in any political race. After the hard lessons of the real-life experience of the Bush administration, voters may be looking not just for toughness but competence. I doubt "pro-torture" is a platform that, in itself, could propel any candidate to the presidency. Theatrics such as Romney vowing to double the size of Gitmo seem laughable now. Maybe they wouldn't have three or four years ago.

Does watching terrorist attacks play out week in/week out make people feel more afraid? Or does the fact that a Jack Bauer exists (even if only in fantasy) make Americans feel safer? Also, if Jack prevails by torturing people, does that, in turn, soften up the American public to the idea that torture is a necessary tool for national security?

I think watching terrorist attacks play out fictionally on TV defuses the fear more than adding to it. I don't think this is because Jack Bauer, a fantasy figure, makes anyone feel safer. Rather it's because the inevitably satisfactory closure provided by a TV serial scenario domesticates the threat, makes it more palatable, and makes it seem more rational and controllable. The viewer can act out the fear psychologically and be assured that it will have a largely happy resolution.

Much of the controversy about the show has focused on the "morality" of torture. But there is another controversial issue getting less play that is arguably just as important—the notion that Americans may need to give up civil liberties in exchange for protection against the threat of terrorism. Can you comment on that?

Certainly that issue is just as important. And it seems that Americans, however much they want to be protected, are also very protective of their civil liberties, in both political parties. The Bush White House has begun to retreat on its more draconian intrusions into Americans' privacy, with even members of the administration itself challenging some of what many (including me) regard as its excesses.

In a 2006 Op-ed, you wrote that the era of Americans' fearing fear itself was over. Do you still stand by that opinion? And, if so, might this be one of the reasons the show lost so many fans during Season 6—or is it that there is a certain ho-hum attitude toward the violence on this show? (OK, says the viewer, they've dropped a nuclear bomb on LA and tossed a severed head on the floor, so what else is new?)

You may have answered your own question. Yes, I still stand by that opinion. I do think we have been desensitized to all the fearmongering, from all quarters. Otherwise a war in Iraq that is constantly sold as a deterrent to terrorism ("Don't let the terrorists follow us home!") wouldn't be so unpopular. Wolf has been cried way too many times. In the case of the Nielsen falloff of *24*, I'm sure some of it is related to the national picture, but some of it may simply be, as you suggest, that the show's producers have begun to run out of ideas and veered into self-parody, much like action movie franchises that do a sequel or two too many. A golden rule of show business remains: Know when to get off the stage! ∎

24 and the
Political/Cultural Zeitgeist

Frank Rich is an op-ed columnist for the New York Times *whose weekly essays on the intersection of culture and news are highly anticipated by over a million readers. Mr. Rich regularly condemns the Bush administration for the way it bamboozled the country into war, cloaked its errant ways in the "politics of fear," and trampled on a wide range of human and civil rights—from the excesses of "enhanced" interrogation to the questionable detention of terrorist suspects in Guantánamo.*

Because of these views, one could easily surmise that Rich would be strongly opposed to a show that finds torture expedient and that is lionized by many conservative politicians and commentators. His views are much more nuanced, however. In the past, he has pointed to 24 *as showing where the real war on terror is: not in Iraq, but at home. He has also written that* 24 *"shows but does not moralize about the use of abuse and torture by Americans interrogating terrorists" and that viewers see that "the results cut both ways."*

In June 2007, he shared his most current thoughts on the show, including his view that 24 *remains a "well-produced and effective TV serial," even as the "tough-guy" persona of its lead character seems less relevant at a time when, he says, our collective fear level has receded and the Jack Bauer–style posturing of politicians has become "something of a sideshow."*

How did Jack Bauer become a hero for our time? Do you think Jack—and 24 in general—would have been so popular if 9/11 had never happened?
I think that the popularity of Jack Bauer very much reflects his time, which is often the case with superheroes (which he is, in essence). Witness the rise of Superman during the Great Depression, of Batman as the clouds gathered for World War II, or, for that matter, the campy TV Batman in the 1960's. Though *24* is a well-produced and effective TV serial, it's hard to imagine that it would have had the same impact had there been no 9/11 and had terrorism still been a remote, abstract concern to most Americans.

A significant number of TV watchers among the American public have spent six years cheering Jack Bauer on as he tortures America to safety—with some among the current crop

Jing Guan and Ben Liaw

24 as Viewed from the
Other Side of the Pacific

24 is aired regularly in more than sixty international markets and has cult followings in some unexpected places. The show has been popular with Scandinavian audiences, for example, even though their cultures are usually thought of as models of nonviolence and peaceful resolution of conflicts. Since a major theme of recent seasons of 24 has been the Chinese as the "bad guys" (Chinese agents kidnapping and torturing Jack and Audrey; the Chinese consul-general in Los Angeles running his own military operations on U.S. soil; the nefarious partnership of the Chinese government and Jack Bauer's traitor father, Phillip; etc.), we thought it would be interesting to find out what a sampling of savvy Chinese viewers in China's most cosmopolitan city thought about the show.

Jing Guan, a Shanghai-based journalist and former senior editor for Newsweek China, *and Ben Liaw, a Shanghai-based technology entrepreneur, went digging and filed this report for* Secrets of 24.

FEW HIGH-QUALITY AMERICAN TV PRODUCTIONS are shown regularly on officially sanctioned Chinese television broadcasting networks. But Chinese fans of *24* and other American TV dramas have access to these shows through informal channels. Chinese fans, especially young people, look to the local DVD street vendor, who carries the latest and greatest international movies and TV dramas for less than $1 per DVD. Even cheaper, easier alternatives are developing with popular BitTorrent peer-to-peer communities and YouTube-esque sites that allow users to download a wealth of programming. All of this with the added bonus of Chinese subtitles at the right price—free.

Chinese viewers are drawn to *24* for many of the same reasons as Americans are. The high production values, the unique filming techniques, the fast-paced structure with an action-packed story unfolding in real time, and the deftly arranged and suspenseful scenes all engage Chinese viewers just as they do entertainment consumers all over the world. But for many Chinese, there is something special about *24*—something worth talking about. The show's cultlike following in China has even given rise to many fan sites and discussion boards, focusing on anything and everything related to *24*.

Telecom engineer Wei Jia avidly watches *24* because he sees the philosophy of the show as being in stark (and positive) contrast to the Chinese ideology of maintaining stability and harmony within society and striving for individuals to be identical and uniform. Wei says that *24* "reflects the spirit of individual heroism." It makes Wei "feel excited and energized," and Jack Bauer has a contagious "spirit that encourages us to reach our full potential."

The plots in the last few seasons involving the Chinese government as an evildoer have certainly not gone unnoticed. Some Chinese intellectuals believe that the writers of *24* are simply looking to spice up the story and capitalize on the China craze. Paul Lu, a director at QiSi Studio, which produces screenplays for movies in China, was attracted to *24* for all the same reasons as other Chinese. But he feels that, by Season 6, the novelty of the show was wearing thin and that "That's why the writers decided to put in something new to recapture the audience's attention: the Chinese government." However, Paul Lu also points out that it is unreasonable to expect other countries and cultures to share the same perspective about your country as you do. He advises, "We should have a open mind and accept others' opinions of China, whether positive or negative."

Chinese people recognize that their country has garnered more than its share of attention on the world stage because of its politics, its approach to human rights, and its surging economy. Ultimately, China is a rising power that will likely challenge America's superpower status in the next half-century. And many also realize that China is seeping into American pop culture in a wide variety of ways, with new stereotypes both positive and negative. Some even watch shows like *24* just to see how the Americans portray the Chinese government and, by extension, its people.

> "In this age of terror and worldwide insecurity, *24* created the illusion of an all-American superagent on whose watch the bad guys, whether Muslims or Russians or shady white men, would inevitably blow off their sorry behinds. It was political comfort food."
>
> —**Andrea Peyser, the *New York Post***

Lin Geng, a reporter from *Securities Times*, a state-owned media outlet, can frequently be found these days in front of his screen watching hit American TV series, including *Prison Break, Lost,* and *Heroes.* Lin says that "the negative portrayal of the Chinese government actually attracts me to watch the show out of curiosity about how foreign countries view China."

As Season 6 unfolded, others contended that the negative portrayal stems from America's love-hate relationship with China. On one hand, the Chinese feel that America looks to China as the "next big thing." But this interest in China is also tempered by the view that China is a threat to and a competitor of the United States. And when America considers a country a competitor, it's not long before that country is depicted on the silver screen as an antagonist. For proof of this, one need look no further than the 007 movies. Historically, the former Soviet Union's KGB agents were James Bond's nemesis. Now in a myriad of ways, "China has replaced the former Soviet Union in the eyes of the West," Lu says, adding, "It demonstrates the mixed feelings of love and hatred

America has toward China." Others, such as Lin Geng, believe the portrayal of China in *24* is off the mark, but not in the traditional sense. The depiction of Chinese agents in *24* shows them as "too efficient and too capable," according to Lin. Speaking about the torture of Jack Bauer at Chinese hands, Lin further points out, "I also doubt that China's intelligence agents would really treat a foreign agent that brutally." Furthermore, he believes that China is sometimes unfairly lumped in with other American enemies and that "Western movies don't differentiate between China and the Middle Eastern countries and the former Soviet Union. They still have a cold war mentality when they look at China nowadays."

Chinese fans of *24* are not about to boycott the series just because some of them don't agree with the way the Chinese government is portrayed in the show. They seem to understand that this is an entertainment product that may be tinged with political messages and cultural biases, but it's overwhelmingly just a good-quality Hollywood production. As one Chinese fan puts it, "I would not refuse to watch *24* just because China is a bad guy in it." ∎

24 and the Fog of Politics:
Is Hollywood Driving Public Policy?

In May 2007, 24 showed up front and center in the runup to the 2008 American presidential election. The next three essays spotlight this unusual confluence of entertainment and politics. At a debate among prospective Republican candidates for the presidency, Fox anchor Brit Hume asked a question designed to elicit the candidates' opinions on counterterrorism and torture: Imagine a scenario in which hundreds of Americans had been killed in three major suicide bombings, but a fourth attack had been averted. The attackers have been captured alive and taken to Guantánamo. U.S. intelligence believes that another attack is planned. "How aggressively would you interrogate" the suspects?

It was an unusual moment in American political debate, maybe even a postmodern watershed: A real-life group of presidential candidates was asked by a Fox news anchor, on a Fox hosted debate, to comment on a hypothetical question torn almost directly out of the script of Fox's TV show, 24. No wonder, perhaps, that the replies ended up invoking Jack Bauer's and other tough guys' tactics.

In the commentaries that follow, we look at three different articles and op-ed columns reporting in different ways on the fluid political boundary lines between reality and fiction, especially when it comes to 24. In the first piece, Colin Freeze of Toronto's Globe and Mail *documents comments by U.S. Supreme Court Justice (and 24 fan) Antonin Scalia at a meeting of judges. Scalia rushed to Bauer's defense, pointing out that since he had saved Los Angeles from nuclear meltdown, he would be unlikely to be tried, let alone convicted, for his practice of torture and other crimes along the way. "Are you going to convict Jack Bauer?" Judge Scalia challenged his fellow judges. "Say that criminal law is against him? 'You have the right to a jury trial?' Is any jury going to convict Jack Bauer? I don't think so."*

Next, we hear from Rosa Brooks, a professor at the Georgetown University Law Center. She comments on the Republican debate and the various answers to Brit Hume's hypothetical scenario, from Republican candidates who appeared to be competing in a Jack Bauer impersonation contest. This theme of "Can you top this?" in support of torture, "enhanced interrogation techniques," waterboarding, and expansion of Guantánamo is further elaborated on in a third piece by Chicago Tribune *columnist Clarence Page.*

Colin Freeze

What Would Jack Bauer Do?

JUSTICE ANTONIN SCALIA is one of the most powerful judges on the planet.

The job of the veteran U.S. Supreme Court judge is to ensure that the superpower lives up to its Constitution. But in his free time, he is a fan of *24*, the popular TV drama where the maverick federal agent Jack Bauer routinely tortures terrorists to save American lives. This much was made clear at a legal conference in Ottawa in June, 2007.

Senior judges from North America and Europe were in the midst of a panel discussion about torture and terrorism law, when a Canadian judge's passing remark—"Thankfully, security agencies in all our countries do not subscribe to the mantra 'What would Jack Bauer do?'"—got the legal bulldog in Judge Scalia barking.

The conservative jurist stuck up for Agent Bauer, arguing that, fictional or not, federal agents require latitude in times of great crisis. "Jack Bauer saved Los Angeles. . . . He saved hundreds of thousands of lives," Judge Scalia said. Then, recalling Season 2, where the agent's rough interrogation tactics saved California from a terrorist nuke, the Supreme Court judge etched a line in the sand.

"Are you going to convict Jack Bauer?" Judge Scalia challenged his fellow judges. "Say that criminal law is against him? 'You have the right to a jury trial?' Is any jury going to convict Jack Bauer? I don't think so.

"So the question is really whether we believe in these absolutes. And ought we believe in these absolutes."

What happened next was like watching the National Security Judges International All-Star Team get into a high-minded version of a conversation that has raged across countless bars and dinner tables, ever since *24* began broadcasting six seasons ago.

Jack Bauer, played by Canadian Kiefer Sutherland, gets meaner as he

> "*24* was well into production when the terrorist attacks on September 11 happened. The effect on the show was that Fox's legal department reviewed the first few episodes and made us recut the sequence where the 747 blows up at 36,000 feet (11,000m). Fox did not want to show the actual plane exploding in the air. It also meant that an extensive aerial sequence which was to have been shot by a second unit downtown was shut down and we had to substitute Glendale for downtown."
>
> —Jon Cassar, director and producer of *24*

Source: Reprinted with permission from *The Globe and Mail* (Toronto).

lurches from crisis to crisis, acting under few legal constraints. "You are going to tell me what I want to know, it's just a matter of how much you want it to hurt," is one of his catchphrases. Every episode poses an implicit question to its viewers: Does the end justify the means if national security is at stake? On *24*, the answer is, invariably, yes.

But sometimes this message proves a little too persuasive. Last November, a U.S. Army brigadier-general, Patrick Finnegan, of West Point, went to California to meet with the show's producers. He asked if the writers would consider reining in Agent Bauer. "The kids see it, and say, 'If torture is wrong, what about *24*?'" he told The New Yorker in February.

He argued that "they should do a show where torture backfires." It's not just the military that's watching *24*. It turns out that the judges who struggle to square the Guantánamo Bay prison camp experiment with the British Habeas Corpus Act of 1679 are watching the show, too. It was Mr. Justice Richard Mosley of the Federal Court of Canada who inadvertently started the debate, with his derogatory drive-by slight against Jack Bauer, the one that so provoked Judge Scalia.

In his day job, the Canadian judge wrestles with the implications of torture. Last winter, for example, Judge Mosley ordered an Osama bin Laden associate freed after seven years in prison and into strict house arrest in Toronto.

Judge Mosley told the panel that rights-respecting governments can't take part in torture or encourage it in any way. "The agents of the state, and the agents of the Canadian state, under the Criminal Code, are very much subject to severe criminal sanction if they would engage in torture," he said.

But the U.S. Supreme Court judge choked on that position, saying it would be folly for laws to dictate that counterterrorism agents must wear kid gloves all the time. While Judge Scalia argued that doomsday scenarios may well lead to the reconsideration of rights, in his legal decisions he has also said that catastrophic attacks and intelligence imperatives do not automatically give the U.S. president a blank cheque—the people have to decide. "If civil rights are to be curtailed during wartime, it must be done openly and democratically, as the Constitution requires, rather than by silent erosion through an opinion of this court," he dissented in a 2004 decision. The judicial majority ruled that a presidential order meant that an American "enemy combatant" wasn't entitled to challenge the conditions of his detention, which happened to be aboard a naval brig.

As they discussed torture in Ottawa, the judicial panelists from outside the United States argued that any implicit or explicit sanction of torture is a slippery slope.

Some said that legal systems might do well to enforce anti-torture laws, even if it meant prosecuting rogue agents. "What if the guy is not the guy who's going to blow up Los Angeles? But some kind of innocent?" asked Lord Carlile of Berriew, a Welshman who acts as the independent reviewer of Britain's terrorism laws.

Torture can lead to false confessions, he said. "How do you protect that person's civil rights from the risk of very serious wrongful conviction?" But Lord Carlile, a barrister by training, added that he was also concerned with Jack Bauer's rights. "I'm sure I could get him off," he said.

One panelist deadpanned that saving Los Angeles from a nuke would likely be a mitigating factor during any sentencing of Jack Bauer.

When the panel opened to questions and commentary from the floor, a senior Canadian government lawyer said: "Maybe saving L.A. is an easy question. How many people are we going to torture to save L.A.?" asked Stanley Cohen, a senior counsel for the Justice Department, who specializes in human rights law. "How much certainty do we get to have that we have the right person in front of us?" Then Lorne Waldman, the lawyer for the famously wronged engineer Maher Arar, emerged from the crowd to say that very little of the conversation sounded hypothetical to him.

Mr. Arar was among a series of Canadian Arabs who emerged from lengthy ordeals in Syrian jails to complain of torture. Their common complaint is that Syrian torture—including beatings with electric cables—flowed from a wrongly premised Canadian investigation after 9/11.

A host of security agents, Mr. Waldman argued, acted with utmost urgency against innocents, after wrongly fearing a bomb plot was afoot.

Generally, the jurists in the room agreed that coerced confessions carry little weight, given that they might be false and are almost never accepted into evidence. But the U.S. Supreme Court judge stressed that he was not speaking about putting together pristine prosecutions, but rather, about allowing agents the freedom to thwart immediate attacks.

"I don't care about holding people. I really don't," Judge Scalia said.

Even if a real terrorist who suffered mistreatment is released because of complaints of abuse, Judge Scalia said, the interruption to the terrorist's plot would have ensured "in Los Angeles everyone is safe." During a break from the panel, Judge Scalia specifically mentioned the segment in Season 2 when Jack Bauer finally figures out how to break the die-hard terrorist intent on nuking L.A. The real genius, the judge said, is that this is primarily done with mental leverage. "There's a great scene where he told a guy that he was going to have his family killed," Judge Scalia said. "They had it on closed circuit television— and it was all staged. . . . They really didn't kill the family." ∎

Rosa Brooks

The GOP's Torture Enthusiasts

IT WASN'T AN EDIFYING spectacle: a group of middle-aged white guys competing with one another to see who could do the best impersonation of Jack Bauer, torture enthusiast and the central character on Fox's hit show "24."

In Tuesday's Republican presidential primary debate, Fox News moderator Brit Hume—who appears to have been watching too much "24" himself—raised "a fictional but we think plausible scenario involving terrorism and the response to it." He then laid out the kind of "ticking-bomb" scenario on which virtually every episode of "24" is premised—precisely the kind that most intelligence experts consider fictional and entirely implausible.

Imagine, Hume told the candidates, that hundreds of Americans have been killed in three major suicide bombings and "a fourth attack has been averted when the attackers were captured . . . and taken to Guantánamo. . . . U.S. intelligence believes that another, larger attack is planned. . . . How aggressively would you interrogate" the captured suspects?

Rudy Giuliani—a man who knows he has a few cross-dressing episodes to live down—didn't hesitate. "I would tell the [interrogators] to use every method. . . . It shouldn't be torture, but every method they can think of."

"Water-boarding?" asked Hume.

"I would. I'd say every method they could think of," affirmed Giuliani.

As governor of the State That Dares Not Speak Its Name—at least not in GOP circles—Mitt Romney naturally had to up the ante. "You said the person's going to be in Guantánamo. I'm glad. . . . Some people have said we ought to close it. My view is, we ought to double Guantánamo." I am politician, hear me roar! And, oh yeah: "Enhanced interrogation techniques have to be used."

Not to be left out, Rep. Duncan Hunter of California boasted that "in terms of getting information that would save American lives, even if it involves very high-pressure techniques," he would offer only "one sentence: Get the information."

And finally, Colorado Rep. Tom Tancredo: "We're wondering about whether water-boarding would be a—a bad thing to do? I'm looking for Jack Bauer at that time, let me tell you."

Ha ha. This remark was greeted by uproarious laughter and applause from the audience because, after all, who doesn't enjoy thinking about a hunky guy threatening to gouge out a detainee's eye with a hunting knife?

Source: This essay was originally published May 18, 2007, as an op-ed piece in the *Los Angeles Times* and is reprinted here by courtesy of the author.

Unlike Hunter and Tancredo, Giuliani and Romney took pains to insist that they didn't favor torture, just . . . you know, "enhanced interrogation." But water-boarding, which neither would disavow, is unquestionably a form of torture. It involves taking a bound, gagged and blindfolded prisoner and pouring water over him or holding him underwater to induce an unbearable sensation of drowning. It was used in the Spanish Inquisition and by Pol Pot's Khmer Rouge—fellas who make Jack Bauer look like a softie.

In Tuesday's debate, only John McCain and Ron Paul bucked the collective swooning over enhanced interrogation. Paul mused about the way that torture has become "enhanced interrogation technique. It sounds like newspeak," he noted, referring to George Orwell's term for totalitarian doubletalk in his novel "1984." Paul obviously never got the memo. For most of the Republican primary candidates, "1984" isn't a cautionary tale, it's a how-to manual.

Only McCain reminded the audience that "it's not about the terrorists, it's about us. It's about what kind of country we are."

McCain's chest-beating Republican rivals would do well to listen to him, and to read the letter Gen. David Petraeus, the top U.S. commander in Iraq, sent May 10 [2007]to all U.S. troops there: "Some may argue that we would be more effective if we sanctioned torture or other expedient methods to obtain information. . . . They would be wrong. Beyond the basic fact that such actions are illegal, history shows that they also are frequently neither useful nor necessary. . . . What sets us apart from our enemies in this fight . . . is how we behave. In everything we do, we must . . . treat noncombatants and detainees with dignity and respect."

> **O**ver six seasons, the enemies depicted on *24* have included mercenaries, Serbian nationalists, Arab terrorists, American oil executives, Mexican drug lords, corrupt British businessmen, the Chinese, pseudo-Chechan terrorists, a vast right-wing conspiracy based in the White House, more Arab terrorists, rogue Russian officials, and, of course, Jack Bauer's own father and brother.

In Tuesday's debate, Tancredo brushed off "theoretical" objections to torture as a luxury we can't afford: If "we go under, Western civilization goes under." And what's a little torture when Western civilization itself is at stake?

But Western civilization isn't about speaking English, or flags, or football or borders. If Western civilization is about anything at all, it's about the arduous, centuries-long struggle to nurture an idea of human dignity that's not dependent on nationality or power. As Petraeus put it, there are some "values and standards that make us who we are."

Tancredo's right about one thing, though. If we embrace the use of torture, we won't need to worry that extremist Islamic terrorists might destroy Western civilization.

We'll have killed it off ourselves. ∎

Memo to the Candidates:
24 is Just a TV Show

TREATMENT OF THE TORTURE ISSUE during the second Republican presidential debate illustrates what's great and what can go terribly wrong with these presidential face-offs.

With the breathless urgency of a racetrack announcer, Fox News' Brit Hume spelled out a hypothetical scenario worthy of Fox TV's Jack Bauer thriller, 24.

Hume's plot involved suicide bombers simultaneously attacking shopping malls, captured suspects being taken to the military's detention camp at Guantánamo Bay, Cuba, and U.S. intelligence agents believing that there are plans for an even larger attack. "How aggressively would you interrogate" the hypothetical captured suspects? Hume asked.

The question triggered a bizarre political version of the old radio show "Can You Top This?"

Former New York City Mayor Rudy Giuliani said he would tell the interrogators to "use every method."

"It shouldn't be torture, but every method they can think of," he said. Including "water-boarding"? Hume asked. Yes, answered Giuliani.

Rep. Duncan Hunter of California said that to get "information that would save American lives, even if it involves very high-pressure techniques," he would tell the defense secretary only one sentence: "Get the information."

Colorado Rep. Tom Tancredo: "We're wondering about whether water-boarding would be a bad thing to do? I'm looking for Jack Bauer at that time, let me tell you."

That thrilled the crowd. Bauer is a fictional counter-terrorist played by Kiefer Sutherland on 24. He is known to employ such tools as fire, rope, electric drills and other sharp objects to hasten his interrogations.

Not to be outdone, Massachusetts Gov. Mitt Romney endorsed "enhanced interrogation techniques" and sparked enthusiastic applause with: "Some people have said we ought to close Guantánamo? My view is, we ought to double Guantánamo."

Ironically, the only person on that stage who was a tortured prisoner of war threw cold water on the Bauer option.

"It's not about the terrorists, it's about us," he said. "It's about what kind of country we are."

No applause. That's what Arizona Sen. John McCain gets for shedding light and not just heat on the question.

Here's a real-life scenario that the presidential candidates should hear about: Last November, Army Brig. Gen. Patrick Finnegan, dean of the U.S. Military Academy at West Point, flew to Southern California to meet with the creative team behind *24*.

Accompanied by three military and FBI interrogators, he described how the show actually was undermining the academy's classroom lessons with the false message that torture is a jim-dandy idea in the real world.

As investigative journalist Jane Mayer reported in the New Yorker in February [2007], the meeting discussed how the show's ticking-time-bomb scenario makes a thrilling hour on TV but is virtually unknown in real life. [See Mayer's story, reprinted in Chapter 1.]

And it would be a big help, the dean told the Hollywood folks, if *24* at least would sometimes show how torture produces false information and actually damages counter-terrorism efforts.

Entertainment Weekly reported that the show's top producer, Joel Surnow, has decided to shy away from torture, not because it is an immoral or impractical technique but because it has been overused as a device in his show. That's showbiz.

As for Guantánamo, researchers at Seton Hall University School of Law went to the trouble last year of reading 517 Guantánamo case files that the Pentagon had released. They found only 8 percent of the detainees were characterized as Al Qaeda fighters and only 5 percent fit President Bush's description of being "picked up on the battlefield"—or anywhere else—by U.S. troops.

Instead, 86 percent were handed over to us by Pakistan or the Afghan Northern Alliance for reasons that are not always quite clear. Many were low-level conscripts, drafted into the service of the Taliban regime. None were Taliban leaders of any note. Yet, in return for bounties of $5,000 to $10,000, a lot of suspects were rounded up, their crimes to be sorted out later.

But as congressional leaders debate whether to shut down Guantánamo, Romney wants to double the number of detainees. Who does he have in mind to be locked up?

The uncomfortable truth is that our side has gotten some suspects right but made big mistakes about others in the fog of war. We don't know how many of the remaining detainees at Guantánamo have actual evidence against them, but there's a way to find out. It's called habeas corpus, the fundamental right of individuals to be protected against arbitrary detention without a trial.

Do our presidential candidates still believe in it? All of them need to be asked that question, although in the heat of a presidential campaign I'm afraid of what they might answer. Sometimes the fog of war is nothing compared to the fog of politics. ∎

A Heritage Foundation Panel, including Rush Limbaugh, James Carafano, David Heyman, Joel Surnow, Robert Cochran, and Howard Gordon

24 and America's Image in Fighting Terrorism: Fact, Fiction, or Does It Matter?

In June 2006, the Heritage Foundation, one of Washington's foremost conservative think tanks, sponsored a high-powered conference called "24 and America's Image in Fighting Terrorism: Fact, Fiction, or Does It Matter?" The conference brought together an A-list of top guns from Washington's "fact-based" war on terrorism with the team from Hollywood's "fiction-based" war for ratings. Michael Chertoff, secretary of Homeland Security, carried the banner for the former; Joel Surnow and Robert Cochran, cocreators of 24, and Howard Gordon, an executive producer, for the latter.

The event turned out to be more love-in than confrontation, with Rush Limbaugh genially presiding over a mutual admiration society that also included terrorism scholars and several actors from the show. The kiss Rush planted foursquare on the lips of Mary Lynn Rajskub, the actress who plays Chloe on 24, became so notorious it even fueled Internet-based rumors that the two were dating.

Almost all the presenters agreed that 24 does reflect aspects of the "real truth," as when, for example, it portrays the way reality often presents us with the urgent need to "make the best choice with a series of bad options," in the words of Secretary Chertoff. (For more on Chertoff's remarks, see Chapter 5.) And, yes, said Howard Gordon, real-world events do "seep into our imaginations," but in the end the goal is highly adrenalized entertainment. "We don't try to represent any real truth . . . we try to present an essential truth, a compressed reality." Actors Mary Lynn Rajskub (Chloe O'Brian) Carlos Bernard (Tony Almeida), and Gregory Itzin (President Charles Logan) each provided colorful anecdotes and reflections on the acting challenge. Rajskub, for example, said her biggest acting challenge was "all the fake typing."

The conference was covered live by C-SPAN and by journalists ranging from television critics to national security reporters. Afterward,

---

Source: Excerpts used with the permission of the Heritage Foundation. The full transcript, which includes remarks from some of the actors on *24*, can be found on the Foundation's Web site at http://www.heritage.org/Press/Events/ev062306.cfm.

commentators all over the political and cultural map parsed its meaning, many of them treating it as a great coming-out party for the show's popularity among an influential group of conservatives, in government and out. Supreme Court Justice Clarence Thomas was in the audience (his wife was an organizer of the day), as was his former law clerk Laura Ingraham, the conservative talk show host. Donald Rumsfeld, Dick Cheney, and other senior political and military leaders in the Bush administration were cited as avid fans.

To best convey the "real time" feel for this extraordinary gathering, we asked the Heritage Foundation for permission to run substantial excerpts from the official transcript, focusing on the remarks by Rush Limbaugh, the think-tank terrorism experts, and 24's creative team. In addition to commentary on the nexus between reality and the portrayal of it, we also learn how Rush got hooked on the show and about his concern that people are trying to discredit it, what impact the show may be having on audiences abroad, the argument for how Jack Bauer represents what's truly in our hearts, and some lessons on what makes for an "adrenalized" TV show. And, of course, the difference between "real truth" and "essential truth."

Rush Limbaugh: Let me tell you how I became familiar with *24*. I went on a troop visit to Afghanistan a year ago February [2005] with Mary Matalin [adviser to Vice President Dick Cheney]. I had never watched *24* but had heard a lot about it. A friend went out and got the first two seasons on DVD, and when I stopped in Washington and picked Mary up, I said, "You ever heard of this show *24*?"

She said, "Ah, people have told me about it."

I said, "You ever watched it?"

She said, "No."

I said, "Well, I've got the first two seasons on DVD. Let's pop a DVD of Season 1 in and see what happens."

Sixteen hours later we landed in Dubai, having watched 18 episodes of Season 1. We did not sleep. After the first four or five episodes, I said, "Mary, let's just watch one more. We've gotta get some sleep. We're going to Afghanistan."

"Okay. We'll just watch one more." And the only reason we stopped is because we landed in Dubai, and the whole week we're in Afghanistan we can't wait to get back to finish the final six episodes of Season 1 and watch Season 2 on the way back. That's how I became familiar with it.

[When I came back] I was telling everybody on my radio program about it. The co-creator of the program, unbeknownst to me, is a huge fan of my program.

He [Joel Surnow] called and thanked me for plugging the show so this relationship started. I've been out there twice, once a set visit while they were actually filming.

The program *24* routinely portrays what people would consider torture. The aspect of torture as portrayed on the program is not the way the media en masse is trying to portray us, which is as evil. What are the connections between that and the people who watch this program? And is the effect of the torture news coverage versus the presentation of this in *24* confusing to viewers?

James Carafano: [terrorism scholar, the Heritage Foundation]: Well, it has nothing to do with reality. I was in the army for 25 years, and I talked to lots of military people who had been in lots of wars; I talked to lots of people in law enforcement. I've never yet ever found anyone that's ever confronted the . . . notion that the bomb is ticking and if we don't get this information from this person right now, then people are going to die; therefore, I'm faced with this enormous moral dilemma: Do I torture them, or do I let people die? That scenario, as far as I can tell, has never even happened in human history. So it's great fiction. It's good drama but it's not the moral dilemma that people normally face.

By inflicting beatings, injections, and the electric shock delivered by a taser gun during an episode in Season 2, the show earned the Parents' Television Council's Least Family-Friendly Program citation for the week. The PTC also calculates that out of the 624 instances of torture on TV from 2002 to 2005, *24* accounted for more than 67 such scenes, making it no. 1 in torture depictions.

The moral dilemma that people normally face is, "Are there ways to get this information legally and lawfully and still support the people who need to act?" That's the real issue. It's not about making a life-threatening decision on some great moral dilemma. It's really about fighting this very slippery slope, when it's a lot easier to say, "Well, you know what? We're getting pushed back on this Gitmo thing; let's just not do that." Or, "You know, every time we arrest somebody we get criticized for picking on whatever, so let's just not do that."

David Heyman: [terrorism scholar, Center for Strategic and International Studies]: I think the show reflects this cultural moment in time. Every generation has it. There's social transformation going. We've got [changing] global forces; we've got the question of how security has changed the way we see the world, domestic policy, foreign policy, domestic intelligence, foreign intelligence. All these things are becoming blurred, as are the questions that we have to face on morality. And the show does a really great job of trying to put those questions on a personal level for all of us. We're all Jack Bauer in our hearts. And you measure up to Jack Bauer by saying, "What would I do if I was in his shoes?" As an individual you want justice—but societies want process—a democratic process. And the show allows us to have both, and that's why we love it.

Rush Limbaugh: Joel, would you like to respond to this? The scholars are interpreting what you're doing. You're creating it.

Joel Surnow: [co-creator of *24*]: The whole conceit of *24* isn't realistic. Writers always like to "put a clock on a story" in the last act to really make it exciting. And the whole concept of *24* is to put a clock on the whole season. So, no, it isn't realistic. But it does allow us to take the most extreme situations and force you to make a decision between, as Secretary of Homeland Security Michael Chertoff said, "a bad decision and a worse decision," and that is where our show lives. I think as we're fighting the war on terror, we are dealing with not-great options. Any time you go to war, it's not a wonderful option. So all our show is an exaggerated sort of expression of that stuff that I think the policymakers in this country have to face every day, but, obviously, in a less intense way.

Rush Limbaugh: How much of the show is written with real-world events as a guide, versus how much of it is just totally made up? Is any of it what you wish the United States was doing? Had the capability to do?

Joel Surnow: Well, every other season we've sort of gone into real-world events. Season 2 and Season 4 dealt with the radical Islam war on terror that we're all facing front and center. Absolutely it's what we wish as a country. . . .

Rush Limbaugh: We know government officials watch this program; can they get creative ideas on dealing with the problems [of terrorism] from this show, or are they strictly fans, do you think?

James Carafano: I think they're strictly fans. This is not how you stop terrorists. Actually, it's the worst thing you'd want—a bunch of guys in a room taking care of the rest of us. Stopping terrorists is very unglorious stuff that takes months and requires a lot of people cooperating over things. And I think that's actually one of the problems with the show. If you think back to [Hurricane] Katrina, for example, Americans related to it on their television. They said, "Oh, my God, there's people down there, do something." And they became very frustrated that their government wasn't able to do that in 24 hours in reality. "You know, I can get instantaneous solutions on television, I can see problems; why can't they fix that?"

Rush Limbaugh: Howard, how conscious are you when you write an episode or a story line, of real-life events? How much do you try to incorporate recent events? Or is it all made up in your head and if it happens to coincide with reality, it's coincidence?

Howard Gordon [executive producer of *24*]: It's a little bit of all of the above. We read the same newspapers that everybody else does, so what's in the ether obviously seeps into our imaginations as well, and we synthesize it. And while we don't try to represent any kind of real truth—the 24-hour format makes that impossible—we try to, I think, present an essential truth, or an essential problem. So when Jack Bauer tortures, it's in a compressed reality. He has to get this information out of somebody, but he also pays a price for it. So we're aware of the price of torture in terms of due process. We try to compress these arguments and these issues and dramatize them in obviously very unreal ways, but hopefully in dramatic and compelling ways. And that's really ultimately our master: making a compelling, "adrenalized" TV show.

Rush Limbaugh: What surprises you most about the reaction that people have had, both audience and government officials?

Joel Surnow: What surprises me, actually, is that we have everybody from Rush Limbaugh to Barbra Streisand like this show, and that's really kind of crazy.

James Carafano: The folks that work at the National Counterterrorism Center say it's their favorite show, too.

Rush Limbaugh: I'm sure it is. Everybody I've met in the government—huge fans. Vice-President Dick Cheney is a huge fan. Secretary of Defense Rumsfeld is a huge fan. That's why I'm fascinated by the show, and I'm sure they are, too.

DVD sales internationally are through the roof. Even countries that would be considered our enemies buy it because America takes it on the chin quite a lot in this show, and these people love seeing that. We're all concerned now with "the image" of America abroad. Some of us aren't concerned about it because we don't care, but a number of people are just wringing their hands: "Oh, my God, what do they think about us!" Internationally, what do you think it does to those people who have an opinion about America pro or con? Does it help it or hurt the image of the United States?

James Carafano: [I was in Europe recently] and everywhere I went . . . I asked people, "Do you watch *24* and what do you think of it?" And remarkably, everywhere I went, everyone I talked to, watches the show—and I think the reason is . . . because it's so damn good. Nobody can compete with the United States; I mean, this is one area where we still rule the world.

Former president Bill Clinton has said he is a big fan of *24*, even though the show is run by "an über right-wing guy" (referring to Joel Surnow). He thinks the show is fair in making both Democrats and Republicans look equally evil.

Now in terms of what they take away, the answer is, quite frankly, people take away what they put into it. If there are people around the world who think ill of us, then they're going to think ill of us regardless. And if they see something on *24*, it just confirms their prejudice. On the other hand, if there are people around the world with us in the war against terrorism, and they see *24*, a lot of times they take the good things out of that. So the American television serves as a mirror for what people already believe, I think.

David Heyman: The show does set expectations in some sense. You've got Jack Bauer as a guy who succeeds by breaking the law, by torturing people, by circumventing the chain of command. God, isn't that great? But you know, maybe that's an image that people have of us and it reinforces it, and maybe that's good; maybe it's not. I don't know. I mean, they loved Rambo. Did that hurt us, help us? I don't know. I think actually on the domestic side, the expectations may be somewhat more difficult in terms of how quickly we can get things done, how easy it is to get things done, and that may be something that represents a complete divergence to what we can do on *24*.

> *24* is a "program-length commercial for one political party [the Republicans]," and "propaganda designed to keep people thinking about domestic terrorism to keep us scared."
>
> —**Keith Olbermann, host of MSNBC's** *Countdown*

Rush Limbaugh: Have you ever come up with any [story lines] you've rejected as just being too unrealistic, couldn't make work, and you would like to admit to?

Robert Cochran: [producer of *24*]: Nothing is too unrealistic for us. We're open to anything.

Rush Limbaugh: Most people have bosses, and I assume you guys do, too. Fox, for example. Do you ever have people say, "Naaaah, you can't do that, or, you've gotta water that down. Nah, that's going too far." How much freedom do you have?

Joel Surnow: The only time in five years that we had anybody from the high levels of News Corporation [owner of the Fox network] tell us not to do something was when we shot down Air Force One in Season 4.

Howard Gordon: Although, in fairness, when we first started the show, they had something to say every day. . . . "That couldn't happen. That's not real," and we had to remind them it was a TV show. But of course, once the ratings started coming in, we got a lot more freedom. As you well know, it works that way.

Rush Limbaugh: Okay, so there is a sense of morality, obviously, in the program. There's a price to pay for everything, even though it ends well and ends optimistic. What's the grand scheme? Are you trying to teach a lesson as well as do an entertaining program? Are you trying to spread values to the audience?

Joel Surnow: We're trying to keep our pool heated. That's all we're trying to do. [Laughter.] And that takes ratings. We're not trying to teach anybody anything. Are we?

Howard Gordon: Umm . . . No. But it's not as simple as that. We do talk a lot about this, both on and off the set, talking about what we are doing and what we're putting out there. So we do take it seriously. We're not just heating our pools. We're also paying for our kids' educations and. . . .

Rush Limbaugh: Back to our scholars from the think tanks. You're taking terrorism extremely seriously; you have both delved deeply into it. What is your reaction as you listen to a discussion like this on a popular culture program as it relates to the effectiveness the country is going to have in dealing with the problem?

David Heyman: The show really brings in an emotional level that we don't always connect with on the policy level, and that is that there is random-ness in death in the war that we're fighting against terrorism. It is tragic. These are people whom we love, and we recognize and embrace that fragility. But the fight continues, and that's the central theme of *24*, and that's what resonates most.

James Carafano: People care about security, people care about terrorism. They invest 24 hours of their life watching this show *24*, and I'd like a census of how many of them spend 24 hours of their life seriously really thinking and reading and studying about the issues that are presented in the show—and, sadly, I don't think that the numbers would be near as high.

Rush Limbaugh: This is a program you will expend energy watching. This is not something that you veg and are doing passively while something else is going on in the house. You can't do that and follow it. You have to keep up with it. And no matter what I think is going to happen next, I'm usually wrong.

People ask these questions. It spawns thought. Your program creates mental energy just from an entertainment standpoint. All the other things about it—"Is it real? Is it going to give people ideas?"—those are just added bonuses. The fact that to me that it's one of the most intelligent programs on the air in tack-ling the subject matter that it does is why I'm captivated by it. ■

"Bauer keeps fighting, of course, but for people, not politics. 24's ideology—Jack Bauerism, if you will—is not so much in between left and right as it is outside them, impatient with both ACLU niceties and Bushian moral absolutes."

—James Poniewozik, *Time* magazine

How Well Does *24* Reflect the Real World?

Throughout *Secrets of 24*, we have pointed out that however fanciful and fantastic the plots and action on *24* may be, a clear element of the show's popularity is that it gives viewers some visceral sense of the new twenty-first-century threats our societies face, a vision of some of the ways those threats manifest themselves, and images—realistic or not—of the ways these new threats are checked and challenged.

From suitcase nukes to dirty bombs, from biowarfare to cyberwarfare, *24* offers case studies, episode by episode, in how the rogue actors in our world can hold the rest of us hostage. The show also gives us a picture of who these rogue actors and stateless terrorists are—jihadists and political revolutionaries, yes, but also Chinese government agents, Russian nationalists, Balkan revanchists, Latin American drug lords, corrupt American politicians, greedy corporations, and immoral businessmen.

Virtually every episode asks its viewers the intractable questions of our times: What would *you* do if you had to choose between your family and your country? In drastic situations, where does our society draw the line between civil liberties and emergency measures? Between the Constitution and the pragmatic necessities of fighting decidedly undemocratic enemies? Between intelligence gathering and torture? And how do we know if we can trust those who are thrusting these unpalatable choices upon us?

With the experience of 9/11 and the war in Iraq so dominant in the politics and culture of the first decade of the twenty-first century, *24* has shown an uncanny ability to provoke our thoughts and push our buttons in this new age of unseen, unknown enemies who can do so much damage so fast with so few resources.

In this chapter, we hear from real-life experts on many of the complex issues involved in responding to terrorism, and also the new enemies and new challenges of our age. Each of them makes the connection between how these issues present themselves in the real world and how the same issues are depicted on *24*. Our cast of characters includes James Woolsey, a former CIA director; William Sessions, a former FBI director; Seymour Hersh, perhaps the leading investigative reporter digging into the Bush administration's conduct of the war in Iraq; Amy Zegart, a top academic expert on counterterrorism; and Shane Harris, a journalist who visits the real-life facility in southern California that comes closest to *24*'s CTU. We lead off the chapter with remarks by Michael Chertoff, U.S. secretary of Homeland Security, on why he thinks *24* resonates so strongly with the public, and how characters' actions, under the auspices of the fictional CTU, do and don't reflect the real work of the Department of Homeland Security.

Chertoff's comments are drawn from a 2006 televised symposium on *24* and its relationship to national security issues, sponsored by the Heritage Foundation. The event also included a panel presided over by radio talk-show host Rush Limbaugh and included a variety of actors and writers from the show, as well as think-tank and public policy experts on terrorism, counterterrorism, and homeland security. (See Chapter 4)

The fact that a pop culture Hollywood creation could sustain a daylong symposium involving thoughtful academic and government luminaries speaks volumes about the raw nerve that *24* has touched. ■

Michael Chertoff

Reflections on *24*
and the Real World

I WANT TO THANK THE HERITAGE FOUNDATION for bringing us all together this morning to talk about the issue of terrorism and its place in American culture. . . . Starting on a serious note, I want to make the point that as we look at the events of the last twenty-four hours in real life [June 23, 2006], not on TV, and as we look at what happened in Canada in the last couple of weeks, where a plot to commit real destruction in Toronto was uncovered, it reminds us of the fact that the issue of terrorism is an international problem. It's not something that is centered in one or two places, but it's a threat that exists throughout the country and throughout the world. And we have to be vigilant across the country, and we have to build our capabilities across the country using risk management as a way of identifying where the priorities are, but also making sure we adequately cover not only the places which have been the subject of plots in the past, but the places that may be the subject of terrorist acts in the future.

In reflecting a little bit about the popularity of the show *24*—and it is popular, and there are a number of senior political and military officials around the country who are fans, and I won't identify them, because they may not want me to do that [laughter]—I was trying to analyze why it's caught such public attention. Obviously, it's a very well-made and very well-acted show, and very exciting. And the premise of a twenty-four-hour period is a novel and, I think, very intriguing premise. But I thought that there was one element of the shows that at least I found very thought-provoking, and I suspect, from talking to people, others do as well.

Typically, in the course of the show, although in a very condensed time period, the actors and the characters are presented with very difficult choices— choices about whether to take drastic and even violent action against a threat, and weighing that against the consequence of not taking the action and the destruction that might otherwise ensue.

In simple terms, whether it's the president in the show or Jack Bauer or the other characters, they're always trying to make the best choice with a series of bad options, where there is no clear magic bullet to solve the problem, and you have to weigh the costs and benefits of a series of unpalatable alternatives. And I think people are attracted to that because, frankly, it reflects real life.

Source: Excerpts from a speech, June 24, 2006, by Secretary of Homeland Security Michael Chertoff. Reprinted with the permission of the Heritage Foundation.

That is what we do every day. That is what we do in the government, that's what we do in private life when we evaluate risks. We recognize that there isn't necessarily a magic bullet that's going to solve the problem easily and without a cost, and that sometimes acting on very imperfect information and running the risk of making a serious mistake, we still have to make a decision because not to make a decision is the worst of all outcomes.

And so I think when people watch the show, it provokes a lot of thinking about what would you do if you were faced with this set of unpalatable alternatives, and what do you do when you make a choice and it turns out to be a mistake because there was something you didn't know. I think that the lesson there is an important one we need to take to heart. It's very easy in hindsight to go back after a decision and inspect it and examine why the decision should have been taken in the other direction. But when you are in the middle of the event, as the characters in *24* are, with very imperfect information and with very little time to make a decision, and with the consequences very high on a wrong decision, you have to be willing to make a decision recognizing that there is a risk of mistake.

> **"W**hat the show tries to do is capture an emotional and psychological reality of living in a world where terrorism is a threat. If you are looking to us for realistic advice on how to fight terrorism, we're all in real trouble."
>
> **—Robert Cochran, co-creator, writer, and producer of *24***

You have to do the best that you can, you have to analyze as best as you can, but at the end of the day you have to act. And I think a little bit of that spirit of understanding of what the decision-makers and the operators face is not a bad tribute to pay to the people in real life who have to make those tough decisions every single day. Of course, there's an element of *24* that is very unrealistic, and that is the idea that we're going to resolve our problems in twenty-four hours. The characters in *24* bring to the challenges they face courage, intelligence, street smarts and determination, but there's one thing they really don't have to bring, because they only have twenty-four hours in which they operate, and that is perseverance and steadfastness over a long period of time.

And yet in the real war on terror, whether it's the war we fight here at home or the war we fight overseas in Iraq and Afghanistan, as important as the courage and the intelligence and the skills is the steadfastness and perseverance. The fact of the matter is, American history shows that we cannot be defeated in a fight unless we lose our nerve or we lose our will. We have only lost those conflicts where we have withdrawn from the field of battle before we prevail, and that perseverance and that resoluteness is the one critical key to our winning this war on terror—which, as we all know, is not going to be resolved in twenty-four hours or twenty-four weeks or even twenty-four months. And so I think as we look at *24* and we consider some of the virtues we see in the characters, it's very important to remember that we owe our operatives and our soldiers and our police and our agents the backing and the perseverance and the resoluteness which are the critical necessity to winning a war like this, that is not going to be resolved in a single day.

Finally, I want to pay tribute to some real heroes, because much as we like the characters, we know that they work hard but they go home every night to be safe in their own beds. But all over the world as we speak, today and over the last days and weeks and months, we've had real American heroes out defending the country. . . . These unsung heroes put themselves at risk every single day, and we don't often know their

> "The show may even work as a kind of inoculation, jolting us with a little dose of manageable terrorism or nuclear threat or biological warfare as a balm to our deeper, unspoken anxieties."
> —**Charles McGrath,** the *New York Times*

names. And the day after they commit an act of heroism, they're out there again doing their job, but I think it's very important whenever we consider the kind of cultural or the public appearance aspect of what we do in the war on terror to realize that the real work and the real courage is shown by the many thousands of people who work not only for the Department of Homeland Security, but for the Department of Justice, the Department of Defense and all the myriad agencies at the federal, state and local government that are charged with protecting our lives and our well-being.

So with that, I'm happy to answer some questions.

What aspects of *24* are most like the real world? Which are most unlike the real world?

CHERTOFF: Well, I can tell you very easily what's not the real world. First of all, I do not have an operations center like CTU. Things do not get resolved in twenty-four hours, and we don't get to get information by using measures that would violate the law. So those are all things that are not like the real world. I think what is like the real world is that you do have very, very hard-working people who put in very long hours sometimes when they have considerable family pressures. . . .

Would it be considered unethical to clone Jack Bauer?

CHERTOFF: We're doing it already. [Laughter.]

In *24*, CTU personnel are greatly aided by satellite technology that can penetrate buildings, even to the desired floor, and provide imagery to assist. How close are we to this? And a related question: Is electromagnetic pulse terrorism fact or fiction?

CHERTOFF: Well, let me say, first of all, that it is true that technology always surprises us, and we find that we have enormous capabilities that we can only dream about. But a year or two later, they come to fruition, and technology is a critical element of what we try to do in Homeland Security. Of course, one thing you don't see on *24* is when the computer's crashing and having to get the IT people to come in to reboot and get the computer working again. [Laughter] . . . As far as electromagnetic pulsating, I don't know if it would shut the entire country down. And there's a lot of scientific data on the circumstances under which it could pose a problem for certain types of systems. Again, we have to build resiliency and redundancy to prevent that kind of a breakdown.

What aspects of the real world of government do you wish resembled *24*?

CHERTOFF: I wish we could have a rapid execution of tasks within twenty-four hours. I think we're a long way from doing that. I wish we could have instant communications. I wish we didn't have systems that sometimes went down and broke. So those are all aspects of *24* I wish we had. On the other hand, there is something that we do have which I think is very satisfying and very important, which is, we have a tremendously dedicated group of men and women who work for us, who have a dedication that I think, frankly, is equal to that of the characters that are portrayed on the television show. . . . [It is my] belief that nowhere, whether in real life or in fiction, can you find a better team than [the] one we have working at all the agencies of government, at all levels of government, to protect homeland security. ■

The Threats Portrayed
on *24* Are Quite Realistic

*J*im Woolsey was director of Central Intelligence from 1993 to 1995. *Always known as a deep thinker, a brilliant strategist, and a consummate Washington insider, Jim Woolsey was an outspoken commentator on the threats faced by the United States before, during, and after his tenure at the CIA.*

In the interview that follows, we asked Woolsey about the dangers depicted on 24. In Woolsey's opinion, the threats shown on 24—discounting for a certain amount of Hollywood hype—are unfortunately all too realistic. "The U.S. really is at risk from smuggled nuclear weapons and dirty bombs, and we really are at war with Islamist totalitarianism," observes Woolsey. He makes a compelling case for moving the United States toward oil and energy independence as one of the most positive and proactive policies Washington could undertake to reduce the power and influence of Islamic extremists. The interview is filled with fascinating insights into the changing real-life global environment that is the context for 24.

How realistic are the threats portrayed on *24*?

Unfortunately, they're quite realistic. The U.S. really is at risk from smuggled nuclear weapons and dirty bombs, and we really are at war with Islamist totalitarianism. Not all of the crazy ideologies out there spring from Islamist totalitarianism, of course, but there's little doubt that it poses the gravest threat. North Korea might prove nutty enough to launch attacks against the U.S.—it once flew missiles over Japan—but at this point it's mostly a threat to regional stability. Russia, for all the thuggishness of the Putin regime, is no longer in the business of sponsoring terrorism, as it was with the Red Army faction and other groups in the '70s and '80s. China could evolve from a trading partner into a military adversary, especially if it were to invade Taiwan, but that's not a foregone conclusion. When it comes to threats against our own safety and the stability of the West, Islamist terrorism is front and center.

Are there terrorist sleeper cells in the United States?

No doubt there are, although there are probably fewer, proportionally speaking, than exist in Great Britain and elsewhere in Europe. In part, that's because American society does a better job of assimilating immigrants, including those from the Muslim world.

It's likely that not all of the cells in the U.S. are affiliated with al Qaeda. Some are probably affiliated with Hezbollah, which is considered the world's most disciplined terrorist organization. Unlike al Qaeda, Hezbollah operates at the behest of the Iranian government, so a military showdown with Tehran might unleash a rash of terrorist acts here at home.

Which specific threats keep you awake at night?

My biggest fear is that a nuclear weapon or a dirty bomb will be detonated in a U.S. city. It's not hard to make a nuclear bomb, once you get a few kilograms of enriched uranium; as countries like Iran and North Korea move ahead with their nuclear programs, the possibility rises that terrorists will get their hands on fissionable material. The second-biggest threat is biological warfare. We got a taste of what that might be like in the aftermath of 9/11, with the spread of anthrax through the mail. My other big worry is that terrorists will disrupt our energy supply, either by blocking the flow of oil to U.S. refineries or by attacking our electrical grid. That would bring our economy to a standstill.

What will it take to defeat the enemy?

Two strategies are key. First, we must cut off the enemy's funding by reducing our dependence on oil. The U.S. spends more than $300 billion a year on imported oil, and a portion of this vast sum goes to Saudi Arabia and other nations where large segments of the populace hate the U.S. In Saudi Arabia, oil brings the Wahhabi sect of Sunni Islam several billion dollars a year. This money is used to support madrassas [religious schools] in Pakistan and elsewhere that teach boys to be suicide bombers. Wahhabism, like al Qaeda, fosters the oppression of girls and women and encourages genocide against Shi'ites, Jews, homosexuals, and apostates.

Another, less direct way that oil wealth promotes fanaticism is by propping up economies that otherwise might topple under the weight of extremely high rates of unemployment. In Saudi Arabia, four-fifths of the people of working age are unemployed. That means there are lots of men with no purpose in life—too poor to marry and extremely frustrated. As these men look for a purpose, some inevitably latch onto fanaticism.

It will be hard to reduce our dependency on oil, but not impossible. Until roughly a century ago, salt was just as much a strategic commodity as oil is today. Wars were waged over it. But once refrigerators appeared and there was another way to preserve meat, salt lost most of its monetary value, along with its geopolitical significance. We must do to oil what refrigeration did to salt. This will require making a major push to develop ethanol and other renewable fuels and plug-in hybrid vehicles.

The other strategy we must pursue is to promote women's rights in the societies hostile to us. Women's rights generally go hand in hand with freedom of speech, freedom of religion, and freedom of the press, and in many parts of the radical Muslim world, girls and women are brutally oppressed. Boys are taught to dominate their sisters. Husbands beat their wives with impunity. Stoning and genital mutilation of women are tolerated. But if we are successful in promoting women's rights, we will be a moderating influence on these societies. To a limited extent, this has already happened in Bahrain, which, not coincidentally, was the first Middle Eastern nation to deplete its oil reserves.

Given how little it costs to mount, say, a suicide bombing, will cutting back on imported oil really help prevent terrorist incidents here at home?
Oil-exporting nations will continue to earn vast wealth from the sale of oil for many years to come. But once oil revenues begin to trend downward, these societies will realize that the U.S. is gaining the upper hand. In effect, we will be saying, "We don't need you anymore." It will be a powerful blow, psychologically as well as financially.

It's been said that the price of oil and the path to freedom run in opposite directions. In other words, the greater a nation's oil wealth, the less likely its government is to meet the needs of its citizens. If you're so rich that you don't need to levy taxes on your citizens, you don't need a legislature, and you probably don't have a system of checks and balances. And just look at the world's oil-producing nations; except for a few, notably Canada and Norway, all are either dictatorships or autocratic kingdoms. The only two democracies in the Middle East are Turkey and Israel, neither of which has any oil to speak of.

What about the argument that poverty breeds terrorism?
There's scant evidence to support that point of view. Osama bin Laden, a former construction executive, is wealthy. His deputy,

Zyman al Zawahiri, is a physician. And his former head of operations, Khalid Sheikh Mohammed, is an engineer. Fifteen of the nineteen terrorists who attacked the World Trade Center and the Pentagon were from Saudi Arabia, one of the world's wealthiest nations. Indeed, in the aftermath of 9/11, Professor Sean Wilentz of Princeton University said, "Now we know the root causes of terrorism: wealth, status and education."

The popularity of *24* stems, in part, from Jack Bauer's dynamism and fearlessness—in short, his heroism. Are his real-world counterparts heroic, or are they bureaucratic functionaries just doing a job?

Our intelligence officers are extraordinary people, and the job they're doing is of unprecedented difficulty. During the cold war, our adversary was comparatively vulnerable to penetration. That was true not only because the Soviet Union was a monolithic bureaucracy with a dead ideology, but also because it was reasonably easy for Americans to blend into Soviet society. If an American intelligence officer was working under official cover of, say, the U.S. Embassy in Moscow, there were many ways in which he or she could mingle unobtrusively with Soviet citizens. The easy interaction between an officer of the U.S. government and, say, a Russian army colonel is virtually impossible with our current foe. If you want to penetrate al Qaeda, you can't be seen as an employee of the State Department or any other U.S. governmental agency. You can't invite terrorists to social events at the U.S. Embassy. The only time al Qaeda is going to come to an American Embassy is to try to blow it up!

To circumvent this problem, U.S. intelligence agencies are increasingly reliant upon nonofficial cover officers, or NOCs, as they are known in the trade. These are men and women who have no U.S. passport or any other apparent link to the U.S. government—and who are able to pass as natives of the region. These people are very brave. They know that if they are caught, they won't simply be kicked out of the country. They'll be executed. So, the simple act of serving in this capacity on a day-to-day basis involves true heroism—even if these officers aren't pulling any Jack Bauer–type exploits.

Jack Bauer often uses torture to get information from terrorists and suspected terrorists. Are there circumstances under which the U.S. government uses or should use torture?

Certainly there are circumstances that call for the use of harsh interrogation techniques, including those that cause extreme emotional distress. However, brutality of the sort employed by Jack Bauer is never permissible. It's against U.S. and international law, and it may not even be especially effective. My understanding is that the most effective interrogation techniques do not involve physical pain or injury, but deception—mind games, in other words.

In at least one episode of *24*, Jack Bauer manipulates a terrorist by falsely convincing him that his wife and daughter have been murdered.

Once you sign on as a terrorist, there's no guarantee against being deceived.

In *24*, agents of the Counter Terrorist Unit seem unfettered by pointless protocol or bureaucratic inefficiencies. In the real world, has our counterterrorism apparatus gotten more efficient—or do roadblocks continue to crop up?

We still aren't quite as efficient as CTU. Given current law, the FBI and other law enforcement agencies are reluctant even to keep files on an individual unless there is clear evidence that he or she poses an imminent threat. Overseas, CIA officers are free to collect information and to recruit spies, of course. But before they can take action to influence events or even to grab a bin Laden, they must have a finding signed by the president and distributed to the appropriate congressional committees. You can't grab someone or blow something up without complying with American law. Most of the things that take place on *24* would never be allowed in the real world.

We have fought three wars on U.S. soil: the Revolutionary War, the War of 1812, and the Civil War. In our current conflict against Islamist totalitarianism, as in the previous three, the U.S. government has taken steps to intercept communications between the enemy and its collaborators here at home. For example, George Washington learned that Benedict Arnold was a British spy after a letter from Arnold's handler, Major André, was surreptitiously opened. I suppose one might consider that letter-opening the eighteenth-century equivalent of intercepting a phone call from al Qaeda in Yemen to someone here in the U.S.

Yes, the National Security Agency is listening in on some such phone conversations. But the notion that the federal government is listening in on everything is nonsense.

Do you believe, as some do, that our conflict with Islamist totalitarianism amounts to "World War IV," after World Wars I and II and the cold war? Or do you prefer the "war on terrorism" appellation?

In my view, the fight against Islamist totalitarianism will resemble the cold war. It makes little sense to call this a war on terrorism, because terrorism is simply a tactic. In World War II, we didn't call the war in the Pacific the "war on kamikaze-ism." And while the conflict will be long and is clearly global in scope, I hesitate to call it "World War IV." That suggests there will be decisive battles, like the invasion of Normandy or the dropping of the bomb on Hiroshima. I think the "long war" may be the least bad title.

In the twentieth century, five great powers tried to destroy us: the German Empire, the Nazis, fascist Italy, imperial Japan, and the Soviet Union. Each of these is gone, and we're still here. There's no doubt that we have a big job ahead of us, but I wouldn't sell us short. ■

An interview with William S. Sessions

I Sleep Well at Night

Judge William S. Sessions was director of the Federal Bureau of Investigation from 1987 to 1993. During his tenure as FBI chief, the Bureau became more focused on the implications of international and terrorist threats to the United States. He is also considered a pioneer in developing standards for the use of DNA fingerprinting technology.

A lawyer who has served in the criminal division of the Department of Justice and was also a chief judge of the Federal District Court in the Western District of Texas before becoming head of the FBI, Judge Sessions is intimately familiar with what goes on inside law enforcement agencies as they attempt to deal with terrorist threats, bomb scares, cyberterror, plots against political leaders, and the like. In the following interview he gives us a sense of real life inside the FBI and other federal agencies, and how this compares to what we see on 24. He also shares his opinions on the current state of the war on terror, stressing his opposition to using torture techniques and his concerns about safeguarding constitutional rights even in the most challenging times. "We must not let our counterterrorism efforts flout the protections established by the Constitution. We must not let law enforcement and intelligence agencies become rogue outfits," warns Sessions in this interview.

It's been six years since 9/11. How secure are we now against terrorist attacks?

I'm encouraged by the steps the government has taken to improve our intelligence networks and secure our borders. The military, the FBI, police forces, and all the other first responders are working diligently to prevent another terrorist attack. We're still a target, of course, and one must presume that there are terrorist cells operating in the U.S. But I certainly don't lie awake at night worrying about the threats against us.

The attacks of 9/11 brought about big changes in the government's approach to fighting terrorism, including the creation of the Department of Homeland Security. Was that a good idea?

I worry about consolidating all those governmental entities into one department, because of the possibility that rivalries might get in the way of information-sharing and because of the potential for problems with coordinating the activities of the various entities. But Congress obviously thought it was a good idea to create DHS. At this point, so do I.

In what ways did the war on terrorism bring about change at the FBI?

It used to be that the Bureau focused primarily on law enforcement—that is, investigating and prosecuting terrorist acts and other crimes that had already occurred. Now, as Director Mueller has said many times, the Bureau is focusing on *preventing* these acts. This is a real sea change for the Bureau. Then again, the FBI is constantly changing. Director William Webster was the one who got the Bureau going on counterterrorism in the first place. Before that, Clarence Kelly started the Bureau's battle against organized crime and white-collar crime. During my tenure as director, the Bureau created the Integrated Automated Fingerprint Identification System. DNA fingerprinting gave us a new and incredibly reliable tool for identifying suspected criminals. It is and will continue to be of enormous value in the war on terrorism.

Can you give an example of how DNA fingerprinting might help catch terrorists?

Let's say a terrorist meets with some of his fellow plotters. There's a good chance that he will leave some of his DNA at the site. And then some cooperative individual gathers it and surrenders it to law enforcement. This DNA can then be analyzed and checked against the DNA of people who are known to be involved in terrorist or criminal activities. The best thing about DNA is that it doesn't die or go away. I mean, we can get DNA from mummies!

What are some of the other high-tech tools that are playing or will play a role in our counterterrorism efforts?

There are now all sorts of ways to identify people—not only by their DNA and their fingerprints but also by their facial features, their voices, their corneas, and so on. Soon these technologies will make it possible to identify people each time they cross the border to come into this country. We can now process vast quantities of information and access huge databases almost instantaneously. As microprocessors get better, our ability to track and identify suspected terrorists will become incomprehensibly fast and efficient.

What do you say to people who fear that growing surveillance by the government is trampling our constitutional right to privacy?

I think that's a valid fear, especially as the technologies become even more invasive. When I drive from Washington to Baltimore, I never know when some surveillance camera is going to catch me speeding through an intersection. The important thing for all Americans is that our government comply with the law. If an agency wants to use a wiretap, for example, it needs to obtain a judge's permission; law enforcement works twenty-four hours a day, so maybe the courts should, too. We must not let our counterterrorism efforts flout the protections established by the Constitution. We must not let law enforcement and intelligence agencies become rogue outfits.

Speaking of rogue outfits, Jack Bauer and his colleagues at the fictional Counter Terrorist Unit don't shy away from the use of torture. Should the U.S. ever use torture to prevent terrorist attacks?
War is always difficult, but I am fundamentally opposed to the use of torture. If the U.S. were to use torture—or even if people *thought* we were using it—we would be putting our own people at tremendous risk. The risk would be far greater than any potential benefit.

Jack Bauer has been celebrated for his resourcefulness and initiative, even if he sometimes plays fast and loose with the rules. Is there a place for Bauerlike agents in the real world?
We certainly need resourceful, creative agents who are able to lie persuasively when they go undercover. These aren't the sorts of guys who come straight from Sunday school. But is there a role for agents who break the rules? No.

Some have criticized *24* for its unflattering portrayal of Muslims. What do you make of that?
One of the biggest mistakes we can make is to point a finger at a group and say they are natural-born enemies of the U.S. After the Oklahoma City bombing in 1995, there was a rush to blame certain groups—wrongly, as it turned out. I warned against this at the time, and I continue to. It's despicable to go on CNN and speculate that the perpetrators of some criminal act are of a particular ethnicity, religion, or nationality. You have to wait for the investigation. You might argue, "Bill, you're ignoring the fact that there are militant groups that do bad things." To which I say, "Yes, that's so, but let's address the threat posed by these groups without regarding all people of the same religion or ethnicity as our enemies." We need to devote more time to learning about the people who oppose us—their languages, their cultures, the way they think. We must have more respect for these people and their ideas. We need to have more country-to-country, people-to-people exchanges—and more diplomacy. Diplomacy involves talking to people you don't agree with. That's the best way to find ways to bridge the gap between us.

What's the biggest threat facing us now?

The biggest threat is our own complacency—an attitude that says, "Oh, well, what will happen will happen." The government must be constantly alert to the threat of terrorism. On the other hand, we can't remain hypervigilant all the time. Basketball teams that try to play full out for the entire game wear themselves out. We shouldn't let that happen to us. ■

Focus on the Real Threat
(It's Not on TV)

*F*ew *outsiders have as much insight into the inner workings of government and its fight against terrorism as Seymour Hersh, the investigative journalist specializing in international affairs and national security for the* New Yorker. *A fellow journalist has referred to Hersh's work as a kind of navigation process, helping readers find their way through the byzantine world of America's overlapping national security bureaucracies. His recent investigative reports form what Hersh himself has taken to calling an "alternative history" of the Bush administration since September 11, 2001.*

Hersh's work first gained worldwide recognition in 1969 when he exposed the My Lai massacre and its cover-up during the Vietnam War. His courageous work on My Lai earned him the Pulitzer Prize in 1970. Relentless in his search for corruption in policy making ever since, he exposed the Abu Ghraib prison scandal in 2003 and, in its wake, the cover-ups of prison abuse he found throughout the chain of military command in Iraq and other fronts of Washington's war on terror. In 2006 Hersh reported that the U.S. military was actively making plans to attack Iran; those plans allegedly called for the use of nuclear weapons.

Obviously, those who formulate the policies Hersh exposes are usually far from pleased with his crusading reports. In 1975, a damaging report about the Nixon administration that he had written for the New York Times *caused then–White House Chief of Staff Donald Rumsfeld to ask his aide, Dick Cheney, to write a memo on a range of options to deal with this nettlesome reporter. The list ranged from an FBI investigation of the paper to doing nothing, but included issuing a search warrant "to go after Hersh papers in his apt." More recently, Richard Perle, who was serving on the Defense Policy Board in 2003 when Hersh wrote about Perle's close connections to a private company trying to sell defense- and security-related technology to Saudi Arabia, lashed out at Hersh, calling him "the closest thing American journalism has to a terrorist."*

So, what might the controversial, dogged, award-winning reporter on national security issues have to say about 24 *and the way it may or may not reflect reality? In our interview, Hersh talks about how little* 24 *has to do with the realities of terrorism and torture in the field. He challenges the assertion that U.S. soldiers are learning their torture techniques from* 24 *or any other television shows, arguing that these abuses are the products of policies, not the imaginations of Hollywood screenwriters.*

Hersh further argues that the way the Bush administration has overplayed its hand in dealing with the threat of terrorism is more dangerous than the threat itself.

Do you think *24* provides an effective discussion of issues of terrorist threats, constriction of civil liberties, and a basis for comparison to the real world?

I think *24* has little to do with the real world. We watch that stuff to get away, not to be informed (at least I do).

In your 2007 New Yorker article, titled "The General's War," you showed that torture is tolerated at the highest levels of the military and even silently endorsed.

I did expand on the notion of higher authority in the series of interviews I did with Antonio Taguba, the major general who conducted the initial Abu Ghraib inquiry for the Pentagon and suffered for it professionally. In all of my interviews on the topic of torture in the military that I did with Taguba and other high-ranking officials, it should be noted that no one mentioned *24* or alluded to it in any way.

Jane Mayer's New Yorker article, "Whatever It Takes" [see Chapter 1], quotes Tony Lagouranis, a former army interrogator in Iraq, as saying to the writers of *24* that he thought soldiers were learning torture techniques from watching the show. What's your response to that?

Actually, I think that is a pretty ludicrous assertion. Torture and mistreatment of the enemy and/or prisoners is a condition of war, and the idea that it is exacerbated or accelerated by a TV show is silly. We all go to the movies and watch TV with a notion of suspended disbelief and we understand that what we are seeing is for entertainment value and has little to do with reality. The notion that a young soldier could be pushed by watching a TV show to be more aggressive and brutal in the treatment of someone under his authority actually undercuts the true horror of war. Is the point that, without *24*, we would be treating detainees better? Or are the people who are making this argument asserting that Americans don't have the same basic instinct to become brutal in warfare, and treat those one has to kill as subhuman?

In a continuing plot thread on *24*, personal emotional involvements and strained interagency relations get in the way of an effective response to the threat of terrorism. What has your reporting shown about this in the real-world context of the FBI, the CIA, and the Department of Homeland Security?

No bureaucracies work together, especially in times of stress. The casual betrayal of fellow Americans, as we see on *24*—always for bureaucratic or personal reasons—is very realistic. But, of course, we don't need another TV show to tell us that this is the way it is. We've had scores of years of cop movies in which the "Feds"—who are always arrogant, stupid, and undercutting—move in with disastrous consequences. This theme is pretty much a cliché, but *24* shows this undercutting more consistently, and better.

Do you think the government downplays security risks or overplays dangers?

Come on! Playing up al Qaeda and the terrorist threat is a core value of the Bush administration. Think how much better off we would be in America if Bush had responded to 9/11 as a crime and not as the rationale for a worldwide war on terrorism. Other great nations have suffered terrorist attacks and moved on with life—I'm referring to the UK and the bombings and other violence from the Irish Republican Army, the French with their Algerian problem, and the Germans and their outbursts from the Baader-Meinhof Gang. Our biggest threat since 9/11 has been the Bush presidency, and its consistently wrongheaded approach to al Qaeda, bin Laden, and other threats. ■

24's Unreality Quotient

*A*my Zegart is a great fan of the genre, but 24 gives her headaches. Her day job, as an associate professor of public policy at UCLA, calls for her to think about how best to organize national security intelligence—so who needs to see images of terrorism when you get home? Besides, she says, the show may deliver great entertainment, but it offers a very poor version of reality. "People whose knowledge of U.S. intelligence comes solely from watching 24, for example, are apt to think that it's an easy game," says Zegart, "when in fact it's really hard." And what makes real-world intelligence gathering "really hard", she says, is the wrongheaded way in which the government has reorganized the homeland security bureaucracy. Its flaws set it up for failure, she believes.

There is still another disconnect between the show and the real world, Zegart says. People may get the impression that our intelligence agencies need less power when, in fact, "the agencies need more power." In her view, Americans should be more worried about how little we know about al Qaeda than giving up "personal information that is already held by Bloomingdale's and the Gap."

Zegart is well qualified to hold these views. Considered one of the nation's leading experts on intelligence reform, she was on the National Security Council during the Clinton administration and then served as an adviser to the Bush-Cheney campaign before holding her present post at UCLA. She has written two books, including Spying Blind: The CIA, the FBI, and the Origins of 9/11.

Readers will find a wealth of information in this interview about our intelligence agencies and the challenges they face internally as well as their overlapping jurisdictions. Zegart also suggests a number of concrete ways in which the system can be fixed. At present, she concludes, "We are not moving fast enough" to minimize the threats we face.

As a professional whose work focuses on matters involving national security and counterterrorism, what do you think of the show?

My husband writes thrillers, so I'm a big fan of that kind of entertainment. But watching 24 makes me a little nutty. My day job involves thinking about terrorism, and I found that I didn't want my evening entertainment to be filled with images of terrorism, too. And my inner monologue kept bothering me about all the unrealistic things in the show.

What sorts of things?
In one episode, for example, Jack Bauer's friends were able to locate a hostage by quickly repositioning a spy satellite to get a bird's eye view of a terrorist hideout. That's totally unrealistic. So are the high-tech gizmos that can be redirected at a moment's notice to read any license plate. The reality about our intelligence agencies is that they are more likely to be incompetent than omnipotent.

In the real world, the National Security Agency is facing chronic problems with its electrical system. The NSA had to delay the installation of new supercomputers because there wasn't enough juice to run them, and the existing computer system will be in serious jeopardy if steps aren't taken to fix the energy shortfall in the next two years. To make matters worse, NSA officials and their congressional overseers have known about this looming electricity shortage since the 1990s. In 2000, the NSA's entire listening system crashed for three days. During that time, we were unable to intercept communications between terrorist groups and other U.S. enemies around the world.

Then there is the human intelligence side of the equation. Anyone who follows the CIA knows that it's extremely difficult to mount human intelligence operations against terrorist groups. In real life, our human intelligence has been a lot less effective than Hollywood would have us believe. The 9/11 Commission found, for example, that the CIA had failed to penetrate al Qaeda's inner circle. And this is no aberration. Declassified documents reveal that we never penetrated the Soviet Union's leadership during the entire cold war, never penetrated the regimes of North Korea or China during the Korean War, never got inside Hanoi's regime during the Vietnam War—the list goes on and on. And yet Jack Bauer is single-handedly able to infiltrate any group, figure out just about every plot, and outmaneuver every menacing force. People whose knowledge of U.S. intelligence comes solely from watching *24* are apt to think that it's an easy game, when in fact it's really hard.

But is that disconnect between public perception and the reality of intelligence work such a bad thing? After all, the show's creators regularly remind us that "it's just entertainment."
I don't want to be the skunk at the dinner party, but I do see a downside to the disconnect between the public perception of our intelli-

gence agencies and the truth about them. The truth is that the agencies need more power, not less, to protect us against terrorism. If lawmakers and their constituents are led to believe that the agencies are already too powerful, it's unlikely that steps will be taken to remedy their deficiencies. We should be more worried about the fact that we haven't been able to penetrate al Qaeda than the possibility that the NSA or FBI might get access to the kind of personal information that is already held by Bloomingdale's and the Gap.

Another thing that bothers me about *24* is that it fuels the misperception, even among Army recruits, that it's permissible to torture detainees. In 2006, a U.S. Army general visited the set of *24* to warn the writers about this problem. Another misperception fueled by the show is that our government is full of evil people who are conspiring to foil the efforts of heroes like Jack Bauer. That's simply not true.

Are there real-life Jack Bauers working for the U.S. government?

If you mean unsung heroes working twenty-four hours a day to keep bad things from happening, then absolutely there are. But if you mean officers and agents who violate the law and torture people, well, I hope not. I don't think there are, either, although we only know what the intelligence community wants us to know. Back in the 1980s, people in the intelligence community joked that CIA director William Casey wouldn't tell you that your coat was on fire unless you asked him.

In a recent *Washington Post* article, you compared the U.S. intelligence community to "a dysfunctional family with no one in charge." Who is supposed to be in charge?

Traditionally, the job fell to the CIA director. But it was hard for one person to run the CIA and oversee the other intelligence agencies. So, in 2004, Congress enacted legislation creating a new position known as the Director of National Intelligence, or DNI. But there's a pretty strong consensus that the DNI has been no more effective than the CIA director at supervising the agencies, and so the debate over who should be in charge goes on. In any case, it's unfair to pin the blame on any one individual. I often say that if Superman were running U.S. intelligence, he'd still be unable to make it work effectively.

The real problem is structural. The federal government has sixteen different intelligence agencies, and it's hard to coordinate their efforts, given all the bureaucracies. In addition to the CIA, there are three big agencies that operate out of the Pentagon: the NSA; the National Reconnaissance Office, which builds and operates the nation's spy satellites; and the National Geospatial-Intelligence Agency, which does imagery intelligence. The State Department has its own intelligence agency, called the Bureau of Intelligence and Research, and similar agencies exist within the departments of Energy, Treasury, and Homeland Security—not to mention each branch of the military.

Turf wars within and between intelligence and law-enforcement agencies are recurrent themes on 24. Do the same sorts of problems crop up in the real world?

Absolutely. *Turf* is the biggest four-letter word in Washington. Until a year or so ago, there was a major turf battle between the CIA and the National Counter Terrorism Center. There is an ongoing battle between the CIA and the Pentagon. And there remains a lack of trust between and within the various agencies involved in counterterrorism. Within the FBI, for example, analysts who sit behind desks are supposed to have the same opportunities and to be accorded the same respect as the special agents who go out into the field and use their guns to catch bad guys. But the Bureau has never treated analysts as first-class citizens. Special agents have tended to look down on them, and FBI regulations render them ineligible for certain top positions.

What's the fix for that kind of a problem?

That's a $64,000 question. First, you have to make sure to hire people who understand the importance of working as a team. Second, you have to train them across agency lines. This is beginning to happen; for the first time ever, FBI special agents are being trained alongside CIA case officers. Third, you have to incentivize the right things, reward the stars for working across agency lines, thinking outside of the box, and doing the valuable thing rather than the easy thing. One example in the CIA is that case officers have historically been rewarded for the numbers of spies they recruit, not the quality of those assets. The same is true with analysts; it's not how smart your report was but how many reports you've churned out. These kinds of incentives need to change if intelligence is to make quantum improvements.

On 24, Jack Bauer is the ultimate antiauthoritarian—someone whose work is disrupted by rivalries and personal relationships. Do these sorts of personality issues play out in real-world intelligence agencies?

Jack Bauer is portrayed in a very personal way—animosities, warts, and all. That's why he's so entertaining. But real intelligence officials pride themselves on being *professionals*. That word *professional* conveys a set of beliefs, values, training, and practices about what is acceptable and expected behavior—and what isn't. A core part of intelligence professionalism is "speaking truth to power," and maintaining a clear distinction between intelligence and policy. Intelligence officials are supposed to provide information. They are never supposed to make policy or policy recommendations. They are supposed to give their best judgments, without prejudice or personal beliefs getting in the way. And they serve all presidents, Democrat and Republican. I think that is often lost in the fictionalized world of TV, where it's far more entertaining to have the maverick good guy breaking all the rules to save the country.

What needs to happen for the nation's counterterrorism apparatus to function properly?
Like former National Security Adviser Brent Scowcroft, I believe that the Pentagon should cede control of its three big intelligence agencies. That would free them up to do more strategic intelligence gathering and analysis. By that, I mean getting a strategic picture of al Qaeda's capabilities and activities, and how the organization is changing, as well as assessing other potential enemies and their intentions. As things now stand, these agencies are so focused on the immediate tactical needs of the war fighter—for example, spotting the target over the next hill—that the big picture gets short shrift. But when General Scrowcroft presented the idea to the White House, it was deep-sixed.

The second thing we need to do is to transfer the domestic intelligence function from the FBI to a new agency or to the Department of Homeland Security. Which organization should perform that role is hard to say, but it's clear that the FBI cannot. If domestic intelligence were removed from the FBI's mission, we'd get two benefits: better intelligence and an FBI focused on what it has always done best, which is fighting crime.

Lastly, we should shrink the staff of the Director of National Intelligence, which now stands at about 1,500. This number, which is far larger than Congress intended, suggests bureaucratic bloat and dysfunction. Generally speaking, smaller is better when it comes to coordinating staffs. The National Security Council staff, which is charged with coordinating foreign policy across the U.S. government, typically has a staff of 50 to 200. A smaller DNI staff would be better able to focus on stopping terrorists and other threats to our national security and less likely to waste time on managing itself.

What will it take to bring about these kinds of reforms?
I'm afraid it's going to take another catastrophic terrorist attack. Even that might not be enough.

That's a pretty bleak assessment.
It is, but we've faced these problems for nearly sixty years, and, despite 9/11, they haven't been solved.

Last year saw the creation of the nation's first multiagency counterterrorism agency, the Joint Regional Intelligence Center (JRIC), in Los Angeles. For those of us on the outside, it sounds a lot like a real-life counterpart to CTU. Is the creation of JRIC a hopeful sign?
JRIC is a great idea. It's not the first so-called fusion center; for some time, the FBI has been operating joint terrorism task forces, or JTTFs, in cities across the country. But JRIC, which is staffed by employees of the FBI, the Los Angeles County Sheriff's Department, and the Los Angeles Police Department, as well as representatives from other agencies and the private sector, is the poster child for a new breed of fusion center. It puts federal, state, and local officials together in the same room to evaluate terrorist threats against targets in southern California.

But there are problems with JRIC, including the fact that it's not staffed around the clock. And it's not entirely clear who is coordinating the efforts of JRIC and the other fusion centers being created across the country. There are other questions, too. Will beat cops get the training that will help them determine which tips and leads to pass along to the analysts at JRIC? Will the analysts get the training—and the necessary computer equipment—to pass along the right information to the federal authorities in Washington? I'm not convinced that they will. A recent report issued by the Congressional Research Service found that there are forty different fusion centers across the U.S. and still no standard way to report the information they get up the line to Washington. Some are now saying that we need to fuse the fusion centers.

Have cubicle-bound analysts of the sort who work at JRIC become more central to our war on terrorism than gun-wielding officers in the field?
Well, I myself am something of a cubicle-bound analyst, so I'll say yes. You can have the best FBI agents in the field, and the best CIA

operatives working abroad, but it's still the analysts who make sense of intelligence and figure out how to use it to protect us. Intelligence is not some set of facts locked away in a vault that suddenly reveal everything. Good intelligence is only as good as the analysis that comes with it. A satellite image of troops massing on a border could mean an imminent attack—or it could be a political bluff or a harmless exercise. Figuring out the truth requires analysts to make judgments and discern patterns from all the information we get.

Analysis also sets collection priorities. Good analysis tells us what we know, what we don't, what gaps are most important, and what information we need to collect to begin filling those gaps. Without analysis, the operators in the field—the people on the pointy tip of the spear—too often are left chasing needles in haystacks.

You've also been critical of JRIC's approach, which involves following up on every credible tip and lead that comes in. Why is that?

JRIC's leave-no-stone-unturned approach to evaluating terrorist threats and preventing terrorist attacks sounds good, but it's fundamentally flawed. In my opinion, the goal shouldn't be to prevent all attacks. The goal should be to prevent those attacks that are most likely to happen and most likely to cause massive damage. In other words, we should focus on the more realistic and achievable goal of managing risk rather than trying to achieve the impossible: eliminating the risk completely. That might mean worrying less about the remote possibility of a suicide bombing at your child's nursery school in North Dakota, which might kill a handful of people, and worrying much more about attacks on major targets in urban areas, which are more likely and which could kill hundreds or thousands. Of course, this is not a very attractive thing to talk about, politically speaking.

Why was JRIC established in Los Angeles rather than in another city likely to be a target of terrorists?

Los Angeles is a leader in cross-jurisdictional cooperation and a model for other cities when it comes to responding to disasters like earthquakes, riots, and terrorist attacks. People here are used to working across agency lines. And we know that, given its huge population and its importance as an economic center, Los Angeles is high on terrorists' target list. In 1999, Customs agents in

Washington state stopped a jihadist named Ahmed Ressam, who was on his way from Canada to bomb Los Angeles International Airport. LAX remains a major target. Another target here is the combined port complex of Los Angeles and Long Beach. These ports share the same harbor, and together they handle more cargo each year than the top ten East Coast ports combined. Even the threat of a major incident at this critical node of the global economy would cause shipping to grind to a halt—not just in the U.S. but around the world. There would be tremendous long-term damage to the economy.

Just how vulnerable is the port?
A recent study by Stanford researchers found that, even under the best of circumstances, there was only a one in four chance that we would be able to detect a nuclear device that had been smuggled into the port inside a shipping container. The same study indicated that the likelihood we would be able to detect such a device as it came into the port was closer to zero. And this is after we had taken steps to beef up security at the port.

Do you think a nuclear attack on the port or elsewhere on U.S. soil is inevitable?
A nuclear attack is not inevitable, but we're not moving fast enough to take the steps needed to minimize that threat. It's a threat that scares the daylights out of me, especially when you consider the abundance of fissile material around the world and Osama bin Laden's stated desire to acquire a nuclear weapon. I'm afraid it's only a matter of time before he gets his hands on one. ■

Shane Harris

The Shadow Hunters: LA's Real CTU

If there is a physical place in the real world that bears any meaningful resemblance to the work done by the fictional CTU of 24, it might be the Joint Regional Intelligence Center (JRIC), an antiterrorism, lead-filtering "fusion center," established in 2004 with the pooled resources of the FBI, the Department of Homeland Security, the Los Angeles Police Department, and other agencies. Now housed in Norwalk—one of those sprawling, anonymous, industrial suburbs of LA, typical of where most of 24's action took place in the first six seasons—the JRIC (pronounced JAY-rick) facility was relaunched in 2006 with a ribbon-cutting ceremony presided over by Secretary of Homeland Security Michael Chertoff.

Shane Harris, a reporter for the National Journal, *got inside JRIC to write the following groundbreaking profile of the behind-the-scenes intelligence work that goes into trying to separate potential hoax from potential horror in the real world of southern California's war on terror. As Harris's report makes clear, this real world is very different from television: Fearful citizens call in reports of "Middle Eastern–looking men" loading potentially explosive fertilizer into a truck in the neighbor's driveway, only to have the incident turn out to be Mexican gardeners doing their jobs. Only a tiny fraction of the hundreds of leads JRIC receives prove to be worth following up on. And, as FBI supervisory special agent Kristen von KleinSmid says, "I wish it were like 24," but "I can't redirect satellites" the way Jack Bauer and his CTU colleagues can.*

In any event, Shane Harris's report on JRIC is required reading for anyone who wants to understand the prosaic daily realities in the real world of counterterrorism.

THE SHADOWY WARNING could have easily been swallowed up in the flow of hundreds of crank calls and sketchy leads about airport attacks and bombs on bridges that flooded government hotlines that year. But this call was different: Al named a place, and a date.

Los Angeles, Thursday, the 29th, Al said. A shopping mall near the Federal Building on Wilshire Boulevard and the close-by campus of UCLA. Al said that a cell of three terrorists would enter the country from Canada. He even gave names. This didn't sound like a crank. Could it be for real? Could this be the one?

Officials in Washington immediately called L.A.'s Joint Terrorism Task Force, a team of FBI agents, Homeland Security officials, and local police and sheriff's officers. The FBI set up dozens of these task forces in cities across the country after 9/11, and they quickly became magnets for bureaucratic turf tussles. But in L.A., partly owing to a long history of cooperating on anti-gang and drug squads, the local cops and the feds got along well. After getting Washington's call about Al, the FBI set up a team within the task force to vet incoming tips, including other bomb threats. The police department's terrorism analysts canceled their weekend plans. Unnoticed in the hustle and flow of city life, L.A. went into terror mode.

At least two big malls were near the Federal Building and UCLA. On busy West Pico Boulevard was the Westside Pavilion, with more than 160 stores. Over in the Fairfax District, a historically Jewish neighborhood, the fashionable outdoor plaza called the Grove beckoned shoppers and moviegoers to its stores and cinemas. Before the Los Angeles Police Department and the mayor told thousands of Angelinos to stay away from these two sites, the authorities needed to know what they were up against.

FBI agents traced Al's call to a prepaid phone card. They tracked down the card seller, who gave agents a log of Al's calls. It turned out that his real name was Zameer Mohamed and that he had called in the bomb threat from Room 308 of a Comfort Inn in Calgary.

Hotel management told agents that a Samier Hussein had rented the room. Authorities ran the name and got a hit in federal records: Mohamed had used *Hussein* as an alias in Texas, where officials had investigated him the year before on a theft charge. Was Mohamed changing names to cover his tracks? That would have helped him if he wanted to evade U.S. authorities or the Qaeda members he had ostensibly just ratted out.

Meanwhile, in Los Angeles, local authorities were analyzing the bomb threat. The city's top terrorism officials were seasoned experts. John Miller, the head of the LAPD's counter-terrorism operation at the time, was a former journalist with deep ties to the FBI. He was also the last Western reporter to interview Osama bin Laden before 9/11. The department's chief, William Bratton, was perhaps the most famous cop in America. He was appointed New York City's police commissioner a year after the 1993 World Trade Center bombing, and he led a dramatic reduction in crime citywide. Miller was Bratton's spokesman then. The two were plugged into those who knew the national threat picture.

No one in Washington had said it publicly yet, but even as Mohamed made his call in April 2004, multiple and credible sources had convinced counter-terrorism officials that Al Qaeda was planning a major attack in the United States. The "chatter" about a strike was at its highest level since 9/11, intelligence agencies calculated.

On Wednesday, the day before the threatened attack, city officials informed the shopping mall owners. On Thursday, Bratton stood before news cameras at the Grove and asked Angelinos for help. "We need the eyes, the ears" of the citizenry, he stressed. He reminded people that bin Laden had recently issued another taped warning promising more violence. Then-Mayor James Hahn said that people should go about their daily business but should be alert to the out-of-place: "a truck that seems to be parked somewhere for too long, or someone . . . wearing bulky clothing on a hot day."

Police stepped up patrols around the two malls and across West Los Angeles. News helicopters whirled above the supposed targets. But by Friday, everything seemed back to normal.

"This just happens all the time. . . . This is no different than any anonymous bomb threat that gets called in," Gene Thompson, the head of corporate security for the Westside Pavilion's owners, told a reporter for the *Los Angeles Times*. "Life goes on," said Tom Miles, the Grove's general manager.

In fact, life did go on, unimpeded by a bomb or any other shopping disruptions. On the day Mohamed had warned that his Qaeda friends would strike, federal authorities apprehended him as he crossed the U.S.-Canadian border into Montana. Mohamed confessed that he'd made the whole thing up. There was no bomb. Those supposed Qaeda operatives were actually friends of his girlfriend. Mohamed had called Homeland Security to get back at her for stealing his paycheck from a Toronto bank where they used to work together. He had asked the three men to help him get the money back, but they had refused. Mohamed said he picked the two malls because he knew the area, having once visited the UCLA law library. Life went on. But the city never really slept.

Mohamed's unusually specific threat inspired a rare frenzy of activity. To be sure, Los Angeles doesn't ramp up to full alert for every lead that comes over the transom. That would be impossible, because, by officials' count, they have received more than 4,000 tips, leads, and other vague insinuations about possible terrorist attacks in the greater L.A. area in just the past three years.

Most of them turn out to be bogus. Anonymous callers see "Arabs" taking photographs of bridges. Electrical plant owners notice a van driving slowly by their security gates. Some concerned citizen sees "Middle Eastern–looking" men loading fertilizer onto a truck in her neighbor's driveway. Authorities have documented literally thousands of such leads in cities across the country, and few of them come to anything. The camera-toting terrorists are actually tourists; the driver of the van was lost; the men loading fertilizer were Mexican gardeners.

Occasionally, of course, the leads are more substantial and are worth investigating. Some are sourced to U.S. intelligence agencies or to the Homeland Security Department, which is nominally tasked with keeping states and localities abreast of threats to their areas.

Today, in L.A. and in more than four dozen other cities across the country, state and local officials, using mostly federal grant money, have built a network of lead-vetting teams to do just that. They call them "fusion centers," and

Bush administration officials, along with powerful members of Congress in both parties, believe that they are one of the best ways to prevent the next attack. Usually run in partnership with federal agencies, such as the FBI and Homeland Security, fusion centers employ teams of terrorism analysts, many of whom are self-educated. They take every lead, hold it up to the light, and ask, Could this be connected to terrorism? .

In L.A., a city that makes its living spinning fact into fiction—the buttoned-down terrorism analyst has morphed into Jack Bauer, terrorist-fighting force of nature on *24*—you might expect the fusion center to pulse at the city's heart. Wrong. To get to the lead-filtering complex—called the Joint Regional Intelligence Center, or "Jay Rick"—you have to leave the beauty bars of the Sunset Strip and the curvy overlooks of the Hollywood Hills. Go south about 10 miles, take the 105 freeway east until it ends, then head down an industrial road, past a taco stand, a car wash, and a movie theater. There, amid a warren of stout office buildings in the industrial L.A. suburb of Norwalk, is a sand-colored 525,000-square-foot edifice. JRIC is on the seventh floor, next to the corporate headquarters of Bally Total Fitness. This is homeland security's next frontier.

JRIC is L.A.'s terrorism "listening post," says Stephen Tidwell, the assistant director in charge of the FBI's Los Angeles field office. Tidwell, LAPD's Bratton, and L.A. County Sheriff Leroy Baca are among JRIC's most enthusiastic supporters. The three men are friends and self-professed true believers in chasing terrorists down at the local level. Their comradeship has caught Washington's attention. When JRIC opened last summer, Homeland Security Secretary Michael Chertoff came out for the ribbon-cutting. Federal officials call JRIC a "model fusion center," one for others to emulate.

JRIC's roster is a bureaucratic potpourri. It contains FBI agents, LAPD officers, L.A. County sheriff's deputies, public health experts, contract analysts who study radical Islam, a liaison from the Homeland Security Department, and officers detailed from other local law enforcement agencies across the Los Angeles region.

At 9 a.m. every Monday through Friday, the JRIC staff sits down and sorts through the daily cache of leads, to make sure that they're vetted and that all agencies are on the same page. If there's a report that terrorists are spiking the water supply with biotoxins, JRIC will ask a microbiologist to take a look. How credible is the threat? Could that toxin actually live in water? How many people might be affected? If there's a call about suspicious activity in Long Beach, the appropriate JRIC officer will run it past his sources. Some have likened the hunt for terrorists to looking for a needle in a haystack. But JRIC members go through haystacks, straw by straw, asking, "Could this be a needle?"

So far, none of the leads has revealed an active terrorist conspiracy in the L.A. region. "Ninety-nine-point-nine percent are false," says Bob Galarneau, a sheriff's department lieutenant and a JRIC program manager. "But we still investigate. . . . Every one is followed up on."

Considering the gravity of the potential threat, one might expect daily life at JRIC to resemble a scene out of a Tom Clancy movie. Wrong again. There are trappings of adventure—wall-mounted televisions turned to cable news channels, including *Al Jazeera*; table tops strewn with copies of *Counterterrorism* magazine. Beyond that, JRIC looks like just another banal workplace. If this were a TV show, it would be *24* meets *The Office*.

"I wish it were like *24*," says Kristen von KleinSmid, the FBI supervisory special agent in charge of the threat squad, a JRIC team that can decide to open investigations on particular leads. "I can't redirect satellites. I'm sure there's someone who can. But I just can't make a phone call and have it done."

The threat squad, also called CT-6, worked the 2004 bomb threat on the shopping malls. Today it comprises about 20 analysts and officers from a variety of federal and local agencies.

"About one out of every 100 leads, there's something good that comes out of that, where really useful information is obtained," von KleinSmid says. Agents "know that a lot of the stuff they're working isn't going to go anywhere."

Which makes one wonder: If nothing will come of most—nearly all—of the leads that have poured into L.A. over the years, why bother chasing down each one? Because, officials say, chasing ghosts and possible hoaxes is the best chance they have of finding a bona fide threat. One time out of thousands, the lead might bear fruit. The terrorist hunters might get lucky. In fact, they say, it has already happened.

In the summer of 2005, police officers in Torrance, south of downtown L.A., investigated an armed robbery at a gas station. It was the latest in a string of heists, and each time the bandits had fled without a trace. But this time one of them dropped his cellphone, giving police a rare lead.

Officers traced the phone to Gregory Vernon Patterson, a 21-year-old local man with no criminal record. They placed him under surveillance. According to a criminal complaint, on the evening of July 5 [2005], Patterson and Levar Haney Washington, who, later investigations showed, was an L.A. gang member, drove to a gas station in Fullerton, east of Torrance in Orange County. Washington, dressed in a dark hooded sweatshirt and carrying a shotgun, robbed the clerk, according to the complaint. Police arrested the two men and then searched Washington's apartment in South Los Angeles.

That search, authorities say, ultimately enabled them to disrupt a major terrorist plot aimed at local military recruiting stations, the Israeli consulate, and other targets across L.A. Torrance police officers found documents outlining an imminent attack, possibly timed for the anniversary of September 11, as well as knives, bulletproof vests, and "jihadist" material that wasn't available from the usual sources on the Internet, investigators said.

More than 200 federal and local investigators worked the case, pursuing leads, tracking evidence, and grilling Washington and Patterson. "Virtually every agency in the area jumped on the hunt," says Tidwell, the FBI assistant director in charge. "It was textbook."

According to an FBI affidavit, Washington told investigators that he led an "Islamic council" that was planning a jihad in the United States, "to respond to the oppression of Muslims in the United States, in Iraq and Afghanistan by the U.S. government." Washington said that his group had scouted targets, to determine whether they should use a bomb or "rifles and inflict as many casualties as possible." Patterson, the affidavit said, had purchased an AR-15 assault rifle and was only days from picking it up at a sporting goods store. Investigators charged that the men commited the gas-station robberies to pay for their citywide offensive. Planning for the attacks, the FBI said that Washington told them, was nearly complete.

Officials later charged that Washington and Patterson acted at the behest of Kevin Lamar James, a Muslim convert doing time in Folsom prison since 1996 for armed robbery in gang-related crimes. Police said that James had founded a radical Islamic cell called Jamiyyat Ul Islam Is Saheeh, or JIS—"The Association of True Islam"—and, from inside Folsom's walls, directed a plot to conduct a violent jihad. Federal officials had warned about the spread of Islamic radicalism in prisons. Local authorities said that Washington and Patterson had met at an area mosque, and had become radicalized by James's vision. On August 31, 2005, a federal grand jury indicted the three men, along with a Pakistani national, on charges of plotting the L.A. attacks.

Ask any of the terrorist hunters in L.A. to cite a plot they've disrupted as a result of their post-9/11 vigilance, and they'll immediately point to JIS. To this day, the FBI calls the incident the closest thing to an "operational" terrorist plot since the September 11 attacks. Miller, the former LAPD counter-terrorism official who is now the FBI's chief spokesman, has called JIS a "home-grown" terrorist cell. He said that it "is the best example of how the threat now is as much out there on our streets, among some disaffected Americans, as are teams of sleeper cells who are sent from faraway training camps."

Before 9/11, officials in L.A. agree, the police officers who searched Washington's apartment might have been alarmed by the weaponry and the jihadist literature but wouldn't have known to immediately call the terrorism task force. The JIS case is proof, they say, that the relentless pursuit of leads, the hyper-alertness, the constant probing of every piece of evidence for a terrorist link, actually prevents attacks.

Many terrorism experts, however, aren't so sure. If the evidence is correct, then Washington and Patterson were clearly capable of violence, and very well may have attacked targets in the city. But is it accurate to call them domestic terrorists, members of a homegrown cell? Are L.A. terrorist hunters so intent on turning over every rock, seeing threats where they don't exist?

Amy Zegart, an associate professor of public policy at UCLA and a leading national authority on counter-terrorism, says that officials are too quick to label as terrorists groups that express some outrage at the government. "When you parade things that clearly aren't at the level of 9/11 as success, you undermine the FBI's credibility with the public," she says. [For more on Amy Zegart's views, see her interview in this chapter.]

Zegart is a prominent FBI skeptic. After she wrote a scathing op-ed in the *Los Angeles Times* last year in which she said that the FBI was "still stupid" about terrorism, the FBI's Tidwell called her to his office for a dressing down.

Still, after examining the city's terrorist-hunting efforts, including JRIC, Zegart says that there's some reason to take heart. "They have a very forward-thinking approach," she said. But there's a flip side to the city's ceaseless pursuit, Zegart says. "What worries me about the follow-every-lead approach is that it is done in a strategic void. I think this is an endemic problem that is true across U.S. intelligence. We're ramping up . . . saying, 'Let's look at today's threat list,'" Zegart says. "The current news cycle and the terrorist threat are putting more pressure on people to focus on the here and now." As a result, counter-terrorism officials might miss the bigger, longer-range picture about terrorism trends, and overlook the new threats that could be emerging below the radar sweep, she fears.

Ask Stephen Tidwell where the FBI and his friends in L.A. are looking for the next terrorist threat, and you'll get no specifics. "We're looking everywhere. . . . We spend hours upon hours," he says. "Got people not sleeping very much. People walking around like zombies. . . . We can't have enough eyes looking."

Considering his obsession with standing vigil over L.A., it's odd that Tidwell's office on the 11th floor of the Federal Building looks not to the south and east, over the city's concrete expanse, but to the northwest, taking in the verdant Santa Monica Mountains, which run east to west, to the Pacific Ocean. It's a vivid reminder that Los Angeles sits in a bowl, surrounded by natural forces that also conspire to wipe the city off the map.

"We game out in our heads multiple suicide bombers or multiple IED attacks," Tidwell says, referring to Iraqi insurgents' weapon of choice, the improvised explosive device. He pauses and glances out the window. What really scares him, Tidwell says, is what happens after the attack. "Eighteen million people, trying to self-evacuate out of here, will collapse this place."

"We're gonna get hit here," Tidwell says. "When it does happen, how are we going to hunt them? How are we going to find them?" By his calculus, every set of eyes, every listening post, every JRIC is one more barrier that terrorists have to overcome. The best chance to save L.A. is to make their job harder. ■

"You don't need to watch 24 as a kind of primer on moral philosophy, but you probably should."
—Brian M. Carney, the *Wall Street Journal*

At the Crossroads of Urgency and Ethics

The reality-versus-fiction debate about *24*, which we covered in the last chapter, is a warm-up for the far more serious question viewers are asked to confront: At what point does the need for our collective security begin to outweigh the most cherished tenets of American civilization? Among them: the fundamental principle of "innocent until proven guilty"; the constitutional injunctions against unwarranted search and seizure; and, the accepted legal doctrines banning wiretapping without a judicial order, prohibiting torture, and requiring due process. *24* runs right up against these most sacred cows of the rule of law and slaughters them in the name of urgency. As Jack Bauer says, "I don't want to bypass the Constitution, but these are extraordinary circumstances." This chapter addresses what might constitute such circumstances and what the right response to them should be.

24 generally leans toward the view that security should trump personal privacy, human and civil rights, and the Geneva Convention. Characters find themselves in desperate circumstances that require desperate responses—albeit sometimes at great emotional cost. Past seasons have brought to life the statement once made by *24* cocreator Joel Surnow: "If there is a bomb about to hit a major U.S. city and you have a person with information . . . if you don't torture that person, that would be one of the most immoral acts you could imagine."

This perspective, shared by a number of our contributors, is decried by *24*'s vocal critics at several levels. First, they say, security may require trade-offs, but privacy and liberty need not be the things always traded off. Second, according to some experienced interrogators and other experts, the show operates on a false premise: Outright torture—or its more euphemistic characterization as "enhanced" interrogation techniques—does not work in practice.

Third, still others say, showing torture on a mainstream TV show as acceptable, even normal, has ethical consequences that should outrage us all. The philosopher, psychologist, and cultural critic Slavoj Žižek maintains in his essay here that *24* asks us to swallow a "lie" by telling us that we can remain human even while carrying out inhuman acts.

Mark Bowden, author of the award-winning book *Black Hawk Down* and a national correspondent for the *Atlantic Monthly*, has probed deeply into the messy realities of violence in the fight against today's terrorists, jihadists, and fanatics. He believes that even though in some extreme cases torture may be necessary, it should be declared illegal and its perpetrators prosecuted. He also talks about the type of interrogation techniques that really do work—rarely are these seen on *24*.

Tony Lagouranis, a former U.S. Army interrogator at Abu Ghraib and other prisons in Iraq, concluded from his experience that not only was excessive torture illegal, but it usually backfired. He also believes that regular viewing of shows like *24* may have prompted impressionable soldiers in the field to mimic some of these techniques. David Danzig, Primetime Torture Project director at Human Rights First, agrees. He had the opportunity to make this case directly to the show's creative team, famously bringing with him Lagouranis and several high-ranking, veteran army interrogators. He shares with us his first-person account of that memorable meeting.

Brian Carney, an editorial writer for the *Wall Street Journal*, starts off the chapter by urging viewers to consider *24* as a welcome primer on moral philosophy. In the real world, he says, right and wrong may be clear only in retrospect: A family may have to suffer or sacrifice for the greater good, and torture may have to be used in extreme cases, in spite of our respect for human and civil rights.

We don't talk much about "moral philosophy" these days, even though we know that the post-9/11 world requires us to think critically about the large issues along the continuum from freedom to security. Our contributors in this chapter remind us of one of the main reasons why *24* is so compelling. While its situations are unrealistically black and white, overly extreme, and excessively urgent, they are nonetheless examples and metaphors for the pressing questions our leaders and our society as a whole must strive to answer. And the answers are neither simple nor easy. ∎

Brian M. Carney

Jack Bauer's Dilemmas—and Ours: Watching *24* As a Primer on Moral Philosophy

THE CURRENT SEASON [Season 6] of Fox's television series "24" began with a dilemma that will be familiar to long-time devotees of the program. A man's wife and child have been taken hostage by a terrorist. If the man does not help [the terrorist] carry out his plans, his family will be killed.

Yes, such a dilemma propels the show's pace and intensifies the dramatic ordeal. But it also points toward difficult ethical puzzles with profound implications for our current real-world moment. You don't need to watch "24" as a kind of primer on moral philosophy, but you probably should.

This season's opening predicament echoes the one into which the show's star, Jack Bauer, was thrust in the series' first season six years ago. Back then, the bad guys tried to compel Bauer, played by Kiefer Sutherland, to assist in the assassination of a presidential candidate. As a result, he was forced both to play along with the terrorists and seek a way to free his family. He succeeded, at least temporarily, in saving both the target of the assassination and his family.

In a variety of forms, the sticky situation with which the series began has formed the heart of the show ever since: Terrorist threats place American civilians and government officials in a position in which they must choose between conflicting loyalties. It is the show's genius, and the key to its enduring appeal, that its writers almost never lapse into thinking that these choices are simple. This is not to say that there are no right and wrong answers. But right and wrong are often only clear—especially to the characters, but even to the viewer—in retrospect.

This season, the kidnapping plot line is reprised, only this time it is the proverbial man on the street who is coerced, and he chooses compliance with the terrorists in the vain hope that if he upholds his end of the bargain, they will too. He does so oblivious to the consequences of abetting a terrorist plot that, as it turns out, results in the detonation of a nuclear bomb in the middle of Los Angeles. Fittingly, the father who made this possible is consumed by the blast. His son, meanwhile, only escapes because the family's mother refuses to rely on the terrorists' goodwill and instead calls in the authorities.

The lesson here is not only that appeasing terrorists is a mug's game. The father's feeling of duty to his family blinds him to the competing claims of his country—and his neighbors. He acts out of simplistic loyalty to family without due consideration of the effects. It is natural to try to save one's family under these circumstances. It would be monstrous not to.

But it is not merely a question of choosing between family and a greater good; or—in other contexts that crop up repeatedly on the show—between civil liberties and national security; or between torture and human rights. It is a failing of our politics that these kinds of questions, in the real world, are presented by both sides as either easy to answer or unnecessary to choose between—or both. It is one achievement of "24" that it treats these tradeoffs as both real and difficult. They are questions that depend on the circumstances in which they are asked.

Which is not to say that the characters in the show always see things as difficult; it would stretch credulity if every character had a knack for moral subtlety. The show's characters—good, bad and in between—can be judged by the extent to which they are able to weigh these countervailing demands. The reputation of Jack Bauer, the counterterrorism officer extraordinaire, has survived episodes in which he threatened to cut out the eye of a presidential aide or shot bad guys in the knees because he never seems to lose sight of the larger goal of saving the country or of resolving the apparent contradictions into which he is sometimes forced in that quest.

> "I just want to see Jack go and kill people."
> —Trent Dilfer, quarterback, expressing disappointment that some episodes of *24* focus too much on character

One of the president's aides, by contrast, reacts to the nuclear blast by suggesting that it's a good opportunity to round up Muslims *en masse*. The callousness of the idea, as much as its content, exposes him as morally obtuse and thus sinister.

In another difficult moment, Bauer was forced to choose between saving the life of a known terrorist and murderer and taking the life of a federal agent and friend. If history is any guide, viewers of the show will presumably be given reason to question whether Jack made the correct decision. But the contrast between Bauer and the agent he had to kill to save the terrorist lies in the ethical realm: Much as he hates to save the bad guy, he knows that the terrorist may be the only hope of preventing even more murders down the road. The agent he kills, by contrast, is motivated purely by the desire for personal revenge.

All these episodes help the show to maintain a realistic moral tone. An enemy that rejects everything we hold dear about our civil society will inevitably force us to make compromises between competing principles and loyalties. The most interesting complications that ensue as a season of "24" unfolds are the moral ones. And the show's great virtue is that it never pretends that these dilemmas are simple or false. ■

An Army Interrogator's Dark Journey Through Iraq

"*Everyone wanted to be a Hollywood interrogator,*" *says Tony Lagouranis, a former U.S. Army interrogator at the infamous Abu Ghraib prison in Iraq. "We didn't have guidance." Since returning from Iraq, Lagouranis has publicly denounced the "enhanced" interrogation techniques designed to break prisoners. He has also observed, "We really had nothing to fall back on, and the only role models we had were from TV and movies. . . . We turned to them to look for ways of interrogating [that worked]: mock executions and mock electrocutions, stress positions, isolation, hypothermia, threatening to execute family members or rape detainees' wives, and things like that." Their behavior might not have been specifically modeled on 24, Lagouranis told the creative team behind the show when he was invited on the set, along with other experienced interrogators in 2006, but such depictions of violence definitely had an "instructional" effect on the interrogators in Iraq, he believes.*

Many of the contributors to this book refer to the depiction of torture on 24, but Specialist Tony Lagouranis brings the voice of experience to this discussion. Trained in the classics in college, he enlisted in the army in early 2001, in part to pursue his goal of learning Arabic. Lagouranis soon found himself deployed to Iraq as an interrogator. His assignment: the prisons of Mosul, North Babel, Fallujah, Abu Ghraib. Lagouranis found a huge disconnect between the rules and training he'd received stateside and the conditions in the field, where "what we learned in military schools didn't apply anymore." Guidance was either nonexistent, he says, or contradictory.

After leaving the army with an honorable discharge, Lagouranis was so haunted by what he had witnessed and so disturbed by the army's lack of interest in investigating his reports that he went public, giving interviews and writing an op-ed piece that appeared in the New York Times *in February 2006. He has also written a book about his experiences, titled* Fear Up Harsh: An Army Interrogator's Dark Journey Through Iraq.

In the interview that follows, Lagouranis shares his experiences in visiting the set of 24 and talking to the writers and producers, his thoughts about the intersection between the show's content and today's political climate, and what it really takes to be a successful interrogator. "Torture is an ugly thing," concludes Lagouranis. "You don't get neat, tidy answers like you do on television."

How did a man who immersed himself in the humanities in college come to be an army interrogator in the infamous Abu Ghraib prison in Iraq?

I went to St. John's College, where the entire course of study is based on reading the "great books" of Western literature. I got very interested in studying ancient Greek, which later led me to study Hebrew on my own. I then wanted to learn Arabic, but it seemed impossible to teach myself. I ended up in Chicago in a white-collar job that I hated, but I took it to pay off my student loans. What I really wanted was to be back in school. The army seemed like a logical step to me: I could learn Arabic and pay off my student loans at the same time. It was early 2001, and it seemed like there was little risk of us going to war. Obviously, everything changed after 9/11, when I was fresh out of basic training. Originally, I tried for a job as a linguist or an interpreter, but I ended up as an interrogator instead. When I got to Abu Ghraib, there were a lot of whispers and rumors about something bad that had happened there, but I never really heard specifics. Although "enhanced interrogation techniques" were still going on, by the time I got there the sexual humiliation we saw all over the news had stopped.

Since leaving the military with an honorable discharge in 2005 after your first tour, you've become outspoken about the abuses that you saw going on in Iraq. What made you decide to do that?

I went to the press and admitted the terrible things I'd seen and I'd done myself as a way to encourage more scrutiny, and maybe influence the public debate about torture. I also volunteered to allow Human Rights First to film me in a training video they were making for West Point cadets about 24 and its effect on interrogations. They were hoping to show it to new army interrogators and to have it distributed to film and television studios to encourage them to be more responsible in how they show torture.

And was it working on this film that led to your meeting with the producers and writers of 24 in Hollywood?

Yes, Human Rights First arranged for me and other former interrogators to meet with the writers of 24 to discuss the torture they portray on the show and the impact it may be having on young soldiers. [For a full account of this meeting, see David Danzig's piece, later in this chapter.] Executive producer Howard Gordon was very interested but the writers were much more resistant. Their main defense was "the show is clearly fantasy, and we're not trying to portray reality. Real interrogators have professional training and aren't influenced by television." I tried to dispel that notion by telling them about my firsthand experiences in the field. However, they really rejected the idea that torture doesn't work and wouldn't be the best method in a ticking time-bomb scenario, or to gain intelligence.

In the end, I felt good about the meeting, but I don't think we changed their minds on the social impact of the show. It always came back to, "We're just trying to make a show that's popular."

You've talked about your feeling that shows like *24* influenced some interrogators in Iraq. Can you give me some examples of that?
The issue here is the difference between what is taught during training and what actually happens out in the field. Take waterboarding, for example, which creates the sensation of drowning. The army never teaches soldiers that. But I remember somebody bringing up the possibility of waterboarding after we had just watched a waterboarding scene on television. We refused to do it; we felt it was illegal. Waterboarding got really popular in movies and TV right after 9/11 and people did use that technique in Iraq, but they definitely didn't get it from any military doctrine. Also, in movies and on TV the interrogator always has an attitude of establishing absolute dominance over a detainee, and then issuing an explicit or implied threat, which is always portrayed as effective. But in the real world, that's not the case.

Why do interrogators seem to be more influenced by the violent torture techniques in the media than by the rules and regulations they were taught in training?
The army did give us specific rules while we were training. As a matter of fact, they told us that torture doesn't work, and that we were not allowed to use torture, with a very broad definition, but here's what goes wrong:

First, the army apparently has no interest in creating a dedicated core of talented and experienced interrogators. The senior people I met who had experience in the first Gulf War and the Balkans were just administrators and we never got to learn from them. All the people who were actually conducting interrogations were privates or specialists who had no idea what they were doing, and the army's promotion process is about how many push-ups you can do and how well you shoot your rifle, not how well you speak Arabic, or how many successful interrogations you've done.

Second, because the privates and specialists they are sending to Iraq as interrogators are not necessarily qualified to be there in the first place—one asked me what the Baath Party was; another asked me whether President Bush was a Democrat or Republican—they are much more susceptible to media and television influences. If you are going into the interrogation booth and you are floundering, you are going to look to anything you can find in order to improve yourself. The role models we had were from movies and television.

Third, we ended up being totally confused about what the rules were. We were taught that in dealing with a detainee there should be no brutality, and no negative repercussions, for example. We were taught that in a combat situation, you go by the rules, not by impulse. But I believe that the Bush administration's definition of torture muddied the waters for us. They said the Geneva Conventions don't apply, so we had no idea what the rules were. They took away our rules and our training, so we really had nothing to fall back on, and the only role models we had were from TV and movies.

Do you think a fourth component of this is that torture may not be just a problem at the unit level, but is condoned all the way up the line, to the highest levels of the military and the government?

To me, that's patently obvious, and I've been saying that ever since I got out of the army. I mean, all of the things that I did that I consider torture, I was told to do by my superiors. The Pentagon issued a memo very specifically telling us that these techniques were legal. It's coming from the Pentagon and filtering down through the entire chain of command. It's systemic. I saw with my own eyes that it was going on all over Iraq. If I thought the methods I'd used were outlawed, I would have refused to do them. I put it all down in official criminal investigation reports, along with torture I'd witnessed that I thought was illegal, but it became clear to me once I was out of Iraq that the army didn't have any interest in investigating prisoner abuse and my reports seemed to be completely ignored.

So if these are the things that don't work, what, in your opinion, are the keys to being a successful interrogator?

One reason our interrogation training was generally inadequate was because we didn't spend much time on approaches, which is the method that you use to break down the detainee's will to resist.

In Iraq, approaches were everything; that's all you did all day long, because people wouldn't give any information.

Another is that there has to be an element of distance: You can't have too much compassion for detainees because ultimately you are going to lie to them. Your job is to get them to betray themselves, their cause, and perhaps their countrymen, so it's obviously tough. In one case I remember bolstering somebody's ego; this guy was sort of a leader in his community and I just kept telling him what a great job he was doing and I sat there and listened to him talk about the things that he had done for the community for a long time. During the course of that, I was able to ask him things that I wanted to know and he told me what I wanted to know without realizing that I was fishing for information. What you have to do is to avoid implicating the prisoner in any crime at all and simply get him talking. Anything that gets him talking works. Even if he is lying to you, you can use that as long as he is giving you a volume of information. Then you can start working out his lies to get to what's true. Torture does not get people talking; torture might get people to say a sentence, but you're not going to get an hour's worth of conversation out of that.

The fact is that the most effective interrogations don't involve any kind of brutality. It's completely unnecessary. Every professional who has done studies on these things has determined that torture does not work when you want to elicit valuable information. It's the White House and civilian leadership that is advocating for it. It's not about getting information; it's about public perception.

Speaking of perception, the storylines on 24 thrive on the image that great threats are imminent and getting information out of a terrorist instantly is the only thing that can save the country. Based on your experience, are there actually ticking time-bomb scenarios?
I could say never, but then this opens up the real danger in allowing an exception to the antitorture rule. People think that if we actually have a ticking time-bomb scenario and you're going to save Los Angeles by torturing someone, people can justify putting an exception on the books. The real problem is that if you make that exception, when I walk into the interrogation booth in Iraq I could have a guy sitting in front of me who is accused of firing mortars at my base. To me, that's a ticking time-bomb scenario, because he can give me the location of the weapons that he was using, he can tell me who he was working with, he can tell me their methods, and I might be able to stop the next attack and save my

own life and save the lives of all the people around me. So is that a time-bomb scenario? Yes. So if you are justifying Jack Bauer torturing in a ticking time-bomb scenario, I am going to be over in Iraq torturing people. That's exactly what went on and that's how people justified it.

Did you encounter any Jack Bauer–like characters with vigilante streaks when you were in the army? Officials have assured the public that if an interrogator used techniques like they do in *24*, such as mock executions or shooting a prisoner in the leg, they'd be arrested. Do you think this is true?
There were people who felt like they were going it alone and they operated above and outside the law. In my book I write about people having their fingers broken, their ribs broken, their feet broken during interrogations. They were burned during interrogations, and received third-degree burns. That's not shooting somebody, but it might as well be. People used horrible methods in Iraq and weren't arrested; usually nothing happened unless a detainee died, and even then there wasn't accountability. When I reported that these things were going on, it was ignored. There was no accountability. But I think the Jack Bauer style ultimately is not effective.

Senator John McCain, who is an outspoken critic of torture, has said, "It's not about who they are, but it's about who we are." What are your thoughts on this?
While I'm not John McCain's biggest fan, I fully agree with him on that point. When I talk about torture, people often say to me, "Look at the tactics that al Qaeda is using when they capture people!" Or they say, "How can you talk about what you did to Iraqis as being torture when if they had been arrested under Saddam Hussein, they would have been hung on a meat hook?" But why are we using Saddam Hussein or al Qaeda as moral benchmarks for the way that we should behave? We really have to look at ourselves; we shouldn't look at ourselves in relation to them. We have to decide who we are and what our moral principles are, and then stick to them no matter how others would treat us or how afraid we are. It's not about getting tough with terrorists in a Jack Bauer style; that doesn't take guts. In my opinion that's cowardly. What takes guts is sticking to your principles no matter what the situation is. ■

Slavoj Žižek

24, Or Himmler in Hollywood

The problem with 24, *says Slavoj Žižek, is that, by presenting torture as a routine counterterrorism technique, it becomes acceptable in an era when every tick of the clock might put us in yet greater danger. The ethical consequences of "normalizing" torture should terrify us, says the Slovenian philosopher. Desperate choices, he says, while sometimes understandable, should not be elevated to a universal principle. When this happens, all sense of horror is lost, creating a moral vacuum in which our actions may become no better than those of Nazi war criminals.*

Žižek is one of the world's leading commentators on what popular culture says about us. He is as comfortable talking about the hidden language of cinema as he is reinterpreting Hegel, Freud, Lenin, Lacan, and other thinkers whose works have had a major impact on politics and culture. Žižek is the international director of the Birkbeck Institute for the Humanities at the University of London. He is the author of The Parallax View *and the presenter in the documentary* The Pervert's Guide to the Cinema, *a film about what psychoanalysis can tell us about cinema.*

The power of 24 *and its global reach into the TV and computer screens of the world's intellectuals has provoked Žižek to write several commentaries on the troubling issues the show raises for him. In this provocative piece he begins by noting that even the way commercials are inserted into the "hour" adds to the shows climate of urgency. He then goes on to address the ethical implications of this sense of urgency and concludes that* 24 *is actually presenting us with a lie: the presumption that it is possible to retain the moral high ground while carrying out acts of torture. Torture, even when done in the name of humanity, remains deeply inhuman, he says.*

THE FIFTH SEASON OF *24* is about the desperate attempt of the LA-based CTU (Counter Terrorist Unit) to prevent a terrorist act of catastrophic magnitude —the explosion of a stolen nuclear weapon. The action takes place among the CTU agents, in the White House, and among the terrorists. The "real-time" nature of the series, with each minute of airtime corresponding to a minute in the lives of the characters, confers on it a strong sense of urgency, emphasized by the ticking of an onscreen digital clock, which appears from time to time. This dynamic is accentuated through a series of formal procedures: from the

Source: An abbreviated form of this essay originally appeared in *The Guardian* (UK) in January 2006. Reprinted with the permission of the author.

frequent use of handheld cameras to the split screens to show the actions of various characters concurrently.

24 is a highly commercial series: Almost one-third of each installment is spent on commercials that break up the show. The way commercials break the continuity of the narrative is in itself unique and contributes to the sense of urgency: A single installment, commercials included, lasts exactly one hour, so that commercial breaks are part of the one-hour temporal continuity of the series. Say, we see the onscreen digital clock signaling that it is "7:46." Then there is a commercial break, after which we return to the series with the same digital clock signaling that it is now "7:51"—the length of the break in our, the spectators', real time is exactly equivalent to the temporal gap in the onscreen narrative. It's as if the commercial breaks miraculously fit into the real-time deployment of the events, that is, as if we were taking a break from the events that nonetheless are going on while we are watching commercials, as if a live transmission were temporarily interrupted. It is thus as if the continuity of the ongoing action is so pressing and urgent, spilling over into the real time of spectators themselves, that it cannot be interrupted, even for the commercial breaks.

And this brings us finally to the crucial point: the ethical dimension of this all-pervasive sense of urgency. The pressure of events is so overbearing, the stakes are so high, that they necessitate a kind of *ethical* suspension of ordinary moral concerns. The CTU collective, as well as its terrorist opponents, live and act in a shadowy space not covered by the law, doing things that "simply have to be done" in order to save our societies from the terrorist threat. This includes not only torturing the terrorists when they are caught, but even torturing the members of CTU itself or their closest relatives if they are suspected of terrorist links.

The CTU agents not only treat terrorists and suspects in this way, they also treat themselves as expendable, always ready to put their own or their colleagues' lives at stake if this will help prevent the terrorist act. Jack Bauer embodies this attitude in its purest form: Without any qualms, he not only tortures others and condones it when his superiors put his own life at stake, but even agrees to be handed over to the People's Republic of China as a scapegoat for a CTU covert operation that killed a Chinese diplomat. Although he knows he will be tortured there and imprisoned for life, he promises not to say anything and never to hurt U.S. interests. The end of the fourth season leaves Jack in a paradigmatic situation: When he is informed by the ex-president of the United States, his close ally, that someone in the government ordered him to be killed, his two closest CTU friends organize his fake death, and then he disappears into nowhere, anonymous, officially nonexisting. Not only the terrorists, but CTU agents themselves operate like what Giorgio Agamben calls *homini sacer*, those who can be killed with impunity since, in the eyes of the law, their life no longer counts. While they continue to act on behalf of the legal power, their acts are no longer covered and constrained by the law—they operate in an empty space within the domain of the law.

It is here that we encounter the series' fundamental ideological lie: In spite of this thorough and ruthless attitude of self-instrumentalization, the CTU agents, especially Jack, remain "warm human beings," loving, caught in the usual emotional dilemmas of us, "normal" people. They love their wives and children, they suffer jealousy—although they are at a moment's notice ready to sacrifice their interests and the lives of their beloved to the necessities of their task. They are something like the psychological equivalent of decaffeinated coffee: doing all the horrible things the situation necessitates, yet without paying the subjective price for it.

Consequently, one should not dismiss *24* as a simple pop cultural companion piece and justification of the problematic methods the United States is resorting to in the "war on terror"—much more is at stake here. Recall the lesson of Coppola's *Apocalypse Now*: The figure of Kurtz is not a remainder of some barbaric past, but the necessary outcome of the modern Western power itself. Kurtz was a perfect soldier—as such, through his overidentification with the military power system, he turned into the excess that the system had to eliminate in an operation that had to imitate what it fights (Willard's mission to kill Kurtz is nonexistent for the official record, "It never happened," as the general who briefs Willard points out).

> "On *24*, there are a few very good people, a few very bad ones and in between, a lot of question marks who can upend the plot (and the political analogies). That may be the biggest lesson of *24* in the Iraq era: don't stubbornly hang on to your preconceptions when the facts on the ground change."
> —*Time* magazine

The problem for those in power is this: how to obtain Kurtz without Kurtz's pathology, how to get people to do the necessary dirty job without turning them into monsters. This was already Heinrich Himmler's dilemma. When confronted with the task of liquidating the Jews of Europe, Himmler, the chief of the SS, adopted the heroic attitude of "somebody has to do the dirty job, so let's do it!" It is easy to do a noble thing for one's country, up to sacrificing one's life for it—it is much more difficult to commit a *crime* for one's country. . . . In *Eichmann in Jerusalem*, Hannah Arendt provided a precise description of this twist the Nazi executioners accomplished in order to be able to endure the horrible acts they performed. Most of them were not simply evil, they were well aware that they were doing things that brought humiliation, suffering, and death to their victims. The way out of this predicament was that, "Instead of saying: What horrible things I did to people!, the murderers would be able to say: What horrible things I had to watch in the pursuance of my duties, how heavily the task weighed upon my shoulders!" In this way, they were able to turn around the logic of resisting temptation: The temptation to be resisted was the very temptation to succumb to the elementary pity and sympathy in the presence of human suffering, and their "ethical" effort was directed toward the task of resisting this temptation *not* to murder, torture, and humiliate. My very violation of spontaneous ethical instincts of pity and compassion is thus turned into the proof of my ethical grandeur: To do my duty, I am ready to assume the heavy burden of inflicting pain on others.

There is a further "ethical problem" here for Himmler: how to make sure that the SS executioners, while performing these terrible acts, will remain human and retain their dignity. His answer was Krishna's message to Arjuna in the *Bhagavad-Gita* (Himmler's sacred book—he always had in his pocket a special leather-bound edition): Carry out your acts with an inner distance, do not get fully involved in them.

Therein also resides the lie of *24*: in the presumption that it is not only pos-

> "I bet Jack will have to torture his own father! AWESOME!! . . . How could they let Assad go? He's a terrorist! . . . No offense to Paul MaCrane but he isn't nearly as hot as Jack. . . . They don't look much like brothers . . . and the tension between Jack and Marilyn is hot. . . . WOW! Jack is kicking his brother's ass. Now he's tying him to the chair. I guess Jack knows he's a bad guy."
> —**Blogger "leora," posting her reactions in real time to Hour 5 of Season 6 on *24* headquarters.com.**

sible to retain human dignity in accomplishing acts of terror, but that when an honest person accomplishes such acts as a heavy duty, this confers on him an additional tragic-ethic grandeur. The very parallel between the CTU agents and the terrorists with regard to this feature (in the fourth season, Marwan, *the* bad guy, is also depicted as a devoted and loving father and husband) is in the service of this lie. But what if such a distance *is* possible? What if we *do* have people who commit terrible acts as part of their job, while, in private, they remain loving husbands, good parents, and fine friends? As Arendt knew, far from redeeming them, the very fact that they were able to retain their normality while committing such acts was the ultimate confirmation of their moral catastrophe.

So what about the popular and seemingly convincing response to this hair-splitting? Some argue that at least the United States is now only more open and less hypocritical about its behavior toward terrorist suspects. To this, one should retort with a simple counterquestion: "If the high representatives of the United States mean only this, *why, then, are they telling us this?* Why don't they just silently go on doing it, as they did it till now?" What is proper to human speech is the irreducible gap between the enunciated content and its act of enunciation. Let us imagine a wife and husband who have a tacit agreement that they can lead discreet extramarital affairs. If, all of a sudden, the husband openly tells his wife about an ongoing affair, she will have good reason to panic: "If it is just an affair, why are you telling me this? It must be something more!" The act of publicly reporting on something is never neutral; it affects the reported content itself.

The same goes for America's recent open admission of torture. When we hear people like Dick Cheney making their obscene statements about the necessity of torture, we should ask them: "If you just want to torture secretly some suspected terrorists, then why are you saying it publicly?" The question to be raised is this: What is there more in this statement that made the speaker enunciate it? This is *24*'s real problem: not its content as such, but the very fact that we are being told openly about it. And that is a sad indication of the deep change in our ethical and political standards. ∎

Is Torture Ever Morally Defensible?

*M*ark *Bowden has been called by the* New York Times *"a master of narrative journalism" for his reporting and writing on the messy reality of violence in the world of heroes, tyrants, and terrorists in theaters of war. Capable of putting us in the heart of a story in a way few other writers can, his best-known work is* Black Hawk Down: A Story of Modern War, *a gripping report on the U.S. military disaster in Mogadishu, subsequently turned into a memorable film.*

In the past few years Bowden has focused his journalism on the fight against Islamic terrorism, highlighted by his much-discussed 2003 Atlantic Monthly *article "The Dark Art of Interrogation." In it, he told the story of Khalid Sheikh Mohammed, widely considered the architect of the World Trade Center attacks. In 2007, Mohammed confessed after being held captive and interrogated by American forces in Guantánamo. This incident led Bowden to ponder the various ways torture is being carried out and the degree to which it works, or not, in the real world.*

Bowden came away from this reporting experience realizing, he says, that in the war against terrorism, where information is everything, harsh interrogation isn't only useful, it's crucial, and he gives us a powerful example. At the same time, Bowden is repelled by the idea of torture and knows it's a dangerous and very slippery slope. Once you allow interrogators to inflict discomfort, Bowden says, it's a very small, short step to inflicting pain. His solution to this quandary would be to ban torture but acknowledge that in certain rare instances it is the right thing to do. Still, it would be unlawful and the perpetrators should be prosecuted. We also asked Bowden to share his views about 24, *which he finds "well made and nicely packaged" with "a pretty accurate portrayal of the way suspects can get slapped around and interrogated with guns pointed at their heads, but* 24 *seems to be the invention of people who have no experience with the military or counterterrorism or even with other cultures."*

What accounts for the continuing popularity of *24*?

At a time when Americans are feeling threatened, it's reassuring to see a heroic character like Jack Bauer protecting us. No matter what sorts of trials and tribulations he encounters, he always prevails. In this sense, *24* functions a lot like the comic book superheroes who were popular during World War II. It reinforces the idea that Americans are the good guys, and that we are constantly under threat from evil. Of course, *24* is also well made and nicely packaged, with a simple narrative and lots of action.

How realistic is the show?

It's certainly true that American agents are working all over the world to monitor and infiltrate terrorist cells, and that their work puts them at grave personal risk. But being a counterterrorism agent isn't nearly as glamorous as Jack Bauer makes it seem. And all those electronic gadgets are a thousand times more effective on *24* than in real life. In these regards, and in the way the show portrays surveillance and other counterterrorism tactics, *24* is a complete fantasy. It seems to be the invention of people who have no experience with the military or counterterrorism or even with other cultures. But the show does give a pretty accurate portrayal of the way suspects can get slapped around and interrogated with guns pointed at their heads. The government can draw up all sorts of rules governing the treatment of detainees, but in the spur of the moment, when emotions are running high, detainees are always subject to abuse. They will always be interrogated harshly. In many instances, they will be tortured.

What's the difference between harsh interrogation and torture?

It is impossible to make a clear distinction. If torture is defined as *any* form of disincentive, as some say, then it could be something as simple as not allowing someone to eat meals with other prisoners. Clearly, there's a big difference between this sort of thing and gouging out eyeballs, cutting off fingers or limbs, and attaching electrodes to the genitals. But it makes no sense to legislate which coercive techniques are permissible and which are not, as Israel did a few years ago. And it was ill-advised for the Bush administration to try to differentiate between torture and a set of interrogation techniques known as *torture lite*. This led CIA and military interrogators to believe that the gloves should be off, which fostered the abuse of detainees in Afghanistan, Iraq, and Guantánamo.

Is torture always morally indefensible?

Not always. In certain rare and extreme circumstances, torture makes sense. I am using the word *torture* in the broad sense of any form of coercion. All of us can imagine situations in which we would be driven to cruelty or would give in to the impulse to cause someone pain. In Germany a few years ago, the police captured a man who had kidnapped a twelve-year-old boy and buried him alive. The kidnapper refused to reveal where the boy was buried until the police chief threatened him with torture. Since it was illegal to make such a threat, the police chief ultimately lost his job. I think that was a fair trade-off. I consider myself moral, and, like the police chief, I would have done anything to save that boy's life. I would also have been willing to face the consequences.

How about torture against a terrorist—for example, Khalid Sheikh Mohammed, one of the masterminds of the 9/11 attacks?
I don't know exactly what was done to Khalid Sheikh Mohammed in the days after his capture. I don't think anyone knows, except for him and the people who did it to him. But since it was likely that he had knowledge of active plots around the world to commit mass murder, it would have been morally defensible to do whatever was necessary to find out what he knew.

What should our government's policy be regarding the use of torture against suspected terrorists?
The only sensible thing is to make it clear that torture is illegal and that anyone who uses it is stepping over the line and is subject to punishment. But, as I said, if coercion seems to be the only way to obtain the information needed to prevent a terrorist attack—to hit them before they hit us—it might be justifiable for an interrogator to use some form of coercion. Of course, if you do use coercion, you are probably damaging your ability to mount a criminal prosecution against that individual. I should also point out that there is a fundamental difference between military intelligence gathering to prevent an attack and the gathering of evidence for a criminal prosecution. You can't torture someone to get evidence to use against them in court.

In recent months, you've written a number of high-profile articles and op-ed pieces on interrogation and torture. What's been the response to these articles?
I've gotten a broad range of responses, from those who enthusiastically agree with me to those who feel that even to discuss the topic seriously is to join forces with Dr. Mengele. Some people in the intelligence field were pleased to see a serious discussion of something that is usually treated superficially. Because my opinion is somewhat complex—ban torture but acknowledge that in certain rare instances it is the right thing to do—it is often misinterpreted.

Which techniques are most effective for obtaining information from detainees?

It depends on the detainee. Sometimes the best approach is to offer some sort of incentive or stroke the ego—or simply to be nice. Fear is usually more effective than pain at coaxing detainees to cooperate. If a subject is afraid that something bad might happen to him or to members of his family, that alone might be sufficient to elicit intelligence. Sometimes the only way is to actually cause physical pain. Because it is true that a person under pressure will sometimes say anything to make it stop, the interrogator must follow up on the information. If it proves to be accurate, the detainee could be rewarded. It could be something as simple as a good meal or access to a family member. If the information proves to be inaccurate, the detainee's situation could be made worse. My point is that if you are in complete control of someone, there are a million ways to make that person's life better or worse.

What does it take to be a good interrogator?

You have to be good at reading people—knowing which buttons to push—and you have to take the time to understand their culture, language, and motivations. Some Islamic fundamentalists are motivated by religion, others by politics. Some are simply nihilists. Others are thugs who use Islam in an attempt to rationalize theft, kidnapping, and rape. Because Americans tend to have little experience with other parts of the world, our view of these people and their cultures tends to be simplistic. *24* reinforces this simplistic view by suggesting that terrorists—whether Islamic fanatics or Ukrainian separatists or Pakistani nationalists—are interchangeable. It's like the way people who watched *The Lone Ranger* could count on any Indian being a villain. Except for Tonto, of course.

Are you concerned about the way *24* portrays Muslims—or the way Muslims are treated in the United States?

Serious people understand that *24* is simply entertainment. I suppose one could complain about the way the show portrays Muslims, but one might as well argue that *Pirates of the Caribbean* maligns pirates. As for the way our society treats Muslims, I believe that our ability to assimilate people from different cultures is one of our nation's greatest attributes—and the main reason that extremist Islam has not gained traction in the U.S. Despite the xenophobes among us, it is possible for immigrants to feel accepted. It was heartening that Arab-Americans were not subjected to vigilantism after 9/11. We passed that test. So far.

How do you characterize the threat posed by Islamic fundamentalism?

The threat is real but overstated. I consider Islamist fundamentalism a passing phenomenon—a fad. It doesn't accurately reflect the aspirations of most Muslims, and its goals run counter to human nature. As I travel the world, I meet few people who are interested in living under religious authoritarianism. Take Iran. Iranians have lived under the mullahs' repressive rule for twenty-five years, and they aren't too happy about it. Since the 1990s, there has been a political movement to topple the government and establish something akin to a real democracy. In its ensuing crackdown, the government has thrown reform-minded politicians out of office, closed down newspapers, locked up student protestors, and become a provocateur in that part of the world.

What about terrorism in this part of the world?

Given the existence of weapons that can kill thousands in a single swipe—whether it's a nuclear or biochemical weapon or a Boeing 767—terrorism is now a serious threat everywhere. Yet the sense of alarm in the U.S. has subsided since 2001. In part, this is because certain actions taken by the U.S. government have made us safer. For example, we've gotten a little more sophisticated at the sort of intelligence gathering that's required to protect our country against terrorist attacks. And as time passes, our sense of the threat posed by radical Islam becomes more realistic. We used to think that Khalid Sheikh Mohammed and Mohammed Atta, the other mastermind of the 9/11 attacks, were typical terrorists. Now we know that they were extremely dedicated and unusually intelligent, and that their audacious attack succeeded far beyond their wildest dreams. Most terrorists are probably more like Richard Reid, the would-be shoe bomber, or the guys accused of plotting to attack Fort Dix. Al Qaeda is a determined adversary, and extravagant acts of horror will continue. But it would surprise me if anything on the level of 9/11 were to happen again. ■

David Danzig

Torture in Prime Time

*O*ne of the strong draws of 24 is the clever way it blurs the line between truth and fiction. The show inhabits its own suspended world, freely borrowing from the realities of a post-9/11 world while helping itself to the scripted fantasies of action/adventure entertainments more commonly seen on television. This is why critics with opposing points of view on the ethical issues behind the program underlying 24's plotlines can both be right: Yes, the show is all too true to life in the way it depicts violations of civil rights and the abuse associated with torture; and, yes, the show is simply entertainment, just like a Jason Bourne or a Jack Ryan flick, so get over it. Which made us all the more curious about the complaint voiced by one human rights group that the show would be better entertainment if it were more realistic.

This is the position taken by the group called *Human Rights First* and its *Primetime Torture Project.* Its director, David Danzig, engineered the much-reported meeting between the creative team behind 24 and a group of experienced army interrogators critical of the show. The core of their argument seems to be that the over-the-top way torture is shown on 24 conveys entirely the wrong impression, because it suggests to the public that such treatment is an effective means of interrogation. The way it's being done on TV is not only the wrong way to depict torture, he says, but, by repeating the torture scenario time and time again, it becomes routine, even boring.

More importantly, Danzig believes, it also provides a negative role model for young and impressionable soldiers who may be tempted to replicate what they see on TV in their own interrogation sessions. To this end, Human Rights First has produced what it calls a corrective DVD, which includes an on-camera interview with Howard Gordon, 24's executive producer. The film drives home the point that 24 and similar shows are meant solely to provide entertainment.

The answer is not censorship, says Danzig. Instead, it's to make torture scenes more realistic; i.e. more process oriented, less bloody, and less likely to have a tidy conclusion. We asked him to give us a firsthand account of the meeting he and his unique group of experienced interrogators had with Howard Gordon and the writers and producers of 24, and to explain the group's position in greater detail. Here is his report.

I ARRIVED IN LOS ANGELES LATE IN THE DAY of August 27, 2006—just in time to watch the end of the Emmy Awards on the television in my hotel room. As a fan of *24*, I was pleased to see Howard Gordon, the executive producer of the show, accept the trophy for Outstanding Drama and hoist it over his head.

Ten hours later a colleague and I were scheduled to meet Gordon at an outdoor café on Sunset Boulevard. We had a mutual acquaintance and Howard Gordon knew that I wanted to talk about human rights and *24*. Given the festivities of the night before, I was dead certain that he would not make our 7:30 a.m. breakfast appointment. I would have forgiven him if he hadn't shown.

But there he was, right on time. "I'm sorry if I seem a bit tired," said Gordon. "I told Kiefer at about 3:00 a.m. that I had to go home and get some sleep because I was going to be meeting two human rights types in the morning."

Over breakfast we told Mr. Gordon that *24* and other action-oriented shows have influenced the way that some junior soldiers in the field in Iraq had behaved. He understood the point and expressed concern about it. He agreed to do what we had come to ask him to do: help us make a training film that the armed services could use to point out that what Jack Bauer does might work on TV, but not in the real world. Gordon also said he would be interested in bringing us together with his writing team to talk to us about the way U.S. intelligence services actually interrogate detainees.

Three months later, with Gordon's support, we returned to Hollywood to visit the set of *24*. This time we brought with us Brigadier General Patrick Finnegan, the dean of the U.S. Military Academy at West Point, plus three seasoned interrogators: Colonel Stuart Herrington, a retired Army intelligence officer who ran the so-called "cage" for high-value detainees in the first Gulf War; Joe Navarro, an interrogator who worked for the FBI for 25 twenty-five years; and Specialist Tony Lagouranis, a former army interrogator who had served in Iraq. [For more about Lagouranis's experiences and views, see his essay earlier in this chapter.]

Our hope was that we might spur the creative team at *24* to portray torture in a more nuanced, less destructive manner.

24 is an extremely creative show. But when it comes to torture, what one sees is almost always the same. Jack Bauer has electrocuted, beaten, suffocated, shot, stabbed and otherwise abused suspects who were previously unwilling to talk. Many of these suspects appear to be willing to die for their cause. But seconds after the abuse begins, they reveal critical secrets. In the real world, there is overwhelming evidence from researchers, law enforcement officers, and military experts that this is not how it works at all. Suspects who are tortured die. They give up false information. They become even more radicalized. Historically, torture is a losing proposition in strategic terms as well—as was demonstrated in the case of Abu Ghraib.

On the set of *24*, Gordon had assembled many of the key writers, including Bob Cochran, one of the show's creators and a main writer. Cochran, a Stanford-trained lawyer who once worked at a corporate law firm and now can come to work everyday in a T-shirt and jeans, began the meeting by getting straight to the point. "I want to know what you would do if you have a guy who planted a bomb that will go off in a matter of hours. Lives are at stake. Lots of them. How would you get the guy to talk?"

Joe Navarro, the retired FBI interrogator, answered Cochran's ticking time-bomb question from a real-world perspective. "These are determined people," he said. "You think they're going to go to all of the trouble to help set off a nuclear bomb over LA and then give up information just hours before they are about to succeed? Do you think they are going to talk because you pull out their fingernails, break some bones, or worse? No way. They are going to lie to you—send you on a wild goose chase."

"Torture is pure amateur hour," added Colonel Herrington. "They expect to be beaten up. If you want real information, you have to use mind games and sophisticated ruses." Herrington then pulled a two-page memo from a file he had prepared for the writers. The memo, he explained, included ploys that had been successful—like the "false flag" trick where a detainee would be broken out of custody by men he believes to be his comrades. His "saviors" get him to tell his story and then reveal that they actually had been working with U.S. forces all the time.

"You're hired," said Howard Gordon jokingly after hearing this.

The meeting broke up amicably. The writers said the interrogators' stories were gripping but that it might be too difficult to portray the sort of complexity and nuance that is often involved in the kind of thorough intelligence work our experts had described.

The next day General Finnegan and I returned to the set to meet with Kiefer Sutherland. Sutherland, like Gordon, was concerned that the show could influence the way young soldiers believe interrogations ought to be conducted. "I say again and again—in almost every media interview that I do—that this is just entertainment," he told us. But at the same time he admitted his frustration that people do seem to get confused. He told the story of how one woman he had seen on the street thought he really was Jack Bauer and begged him not to hurt her.

Ironically, while we were on the set, we saw firsthand how the blend of pure fantasy and authenticity on the show can be confusing. Earlier in the day, an actor dressed as a Los Angeles police officer approached General Finnegan, who was wearing a formal military uniform complete with ribbons and medals. He playfully punched the general on the shoulder to get his attention. "When is first call?" the actor said. Apparently, he thought General Finnegan was an extra.

Ultimately, of course, the responsibility for ensuring that members of the armed services do not act like Jack Bauer rests with military leaders. And it should be acknowledged that since Abu Ghraib and other abuses have come to light the armed services have clarified procedures. In September 2006, for example, the army updated and re-released its interrogation field manual—known as *"the Bible"* by intelligence officers—to be crystal clear that torture and cruelty were considered off-limits. Still, many military educators acknowledge that some of their students believe it is appropriate to cross the line and do "whatever it takes" to save lives.

Rather than exacerbate the training challenge military educators face, *24* could help by portraying torture in a more nuanced, realistic fashion. It comes as no surprise that young soldiers—like a lot of eighteen, nineteen, and twenty-year-olds everywhere—look up to Jack Bauer. What he does, they want to do. What they do not realize is that they almost certainly will not generate the same results.

In February 2007, Gordon told the *Philadelphia Inquirer* that *24* would change the way it showed torture. He explained that "what once was an extraordinary or exceptional moment is starting to feel a little trite."

It was a significant admission. *24* has shown so much torture—in almost exactly the same way—that the audience knew what was going to happen before it even took place. What's troubling about this from a human rights perspective is not so much that torture is shown, but that it is shown over and over again in a way that suggests that these methods work. The audience is not only bored, but they are left with the impression that these tactics are effective virtually every time.

TV does not have to be this way. There are programs that show realistic repercussions of torture, rather than reinforcing mistaken beliefs about the practice. The *Shield* on FX, for example, follows Vic Mackey, an ends-justifies-the-means cop. Mackey gets rough with suspects, but torture does not always work for him. This past season he tortured, and then shot, the wrong guy. Mackey finds that he has closed a case that actually remains wide open. The resulting drama unfolds in large part because Mackey has made a huge mistake.

This sort of nuance has rarely, if ever, appeared on *24*. A more thoughtful portrayal of abusive interrogation techniques would leave the audience with a more sophisticated understanding of the problems associated with combining physical abuse and interrogation, and it would probably also make for more interesting TV. We'll be watching *24* next season, staying particularly tuned in to see how this issue unfolds. ■

Next Threat: The Battles in Jack Bauer's Future

Central to many elements that blend together to create *24*'s riveting appeal to audiences is the way the show's creators evoke the look and feel of the future. This is not the distant future of science fiction, but the future that lies just on the edge of tomorrow, the near future, the future of social fiction. It is a dystopian tomorrow, vaguely resonant of the sensibility of Ridley Scott's famous *Blade Runner* film, now twenty-five years old, which set the agenda for the postmodern, onscreen aesthetics in a world of anxiety, uncertainty, and fear.

Watching *24*, we see the surveillance, satellite, videoconferencing, and database technology that is available today—or may be available tomorrow. We confront the workplace layouts and power struggles that we all know are in our collective future in the age of the collaborative organization. We experience the attention-deficit–inducing, 24/7 pressures on people's personal lives. Everywhere, it seems, big brother, traitorous moles, or merely morally challenged coworkers are watching our every move. Most important, of course, *24* exposes us viscerally to the multitude of doomsday threats facing our globalizing world. We have a front-row seat as some of the possible terrorist plots unfold in fiction, knowing all the while that reasonable facsimiles might actually be news reports in our future.

In this chapter, we turn to several experts on technology, the future of warfare, and the future itself to think out loud about *24* in the broadest sense. The commentators assembled here represent some of the world's most cogent thinkers about the future: John Robb, a former counterterrorism officer and one of the most incisive experts on the future of warfare; Alvin Toffler, author of the pioneering classic of futurism, *Future Shock;* Laura Holgate, a national security expert who has worked for years with former Senator Sam Nunn (D-Ga.) on the intractable challenges left over from the cold war's legacy of nuclear technology proliferation; and David Shugarts, who offers a wise and witty look at real-life, state-of-the-art technology and how it is depicted on *24*.

There is arguably no better example of the way *24* looks at the present-as-future than in the way it portrays the vast changes in the nature of warfare. The audience sees "firsthand" how a small group of committed terrorists can now produce destructive results that far exceed any that a small band could have accomplished in years past. Moreover, we witness how the new dynamics of globalization rapidly escalate the chances that "a single match can light a prairie fire," to use Chairman Mao's apt phrase. In Season 6, for example, a suitcase bomb detonated by a group of apparently Middle Eastern terrorists in Los Angeles leads to an eyeball-to-eyeball confrontation with the Russians, all because the Chinese are after the secrets of the Russian bomb codes carried by American traitors (who happen to be Jack's brother and father).

John Robb, whose insights into the new warfare open this chapter, sums it up in a startling way: "Over time, perhaps in as little as twenty years, and as the leverage provided by technology increases, this threshold will finally reach its culmination—*with the ability of one man to declare war on the world and win.*" Robb goes on to explain, "We are now into a fourth-generation type of warfare, characterized by an open-source framework of loose organizations." There are no longer cohesive centralized movements to fight, as in the cold war. No wars of liberation *à la* the guerrilla war in Vietnam. This is a ground-up, "wiki-war" and it isn't restricted to Islamic terrorism. It's happening from Brazil to Nigeria to Chechnya.

Here we reprint the first chapter of Robb's important new book, *Brave New War*. It will give you a whole new understanding of terms like *defense, offense, aggression,* and *security.* Robb will also acquaint you with black swans (rapid, chaotic, and unexpected events, which are ever more likely), and explain why our current homeland security apparatus is completely inadequate for its tasks (an opinion shared by Alvin Toffler in his interview) and why our country needs to focus on "dynamic, decentralized resilience platforms." Welcome to the Brave New War of the Worlds. ■

John Robb

Brave New War: The Next Stage of Terrorism

THE NEAR FUTURE HOLDS MIND-BENDING promise for American business. Globalization is prying open vast new markets. Technology is plowing ahead, fueling—and transforming entire industries, creating services we never thought possible. Clever people worldwide are capitalizing every which way. But because globalization and technology are morally neutral forces, they can also drive change of a different sort. We saw this very clearly on September 11, 2001, and are seeing it now in Iraq and in conflicts around the world. In short, despite the aura of limitless possibility, our lives are evolving in ways we can control only if we recognize the new landscape. It's time to take an unblinking look.

We have entered the age of the faceless, agile enemy. From London to Madrid to Nigeria to Russia, stateless terrorist groups have emerged to score blow after blow against us. Driven by cultural fragmentation, schooled in the most sophisticated technologies, and fueled by transnational crime, these groups are forcing corporations and individuals to develop new ways of defending themselves. The end result of this struggle will be a new, more resilient approach to national security, one built not around the state but around private citizens and companies. That new system will change how we live and work—for the better, in many ways—but the road getting there may seem long at times.

The conflict in Iraq has foreshadowed the future of global security in much the same way that the Spanish civil war prefigured World War II: it's become a testing ground, a dry run for something much larger. Unlike previous insurgencies, the one in Iraq comprises seventy-five to one hundred small, diverse, and autonomous groups of zealots, patriots, and criminals alike. These groups, of course, have access to many of the same tools we do—from satellite phones to engineering degrees—and they use them every bit as effectively. But their single most important asset is their organizational structure, an open-source community network—one that seems to me quite similar to what we see in the software industry. That's how they're able to continually stay one step ahead of us. It is an extremely innovative structure, sadly, and it

Source: John Robb, *Brave New War: The Next Stage of Terrorism and the End of Globalization*, Chapter 1, "The Superempowered Competition." © 2007 by John Robb. Reprinted with permission of John Wiley & Sons, Inc.

results in decision-making cycles much shorter than those of the U.S. military. Indeed, because the insurgents in Iraq lack a recognizable center of gravity—a leadership structure or an ideology—they are nearly immune to the application of conventional military force. Like Microsoft, the software superpower, the United States hasn't found its match in a Goliath competitor similar to itself, but in a loose, self-tuning network.

In Iraq, we've also witnessed the convergence of international crime and terrorism as they provide ample fuel and a global platform for these new enemies. Al-Qaeda's attack on Madrid, for example, was funded by the sale of the drug ecstasy. Moisés Naim, a former Venezuelan minister of trade and industry and the editor and publisher of the magazine *Foreign Policy*, documented this trend in his insightful book *Illicit: How Smugglers, Traffickers, and Copycats Are Hijacking the Global Economy*. Globalization has fostered the development of a huge criminal economy that boasts a technologically leveraged global supply chain (like Wal-Mart's) and can handle everything from human trafficking (Eastern Europe) to illicit drugs (Asia and South America), pirated goods (Southeast Asia), arms (Central Asia), and money laundering (everywhere). Naim puts the value of that economy at between $2 and $3 trillion a year. He says it is expanding at *seven times* the rate of legitimate world trade.

This terrorist-criminal symbiosis becomes even more powerful when considered next to the most disturbing sign coming out of Iraq: the terrorists have developed the ability to fight nation-states strategically—without weapons of mass destruction. This new method is called *systems disruption*, a simple way of attacking the critical networks (electricity, oil, gas, water, communications, and transportation) that underpin modern life. Such disruptions are designed to erode the target state's legitimacy, to drive it to failure by keeping it from providing the services it must deliver in order to command the allegiance of its citizens. Over the past two years, attacks on the oil and electricity networks in Iraq have reduced and held delivery of these critical services below prewar levels, with a disastrous effect on the country, its people, and its economy.

The early examples of systems disruption in Iraq and elsewhere are ominous. If these techniques are even lightly applied to the fragile electrical and oil-gas systems in Russia, Saudi Arabia, or anywhere in the target-rich West, we could see a rapid onset of economic and political chaos unmatched since the advent of the blitzkrieg. (India's January [2007] arrest of militants with explosives in Hyderabad suggests that the country's high-tech industry could be a new target.) It's even worse when we consider the asymmetry of the economics involved: one small attack on an oil pipeline in southeast Iraq, conducted for an estimated $2,000, cost the Iraqi government more than $500 million in lost oil revenues. That is a return on investment of 25 million percent.

Now that the tipping point has been reached, the rise of global virtual states—with their thriving criminal economies, innovative networks, and hyper-efficient war craft—will rapidly undermine public confidence in our national security systems. . . . As disruptions continue, the damage will spill over into the very structure of our society. Our profligate U.S. Department of Defense, reeling from its inability to defend our borders on 9/11 or to pacify even a small country like Iraq, will increasingly be seen as obsolete.

Technological Multipliers

From a security perspective, the most disturbing aspect of 9/11 wasn't the horrible destruction, but that the men who attacked us on that day didn't even factor the opposition of the U.S. military into their planning. Despite tens of trillions of dollars spent on defense over the last decades, this military force proved ineffectual as a deterrent at the point when we needed it most.

Worse yet, nothing has changed since then. The U.S. military, in budget after budget since 9/11, has continued to plan, build, and fund forces dedicated to fighting a great power war—with an increasing emphasis on China and to a lesser extent on Iran. Even the guerrilla war in Iraq hasn't forced any substantive changes to our defense structure. This isn't due to a nefarious plot at the highest levels of government. It is due to the fundamental inability of the nation-state to conceptualize a role that makes sense in fighting and deterring the emerging threat.

The real threat, as seen in the rapid rise in global terrorism over the past five years, is that this threat isn't another state but rather the superempowered group. This group, riding on the leverage provided by rapid technology improvement and global integration, is and will remain the major threat to our way of life.

To really understand this future, you need to discard the idea of state-versus-state conflict. That age is over. It ended with the rise of nuclear weapons, the integration of the world's economies, and the end of the cold war. Wars between states are now, for all intents and purposes, obsolete. The real remaining threat posed by wars between states, in those rare cases when they do occur by choice, is that they will create a vacuum within which these non-state groups can thrive. Every time we shuffle the playing cards with state-versus-state conflict, we will find that we are ultimately less well off than before it occurred.

Given the withering away of state-versus-state conflict, we shouldn't assume that the reasons for warfare have departed with it. All the economic, environmental, social, religious, and ethnic drivers of conflict are still in place. In fact, there is every reason to believe they actually may be strengthening, given the fragmenting power of the Internet. The real change is that wars fought over these issues won't be fought by states, but at a level below that of the state.

Within this larger context, the conflict we are currently engaged in is merely a waypoint on this trend line. The threshold necessary for small groups to conduct warfare has finally been breached, and we are only starting to feel its effects. Over time, perhaps in as little as twenty years, and as the leverage provided by technology increases, this threshold will finally reach its culmination—*with the ability of one man to declare war on the world and win*. Now, with every improvement in genetic engineering and nanotechnology (only some of many potential threats), we come closer to the day when a single individual will have the budget, the knowledge, and the tools necessary to make this future possible. . . . Over the last twenty years or so, the ability to manipulate and use technology has decentralized to become widely accessible. Not only are the tools accelerating in power but also the breadth of access to these tools has become nearly universal.

Technology's Paradox

It's well known that technology can be used for both good and bad ends. The classic example of this is nuclear power (although many would argue that it is entirely bad). Under the classic rules of this paradox, these rogue technologies occurred only rarely and required a nation-state to produce them.

Today's rules are different. Technology is now rapidly advancing across a broad front, and the barriers to usage have dropped to nothing. A recent example of this new rule set is Japan's realization that Sony's PlayStation 2 console has sufficient graphics-crunching capability to pilot a missile to its desired target. In essence, anyone can now buy a critical component for an advanced weapons guidance system on eBay for $200.

> "There are lots of threats to you in the world. There's the threat of a heart attack for genetic reasons. You can't sit there and worry about everything. Get a life."
>
> **—New York City Mayor Michael Bloomberg, reacting to what turned out to be a less-than-advertised plot to set off a bomb at New York's John F. Kennedy Airport in June 2007**

The reason for this breakout from technology's historically glacial and seemingly linear pace of improvement is Moore's law. Named for a claim made by Gordon E. Moore, the cofounder of Intel in the 1960s, Moore's law states that the number of transistors on a computer chip (integrated circuit) doubles every eighteen months.

Moore was right, and this exponential pace of improvement has been holding steady within this technology cycle since the middle of the twentieth century. In fact, the technologist Ray Kurzweil has shown that it reaches back to technology cycles before the integrated circuit as well. It is only now making its effects known, as the curve of this exponential rate of improvement breaks above the horizon of linear progress.

Furthermore, since this improvement was packaged in a product that is globally accessible (the computer chip), Moore's law has not begun to permeate every field of technology. For the purposes of our discussion, the fact that Moore's law is packaged in an affordable form means that the tools available to individuals are also improving at an exponential pace. You can now run programs on your laptop that previously would have taken a team of accountants, a laboratory of biologists, a pool of secretaries, or a group of engineers to accomplish.

Right behind Moore's law is a second inexorable trend. The trend is the increasing power and complexity provided by a ubiquitous global network. That network, of course, is the Internet, and its most important application, the World Wide Web, is an example of the reverse of the dual use of technology since the Internet started within the Department of Defense. Again, within economic terms this is a cornucopia of plenty, powering a bewilderingly complex array of global goods and services. Within the context of warfare, however, it takes a different form altogether.

The leverage provided by these technologies has finally reached a point where small superempowered groups, and not yet individuals, now have the capability to challenge the state in warfare and win. For the most part, these non-state groups have been using these new technologies mostly as a means to recruit, train, equip, and mobilize decentralized organizations. A more ominous trend has developed, however. These groups are quickly learning to use—against us—the technologies we use daily.

> "We certainly can't say with any certainty that cyberterrorism doesn't exist, and can't say it didn't occur . . . but there is little doubt in my mind that, years from now, this will be a primary method of attack, a primary theater of operations, if you will."
> —Amit Yoran, vice president of managed security services operations, Symantec Corporation

Airplanes are being turned into flying bombs, cell phone networks are being used to simultaneously detonate bombs from miles away, and critical computer networks are being hacked. More important, a growing number of attacks are being made on the underlying computerized networks that support our very economic fabric: from the oil distribution system to electricity grids. If this is what we are already seeing with the first iteration of this trend, then it is a safe bet that the capability to instantly leverage the rapid technological progress under way will soon be dangerous enough to threaten the world with catastrophe.

It's my belief that our response to the threats posed by the superempowered groups that we face today will define our survivability against the threat of extermination in the future. If we continue to expect the next major terrorist attack to look just like the last one, the odds will not be in our favor. ■

Why the Department of Homeland Security Should Be Dismantled

*A*lvin Toffler *defined the visionary type of commentary we now know as* futurism *with his pathbreaking global best-seller,* Future Shock, *which appeared almost four decades ago. In* Future Shock *and numerous other thought-provoking best-sellers since, written with Heidi Toffler, his wife and collaborator, Toffler has been among the first to describe social, cultural, business, technological, and economic trends that have subsequently come to dominate our lives. From the rise of the Internet to telecommuting, from changes in family structures to changes in political systems in America and around the world, the Tofflers have established an amazing track record of understanding where our society is going before it gets there.*

24 is a case study in many of the issues the Tofflers have written about since the 1960s—changing relationships in the family, changing relationships in the workplace, shifting ethics and morals, the need for institutions to speed up their response time to new kinds of threats and challenges, changing social perceptions of time, the increasingly 24/7 world, the power of information technology, the diffusion and diversity of security challenges to the peace and stability of our society—and much more. Even the decision to set 24 in Los Angeles for the first six seasons is no surprise to Toffler who, for decades, has been noting the rise and influence of Pacific Rim countries and the rise of California as the epicenter of change in the global economy.

One of the main principles of Toffler's analysis is that we currently inhabit the Third Wave of civilization. Agricultural societies were the First Wave, industrial societies the Second Wave, and information and knowledge-oriented societies are the Third Wave. This Third Wave is fundamentally different, in every respect from Second Wave societies. The problems are different and so too are their solutions. Yet our politicians are often trying to address Third Wave challenges with Second Wave solutions. Case in point, says Toffler, is our current approach to homeland defense. In that context, we sat down with Alvin Toffler to talk about 24, national security, nuclear technology, and much more.

One of the aspects that makes *24* unusual is its use of real time and the conceit that the course of a season covers a single twenty-four-hour day. As someone who has written about society's relationship to time, what are your thoughts on this?
This show's creative manipulation of time is obviously an innovation in the history of television and pop culture, by breaking time into chunks of twenty-four hours, and not telling the entire story in thirty minutes or an hour. This is indicative of how the media is changing on many levels in its use of time. We now have advertisers who are talking not just about five-second commercials, but also about two-second commercials. So everything is being crammed into faster-paced time, and time is being manipulated in many ways. *24* is one experiment with how time can be used differently from its traditional compartmentalization and contours.

One theme *24* deals with is the shift from a cold war mentality of having one monolithic enemy to a world in which we have dozens or perhaps thousands of diverse enemies, many of which we can't "see" and most of which we don't really understand. How do people live in a world like that?
I don't think the public gets it yet; at least not the American public. I think they're still thinking in terms of one central enemy: In the case of 9/11, it was deemed to be Osama bin Laden. We made a side venture against Saddam Hussein, and President George W. Bush is being criticized for doing that, because it took his eye off the single ball. The problem is that, in the future, it's not going to be a single ball that's thrown. There will be many pitches and games going on all over the field. It will also be more likely that we'll have convergent crises, not just one crisis. And what's happening is that you have nonstate actors multiplying in different forms, from bin Laden and his metastasizing pals, to a whole variety of nonnational, nonstate actors on the scene. They are going to have access to weapons of mass destruction, because it's clear we can't keep the nuclear stuff bottled up. I think we are heading into a period that will be very dangerous, so we'll need more assets of society devoted to security. And it must begin with the dismantling of the Department of Homeland Security.

Dismantling? But it was just put together! Would you like to elaborate on that?
When we were hit on 9/11, we decided we had to do something about it. So we took somewhere between fifteen and twenty-two small agencies and put them into one superbureaucracy called the

Department of Homeland Security. But the people we're fighting—and those we are going to be fighting in the future—are organized differently. They can move faster, they don't have to get permission from many hierarchical levels, and so forth. Because it is so big and bureaucratic, the Department of Homeland Security can't respond quickly and with agility to these kinds of threats. I think a perfect example of the failure of the large bureaucracy is FEMA during Katrina. FEMA is a giant bureaucracy embedded within a giant bureaucracy, and it absolutely died when it came to doing what it needed to do. Our institutions and our technologies are so radically out of sync that they're going to fail as they try to deal with institutional Katrinas. The existing superbureaucracies are beyond help. They can't be reformed. They have to be replaced.

Do you think this is the same for the military?
Many of our military leaders are, as far as I can judge, far better educated than our "smart" businessmen, the CEOs who are glorified on the pages of the *Wall Street Journal*. However, they are part of a larger system, and they don't run the country (and I'm glad they don't). But the fact is that they are subject to orders from the political system and, in effect, if the orders are stupid, their job is to carry them out even if they are uncomfortable with doing so. I was in the army briefly during the Korean War, and later my work as a journalist also brought me in touch with many military men. These experiences challenged my stereotypes about people in the army not being smart or the assumption that they are all politically uniform. I think that our military people are pretty smart, but they are also part of the biggest and most rigid bureaucracy that exists, and they basically do what they are told to do.

24 draws considerable heat for its depictions of torture, which taps into the current national debate on whether torturing military detainees is acceptable. What are your thoughts on that?
Years ago, I visited what was at that time the only institute for the rehabilitation of the tortured. At this European institute, they had an absolutist position, which was that under no circumstances anywhere at anytime should there be torture. I can't share that opinion. Quite a few years ago, the then-chief of staff of the Canadian military told me a story. He said, "When I was in World War II, I was leading a line of tanks up a road and we were surrounded by hundreds of refugees and we asked them to get out of the way because we knew that the Germans were going to bomb

that intersection in three minutes. When we saw that they would not get out of the way, we knew our tanks would have to move on. I can still hear the baby crunching under my tank treads." What this story illustrates to me is that you can't believe in absolutes. There can't, in my view, be an absolute ban on torture or other kinds of horrible violence. Sometimes a few must be sacrificed to prevent a disaster for many.

Much of the action in *24* to date has been set in Los Angeles. Since you live in southern California, what are your thoughts on the "Los Angelization" of mankind?
Well, I think that it was a mistake to put the nation's capital permanently in Washington, D.C. I think the capital should have been moved west in every generation until it got to California, in which case by now our leading politicians might know how to spell *Asia*. These last two administrations didn't know that Asia existed except for China. I think there are serious consequences to this, especially with regard to nuclearization. North Korea now has nuclear capability. China and Japan either have or can have nuclear capability as well. And I believe that we are going to see the reunification of Korea. In the end, South Korea is going to inherit a nuclear weapon, which will complete the nuclearization of practically all major countries in Asia.

What do you think are the implications of a future with more nuclear proliferation?
In addition to the obvious danger that a nuclear Asia poses, there are more subtle dangers. Traditional nuclear bombs and their traditional missile delivery systems are an awfully complicated, expensive way for a country to gain power, so we're also going to have much cheaper forms of nuclear and other extremely lethal weaponry. Therefore, these kinds of weapons—suitcase bombs, chemical weapons, etc.—will be more available to many different potential buyers at smaller scales. And as the North Korean case underscores, you don't have to be a superpower to have nukes. I think we're going to live in a world in which there's a lot of weaponry, much of it unrecognized by us now and we're going to have to learn how to cope with and live in a world like that. Unfortunately, the answers are much more complicated than just sending in Jack Bauer to deal with a twenty-four-hour crisis. ∎

24's Suitcase Nuke Scenario: A Real-World Worry

*A*mong the many dangers 24 has consistently rendered clear and present is that of advanced nuclear technology falling into rogue hands and being used by terrorists against the United States. This is, of course, a real-life, real-world issue, and one that has provoked concern in the national security community for years.

Back in 1981, Senator Sam Nunn, the highly respected "defense policy wonk" from Georgia, who was then serving as chairman of the Senate Armed Services Committee, asked a question that alerted the world to the possibility of a new kind of terrorism. Suppose a nuclear device were detonated in and destroyed an American city, he asked the head of the Strategic Air Command. Could the United States ascertain who was responsible in order to decide how and whether to retaliate? The answer was disquieting: No, the general told Nunn, because we might not be able to determine who had launched it. The attack might have come from what was then the Soviet Union, or it might have come from terrorists acting independently.

Congress took up the issue in 1987, establishing "risk reduction centers" tasked to do contingency planning in two areas: (1) to lower the chance of unintended wars getting started because of miscalculations between the two superpowers and (2) to try to prevent nuclear technology from falling into the hands of terrorists—a dire scenario virtually tailor-made for 24. With the collapse of the Soviet Union in 1989, Russian nuclear weapons facilities were no longer under the control of a central authority, however. This prompted Congress to expand the program by establishing the Cooperative Threat Reduction Program in 1991 within the Department of Defense, a program designed to broaden the original mission of the risk reduction centers by expanding it to the States now freed from Russian control. Since then, and with the cooperation of the governments involved, the Nunn-Lugar program—as it became known in honor of sponsors Nunn (a Democrat) and Richard Lugar of Indiana (a Republican)—has dismantled and destroyed more nuclear weapons than there are in the combined arsenals of China, France, and Great Britain.

While this reduced the risk of fissile materials falling into the wrong hands, it far from eliminated it. Consequently, when Nunn left Congress in 1996, he began thinking about supplementing the Nunn-Lugar program with a privately funded, nonprofit organization whose mission

would dovetail with that of the program he had cofounded and placed
under the auspices of the Department of Defense. With support from pri-
vate citizens like Ted Turner, who became cochairman with Nunn, the
Nuclear Threat Initiative (NTI) was born.

In addition to initiating direct action to reduce the very real threat of
nuclear terrorism, the Nuclear Threat Initiative also seeks to raise public
awareness of the issues it addresses. It is in this context that we asked Laura
Holgate, a vice president of NTI, to give us a progress report on our ability
to answer the question posed by Senator Nunn more than a quarter of a
century ago: Despite the many measures in place to prevent it, are we
really as close to a 24-type scenario (in which a renegade Russian general
and a willing terrorist organization smuggle suitcase bombs into the
country) as it seems? Once again the answer is disquieting.

24 may be fiction, but reality seems to be catching up quickly:
The idea of terrorists with suitcase nuclear weapons, deter-
mined to detonate them in American cities, is actually some-
thing you worry about, right?
Certainly there is a higher potential for nuclear weapons falling in
the hands of terrorists than ever. There are a number of reasons for
this. One is that communication technology now allows the unfettered spread of information—even the physics behind the design of
nuclear weapons. Another big change, of course, is the fall of the
Soviet Union and the resulting concerns about security for their
vast amounts of weapons and materials in that aftermath. Many of
those risks have been reduced, but challenges remain. Then there
is the development of nuclear weapons programs in countries like
India, Pakistan, and North Korea. The last two are known to have
shared weapons-related technology with other countries,
including Iran. Given the political instability in Pakistan, and the
sheer amount of nuclear material in Russia, the odds of such
weapons falling into the hands of stateless terrorists increases.

Finally, the nature of terrorism itself has changed. Terrorist acts
have evolved from a tool used against targets within a country to
achieve political demands—the IRA and Basque terrorist groups,
for example—to one that seeks mass death as an end goal in itself.

In Season 6 of 24, a Russian general with access to the
country's nuclear arsenal pilfered five bombs and passed
them on to Middle Eastern–based terrorists. How easy would
that be?
That situation would have been easier to imagine in the early '90s,
when controls in Russia were more lax. Back then you might have

been able to steal a relevant quantity of highly enriched uranium just by using a pair of bolt cutters. Fortunately, we have had fifteen years of good U.S.–Russian cooperation on nuclear security programs, even in periods when government relations were disrupted. But I *am* worried about the growing authoritarian strain within Russia that has resulted in increased restrictions on access formerly granted to foreigners working on security issues. We try continually to remind Russia's leaders that their country, too, is a target for terrorism and thus they should have every incentive to carry out high-quality protection at those facilities.

Also worrisome is that while facilities both in Russia and the former satellite nations have high-quality security equipment, there is evidence that the people who are operating that equipment are not using it consistently, or well. They are turning off detectors because there are so many false alarms, for example, or allowing bosses to go around checkpoints because, well, they are the bosses. We are talking about a group of countries where corruption is endemic, where petty theft occurs regularly at military facilities, and where organized crime has penetrated even some of the "closed cities" where these nuclear resources are still active.

So where should lax controls in Russia fall on our list of big issues to worry about?
Russia is important because of the sheer quantity of material there, as well as some of the governance issues, of course. But it's Pakistan that is at the top of my list because of the extraordinary level of unrest in that region. In its 2007 report on the threat of the political disintegration of Pakistan, the American National Intelligence Estimate cites the known presence of al Qaeda leadership in that country, the weakness of the Musharraf government, and the potential for a coup by radical Islamic factions. If those factions ever took over, they would have control not just of nuclear weapons but of the whole nuclear enterprise in Pakistan. I would say it leads to very significant concerns.

Where else can terrorists go shopping?
At MIT. In all seriousness, a less well understood risk is that posed by civilian research reactors that use highly enriched uranium. There are more than one hundred of these facilities in forty countries around the world. There is one at Chalk River in Canada, and at Petten in the Netherlands. There is a large research reactor in Germany called FRM-2 that uses highly enriched uranium. There are dozens of civilian reactors in Russia. And many of these facilities can be found in university environments where people without

proper, or in some cases, any background checks may be working or have access.

Most of these research reactors have enough material to make a bomb. But we tend to overlook them because they are located typically at universities or institutes outside of a military structure. These facilities have nothing to do with any weapons program, but they do have weapons-usable material.

The good news is that the material in these facilities is not very radioactive, so it wouldn't be of much use in the making of a dirty bomb. But the bad news is that the material could easily be carried off by a terrorist without any near-term impact on his health. With a little chemistry and physics, it could be used to manufacture a nuclear weapon at some clandestine facility. The bomb would most likely be based on the "old" Hiroshima design and could create that scale of devastation.

You have outlined two scenarios: One is the theft of a near-ready-to-go weapon; the other is the surreptitious acquisition of weapons-grade material. Which of these might a terrorist group focus on?

The first scenario is not out of the question. But there is a challenge. These weapons are difficult to use and they generally do not come with an instruction manual. In many ways it can be easier to build and fire your own weapon than it is to steal one and then figure out how to use it. Say, for example, a terrorist goes after fifty kilograms of highly enriched uranium that could be used to manufacture a weapon. The terrorist would be able to design it using rudimentary physics techniques. And, of course, he or she would need a team of experts to put it together. Having built it himself, he would know exactly how it works. But the elapsed time from theft to having a manufactured bomb could be only on the order of a few weeks. It could be delivered in a truck or a boat or a shipping container. And this is all doable. I don't want to say it's likely, I don't want to say it's easy, but once the terrorists have that material, your chances of disrupting anything they wish to do declines.

Wouldn't you catch something like this, with all of these monitors we've been putting in ports and airports and seaports and border crossings?

Highly enriched uranium—despite the words *highly enriched*—doesn't mean highly radioactive. In fact, it is barely radioactive and quite difficult to detect. One of the entirely plausible scenarios we included in our movie *Last Best Chance* posited a small fishing craft with a highly enriched uranium bomb aboard, sailing up the Potomac right into the heart of the capital. Nothing would be likely to impede the progress of such a boat.

Aren't the radiation detectors that are in place capable of picking up all nuclear materials?
No. Technology simply has not progressed to the point of being able to reliably find very low-radioactivity components. The signature highly enriched uranium emits is too weak to be easily detected. Do remember, however, that things are different when it comes to smuggling a dirty bomb. The whole premise of a dirty bomb is that it is highly radioactive. So these would be much easier to discover with the detection technologies in place today. But the people who say that these technologies are preventing the smuggling of any kind of nuclear weapon into the U.S. are fooling themselves.

So, to sum up, how plausible is it that a nuclear attack could take place on American soil?
I think it is preventable. But if we keep doing the inadequate job we are doing today, it's much more likely to happen. We are not moving fast enough and the risk is not well enough understood on a global basis to get the cooperation we need. A huge missing piece is a coordinated *global* approach. The security chain is only as strong as its weakest link. If you are successful in establishing controls everywhere but in Pakistan, for example, we are all still hugely vulnerable.

If there is a hope for the prevention of a nuclear device falling into the hands of terrorists, it is devising a global solution, with global participation. If we change our approach to deal with that challenge, we can prevent this. But we certainly cannot say today that we are doing all we can to prevent acts of nuclear terrorism from taking place in the United States or elsewhere. ■

David A. Shugarts

The Technology of *24*:
Real and Imagined,
Fiction and Nonfiction

David A. Shugarts is a veteran journalist with a passion for technology and for probing the inner workings of devices. Over the last several years, Shugarts has served as the chief investigative reporter for the Secrets book series, often delving into the ways in which the creators of pop culture works use a mix of fact and fantasy, even in books, films, and TV shows that are supposed to be meticulously researched and highly realistic. For our 2004 book, Secrets of the Code, *Shugarts analyzed the many plot flaws of* The Da Vinci Code *in a commentary that became the gold standard for fact-based* Da Vinci Code *debunking. Indeed, Shugarts was able to go so deeply into the thought process of* Da Vinci Code *author Dan Brown, that he produced a book-length work (*Secrets of the Widow's Son*) about what Dan Brown's next book might be about—before Brown even published it.*

We asked Shugarts to tell us a bit about what's real and what's not concerning the technology and gadgetry we see on 24. *His fascinating report follows.*

THE SALIENT POINT ABOUT JACK BAUER and his use of technology is that while he uses many devices, he doesn't actually *require* any of these techie toys at all. He uses whatever is available. If a device is handy, it's a convenience, not a necessity.

This is different from James Bond, where there is always a scene in which the technology supply sergeant, "Q," shows James the toys (and James fiddles with them and breaks something). Once we have seen Q give the demo, we are simply waiting for the other shoe to drop. We patiently keep tabs until the end of the film for James to get around to using all the devices he has been carrying. The last device is also the one that is crucial in getting 007 out of the final predicament of the film.

By contrast, Jack Bauer carries a gun, a knife, a cell phone, and a PDA. Sometimes he doesn't bother with these things, though, or they are stripped from him. What we have learned over the various seasons is that Jack is probably at his most dangerous without the toys. That's because possibly the most potent tech weapon of all is Jack's mind. Jack is the fanatic who will not quit, who will sacrifice himself totally for the cause, and who is infinitely adaptable.

But the other side of "Jack tech" is that he knows tech stuff intuitively.

Every tech item he touches bends to his indomitable will. Most of us poor slobs have to invest hours of sweat and study just to get familiar with one major program, like Microsoft Excel or Outlook. How many people do you know who still can't reliably send an e-mail attachment? Jack, by contrast, sits down at any computerlike device, anywhere, under any conditions, dials up CTU on the phone, and, after three keystrokes, announces, "I'm uploading the file to you now!" Jack can operate any weapon, fly any plane or helicopter, and eavesdrop on terrorist plots in several languages. He surely must be both a genius and some kind of closet techie.

Of course, Jack cannot take all the credit, since there are something like four hundred people at CTU's Los Angeles facility, as well as others around the world, who comprise a giant tech support engine, ready to assist Jack at the phizzt of a photon. All of them scurry around doing highly technical stuff. And they have true wizards among them, characters like Adam and Milo and Morris and Edgar and Chloe, who are doing the impossible stuff.

So let's look at some highlights from the wide range of "24 Tech" that is used by Jack and the CTU team:

Jack's Gear

Jack's Knife The knife that Jack carries is a Microtech Halo III. This is a very specialized knife costing upwards of $350. At the touch of a button, the blade jumps out the end of the handle—clearly not for people who fidget with things in their pockets. Generally speaking, it would be classified as a *switchblade* and banned in many states. The handle and the blade are usually black, and the name recalls the acronym for High Altitude Low Opening, the Special Forces method of dropping into occupied territory by parachute. Thus, if you are a "black ops" kind of guy, this knife is for you. The blade shape of the Halo III is wicked-looking. It is shaped like a miniature Japanese sword. Jack uses it in Day 5 (12:00 p.m.) to threaten to cut out Walt Cummings's eyes. (It works great for that.) Actually, the Halo knife comes up much earlier, in Day 1 (10:00 a.m.), when a terrorist agent, posing as a businessman, has one. Fortunately, Jack recognizes that the guy's Halo is no ordinary pocketknife.

Jack's Gun Although Jack uses any gun within reach at any moment, he settled on carrying the HK (Heckler & Koch) USP 9 Compact from Day 3 through Day 6. This all-black, semiautomatic, nine-millimeter pistol holds up to thirteen rounds. Its frame is made of polymer, and it has been made more "concealable" by its compact design. However, this is not a "stealth" gun, since it has many metal parts and would definitely trigger a metal detector. It is not standard issue in most Special Ops forces or police special units.

Click-click In Hollywood, this is the sound that a pistol always makes when it's empty but the shooter keeps trying to fire it. It comes from the days of the Westerns, where cowboys fired revolvers. Semiautomatic pistols, such as Jack

Bauer's HK USP 9C, typically don't make a sound after the last round. You can't really pull the trigger because it's gone all the way back and will not reset itself. Film directors are aware of this, but they keep putting the click-click into the sound track because the audience expects it. The directors of 24 are no exception, so even Jack gets caught doing this.

Jack's Wristwatch Since at least Day 5, Jack has been wearing a truly remarkable watch. It is the Black Hawk, or Special Ops watch, built by American Watch Co., a division of MTM, Inc., of Los Angeles. The all-black, $450 watch has a case of solid stainless steel, with a unique system for electromagnetic recharging of its lithium battery. This allows the watch to remain sealed so that it is waterproof to 100 meters (330 feet). Not only does the watch have an illuminated dial, but it also features a lighting system for illuminating maps or for signaling at night, at distances of up to a mile (1.6km). It has been used by a wide range of U.S. Special Forces, from Army Rangers to Navy SEALS.

Jack's PDA/Phone In Day 1, Jack calls his personal digital assistant (PDA) a "Palm Pilot," which at that time was the very essence of a PDA, used for such things as keeping track of meetings and people's phone numbers. As the seasons marched by, it became much more common to have features of the PDA combined with cell phones and e-mailing or texting devices. Jack was later seen using the Palm Treo, now called a "smartphone." (But in Day 6, Jack switched to a Motorola i880 that he confiscated.) What is a bit odd here is that we don't see the BlackBerry, a phone/PDA combo that also browses and e-mails. It is one of the most common units found in government circles, and ubiquitous in the business world, on Capitol Hill, and in Hollywood. It will be interesting to see whether Jack can keep his hands off an iPhone in the future. The iPhone made its debut around the time Day 6 wrapped up, and Apple products have shown up a lot, perhaps as the result of product placement strategies.

How-Low-Can-You-Go Tech

Rag and Bag When Jack goes to torture you, he can get completely no-tech. In Day 1 (10:00 a.m.), he threatens Ted Cofell by describing a Russian torture: They stuff a rag down your throat, all the way to your stomach, wait for it to begin digestion, then pull it out. Jack himself has undergone waterboarding, which doesn't require any special tools, just a way to tie the victim down and pour enough water on his face to simulate drowning. In Day 6 (10:00 a.m.), Jack begins his preliminary interrogation of his brother Graem by putting a plastic bag over his head.

Rolodex Despite all the technical gear and the massive computing power of CTU, when Jack goes to find some phone numbers on Day 1 (12:00 a.m.), he uses an ordinary Rolodex.

Hacksaw, Fire Ax, Wire Cutters These are common tools to most people, but Jack finds new uses for them, mostly gruesome ones. In Day 3 (12:00 p.m.), he needs to save Chase, who has clamped the cordilla virus device to his arm. So he uses a fire ax to cut off Chase's arm. In Day 2 (8:00 a.m.), Jack has a prisoner brought in and suddenly shoots him dead. "I'm going to need a hacksaw," says Jack. He later presents the prisoner's head to a gang leader. In Day 1 (1:00 a.m.), Jack cuts off a finger from a dead man's hand in order to retrieve it for fingerprinting. And in Day 6 (5:00 p.m.), Jack uses a cigar cutter to lop off an interrogation subject's pinkie.

Keeping an Eye Out

Infrared Satellite, Infrared Surveillance In Day 6 (1:00 p.m.), Jack and a CTU team surround an apartment building where the terrorists are holding Morris. Jack asks what can be seen on "infrared satellite." CTU tells him, "The latest scan shows 215 people in the building, spread out over six floors and 112 apartments." This is a completely fictional use of today's satellite surveillance technology. Although there are lots of infrared satellites (mainly weather satellites), there are no satellites that can see down into buildings using infrared technology, in the manner portrayed in that episode. That's because the satellites are geared for using light that is reflected off the surfaces and clouds here on earth (the main light source being the sun). The sensors focus on the portion of the spectrum just outside the range of visible light, the "near-infrared." This achieves a better contrast for certain weather features. If the sun is not available, an infrared surveillance camera is often accompanied by an infrared light source to light up the area. When surveillance gear is much closer than a satellite (i.e., at street level) this kind of rig can provide good, low-cost night surveillance, even in dark areas where there are no conventional lights (thieves don't notice the invisible infrared lighting). However, the cameras cannot see through walls or roofs. (But there are related surveillance technologies of interest. See *Thermal Imaging, Night Vision,* and *Through-the-Wall Surveillance,* below.)

Thermal Imaging Often conflated with "infrared surveillance," thermal imaging detects heat radiating from an object, as opposed to near-infrared *light* reflected off an object. The thermal detection method makes the field of view pretty dark, except where warm objects or people create bright areas, which makes these items stand out. The technique does work through fog and smoke. Thermal imaging has been used to look at buildings and detect areas of heat loss, or indistinct indications of things below the surface. It has been tested in hopes of detecting people inside buildings, but many other heat sources can confuse the sensors. CTU has used thermal imaging, as have many police departments, to capture images of people in bushes, under trees, and so on. The police have great examples of finding the criminal, and then finding the (hot) smoking gun, thrown into dark bushes. Firemen now commonly use this gear (tuned for the proper heat range) for finding people in smoky buildings.

Night Vision The principle of night vision is to be able to use the dimmest of ambient conditions, such as starlight alone, to illuminate a scene. Today's night vision viewers receive the tiny signals of light or heat and they may use either infrared sensing and/or thermal imaging to compose a picture for the user. Night vision goggles give our troops overseas the ability to fight in the dark routinely, and the CTU teams in *24* sometimes use them, although Jack doesn't ever seem to need such gear. The terrorists of *24* also know where to shop for night vision goggles when needed.

Through-the-Wall Surveillance Infrared and thermal imaging have been represented as being able to "see" inside buildings, but this capability has been eluding law enforcement officials for a long time, and Hollywood has been regularly jumping the gun in depicting it. Hitherto it has been mainly theoretical and experimental. But there is a promising technology using a form of radar. The U.S. military and the Department of Homeland Security (if CTU were a real-life agency, it would be operating under the umbrella of DHS) have actually been working hard on "through-the-wall surveillance" (TWS) that detects human beings and other recognizable shapes, even behind concrete walls. It can also be calibrated to zero in on a person's breathing and heartbeat.

Nuclear Threats

Nuclear Warheads In Day 2, the big threat is a nuclear warhead carried in a drone that will be exploded at about five hundred feet (174m) over Los Angeles, except that Jack and Mason fly it out to the desert. In Day 2 (8:00 a.m.) we learn that it may be a "dirty" bomb but also we are given projections of one million dead if it exploded over a city like LA. This is a contradiction in nuclear bomb terms because a "dirty" bomb implies a conventional explosion that scatters nuclear material but doesn't destroy much. (See *Dirty Bomb*, below). Later on, enough information comes into CTU to indicate that it is a nuclear device, probably a missile warhead, of about ten kilotons, a size much more akin to that of an actual weapon, although at the very low end of nuclear yields. (The really big nuclear devices have yields in the tens of megatons, a thousand times as big, which could wipe out entire metropolitan areas.) As is customary in Hollywood, it is assumed that the weapon was stolen or bought from the Russians. In actuality, while there have been security problems at Russian nuclear sites, there is no documented case of an actual warhead falling into terrorist hands. [For more on this issue, see the interview with Laura Holgate of the National Threat Initiative, earlier in this chapter.] The figure of a million dead seems very plausible for ten kilotons. The concept of exploding it at five hundred feet (174m) is well founded in the physics of explosions, designed to maximize the destruction from the blast. Later, CTU must choose between flying the bomb out over the Pacific or over the Mojave Desert. They conclude that exploding the bomb over the Pacific would mean the loss of eighty commercial ships as well as untold environmental damage, while the desert option would just kill a few campers, more or less. This is a vast oversimplification, but there is a certain logic to it.

"Nucular" Bomb This is a mispronunciation of *nuclear*. In Day 2, Jack has no problem correctly pronouncing nuclear both times he uses it. However, that was before lots of people began calling attention to President George W. Bush's mispronouncing it as *nucular*, which he has consistently done for his entire two terms, despite growing ridicule. By Day 6 (12:00 p.m.), Jack, too, says "nucular." Could this be a Fox production value?

"Dirty" Bomb The aim of a "dirty" nuke is not to create a nuclear explosion. Rather, it is to use an ordinary explosion to scatter radioactive material. The number of people who might be harmed by the blast itself is relatively small, and the fallout would be limited. The value of a dirty nuke to a terrorist is that it is comparatively compact, relatively easy to bring into a major city, and could cause substantial panic, chaos, and death in a metropolitan area if deployed successfully. If a dirty nuke were detonated in a downtown business district, for instance, it could stop commerce there for years. Two big advantages to terrorists of the dirty nuke are that it doesn't require any significant technical abilities, and any grade of nuclear material (not necessarily weapons grade) will suffice. Unfortunately, the real-life threat of a terrorist organization obtaining nuclear material and detonating a dirty bomb in a major U.S. city is very real. (See also *Suitcase Nuke* and *Nuclear Warheads*.)

Suitcase Nuke The Big Threat in Day 6 is a set of five suitcase nuclear bombs, one of which is detonated in Valencia, a suburban area just north of Los Angeles. CTU estimates that twelve thousand people are killed in the blast, but luckily, the wind is blowing the fallout northward, away from LA. Despite localized pandemonium, the directors of *24* paint nearby LA as relatively unaffected. They allow CTU personnel to drive freely around the city in conditions of light traffic just a few hours after the blast. The idea that traffic would flow freely a few hours after a suitcase nuke exploded just a few miles away requires extreme suspension of disbelief.

No one knows for sure that Russian suitcase nukes even exist, but it's widely believed that they do, especially after testimony in 1996 from a former Soviet official who said several dozen of these devices were missing and may have fallen into the hands of Chechens. *Suitcase* itself is a bit of an exaggeration, though: The size would be more like a small footlocker weighing about 120 to 150 pounds (54.5–68kg). The United States had also developed nuclear weapons of this approximate size; they generally are in yield ranges of one to ten kilotons. The worst aspect of the Russian suitcase nuke scenario is that a number of these devices are said to have been sold to Osama bin Laden. Thus, although it is portrayed almost as just another explosion in *24*, to be sloughed off as total fiction, perhaps a serious debate should center on whether we have sufficient plans in place to deal with a nuke of any size exploding in an American city.

Network Stuff

Virtual Private Network, Point-to-Point Protocols   In *24*, like nowhere else in television, you find that people send electronic files to other people through all sorts of odd connections. They use terms like "I'm piping it to you" and the data shows up at the destination, without the recipient doing anything in particular. It's true that there are ways to accomplish this, but you would think that an intelligence-reliant outfit like CTU would have better control and coordination of such file transfers. To do otherwise would invite various forms of computer attack. But wait—that's exactly what *does* happen when Nina Myers gets Jack to call a "Felco" number and release a devastating computer worm into the CTU facility on Day 3 (1:00 a.m.). Anyway, well-known methods of transfer include File Transfer Protocol (FTP), routinely employed by millions of computers daily, and the lesser known Point-to-Point Tunneling Protocol, the essential ingredient of what is fairly well known as Virtual Private Networking (VPN). Through VPN connections, computers can be remotely operated, form teleconference groups, etc. The wizards at CTU—especially Chloe—are so good at this kind of thing that they can send live video feeds to Jack's cell phone this way.

Apple versus PC   In many Hollywood productions, it's common to see Apple computers, much more than any other brand. This has been the case in *24* as well. Perhaps that's because Apple has been careful to make its designs distinctive, with large and backlit Apple logos, whereas lots of PCs are faceless. Perhaps it's due to a "product placement" agreement. If you follow *24* carefully, you'll see that even the president of the United States chooses an Apple laptop. From the very first episode of *24*, Jack Bauer's office was fully configured with various new Macintosh models, and there are always plenty of them strewn around at CTU. Occasionally, Dells appear, along with a lot of nondescript hardware.

Packets and Other Lingo   When computers are networked, they "talk" to each other by breaking up the information and sending it in small hunks called packets. In a flow of data, packets are like the individual droplets of water going over Niagara Falls. Nobody would ever try to follow the progress of an individual packet—except at CTU. (However, there are now dedicated chips coming on the market that security-check packets in a high-speed, automated way.) Talk of packets is just one example of a bunch of pseudocomputer lingo that Chloe and the gang sling. For instance, in Day 6 (1:00 p.m.), Milo says, "You're not resyncing the core nodes correctly," and Chloe snaps, "I know what I'm doing!" Some of this is closer to reality than we might think. For instance, Michelle says in Day 3 (1:00 p.m.), "You know, it could be that you forgot to set the group permission. Someone who knows the tree structure changed the ownership." This is essentially a basic Linux operating system procedure—hardly news to the CTU geeks—but it is a recognizable script from the language of computerspeak that might actually occur among IT professionals.

Biohazard Threats

Nerve Gas   In Day 5, the terrorists release a nerve gas, dubbed Sentox VX-1, at various locations, including the CTU facility itself. This is clearly intended to represent the actual nerve gas known as VX, which is very nasty stuff indeed. It kills within minutes, basically by disabling the body's nervous system. Fluids are instantly secreted from every part of the body and then there are spasms, convulsions, and death. Certain drugs, such as atropine, can counteract nerve gas but are dangerous poisons themselves. In use, VX is a gas that dissipates and settles as an oily residue, which can still be very harmful if it comes in contact with the skin. Although quite a number of deadly nerve agents were developed by the Germans (sarin among them, infamously and murderously used by local Japanese terrorists in the Tokyo subway system in 1995), the V series is about ten times as toxic, and VX itself was developed by the British. The VX technology was later traded by Britain in exchange for U.S. nuclear weapons technology, and the United States subsequently became one of the largest manufacturers of VX. When the terrorists release the Sentox in the CTU air ducts, certain rooms can be sealed off, but the team then learns that the Sentox was supposedly laced with acid, which is breaking down the door seals. This is an unrealistic gilding of the terrorist lily. The concentration of any acid would be minuscule. When Jack enters a gassed room, he merely holds his breath and pulls his hood up. This would not protect him in reality, since VX can be absorbed through the skin. Later, when ventilation in the CTU is restored and the gas clears, they assume it's safe to walk around. But no: By one logic there is an oily residue of VX everywhere, and by another logic there is acid everywhere. Acid really eats at electronic equipment, and practically everything at CTU is electronic.

Cordilla Virus   As invented by the writers of *24*, the cordilla virus in Day 3 appears to be similar to the scientifically known and medically diagnosed hantavirus, a genuine pulmonary disease that was first noticed in 1993 and comes from rodents. Initial symptoms of hantavirus are muscle aches, fever, and fatigue. The late stage involves lungs that fill up with fluid, killing the victim. There is no known cure, except that some survive when given intensive care measures like oxygen and intubation. The fictional cordilla virus in *24* is described as a pneumopulmonary virus, but symptoms are nosebleeds, hemorrhaging, skin abscesses, and eventually death. There's no cure, but some people are immune to it. That aspect makes cordilla sound much closer to ebola (hemorrhagic fever). In *24*, the cordilla is "weaponized" by shortening the incubation period from its already short fourteen hours, apparently to less than an hour, based on the evidence of what happens when people at the Chandler Plaza Hotel are exposed. The virus is released at 3:58 a.m. and the first symptoms are seen in Gael at 4:23 a.m., a mere twenty-five minutes later. Great for *24*'s dramatic narrative and ticking time clock, but again, quite unrealistic. All the known horrific viruses like ebola and hanta take days, even weeks, to induce death. Similarly, the discussion at CTU of projections showing that millions of people will die within the first forty-eight hours from cordilla are dramatically overstated when compared to the loss of life projected by even the most worried real-life experts on how fast, widespread, and deadly the effects of most viruses deployed in a bioterror mode might be.

Weaponized The writers of *24* are able to make the extremely nasty cordilla virus sound even worse because it is said to be *weaponized*. The word entered the public mind with the anthrax attacks that followed swiftly on the heels of 9/11. The first attack involved a brownish granular substance, sent to various news media, which caused a skin infection of anthrax. This was bad, but then things got worse. The second wave involved a finely processed white powder, sent to two U.S. senators' offices, which caused a respiratory anthrax infection. Anthrax (a bacterium) is a sludgy substance when cultivated, so it had to be processed into the fine powder to make it more likely to be inhaled. This is what it means to *weaponize* it. (It's all in the delivery system.) What the nefarious villain Marcus Alvers did in Day 3 of *24* was to genetically modify the cordilla virus to give it a much shorter incubation period than the original fourteen hours. This isn't *weaponizing* it, just accelerating its deadly performance.

Truth, Lies, Torture Techniques

Truth Serum In most cases when Jack wants to get the truth out of a reluctant suspect quickly, the "truth drug" of choice is something that *24* calls *hyoscine pentothal*, a fictional drug that is a conflation of two real drugs, hyoscine (also known as scopolamine) and sodium thiopental (trade name: sodium pentothal). The two real drugs are classed as depressants, while the description on *24* of hyoscine pentothal as a "neuroinflammatory" ("makes your whole body feel like it's on fire") makes it more of a torture drug than a truth serum. This distinction—truth inducement versus torture—makes all the difference. If a truth-inducing drug were developed, the suspect would give up his secrets willingly, saving time and suffering. But the search for a really good truth serum has been going on for hundreds of years, and so far nothing effective has been found. Historically, the most likely candidates have been alcohol, scopolamine, and sodium thiopental. None is completely effective and some other drugs that have been tried, such as LSD, are somewhat counterproductive or unpredictable. Recent experiments have focused on the possibility that, under the right conditions, a drug can assist in getting the subject to trust and confide in someone (perhaps a cellmate). One trust-inducing drug under investigation is the hormone oxytocin (tradenamed pitocin), commonly used for stimulating contractions in childbirth. By contrast, hyoscine pentothal, the torture drug used in *24*, is not markedly different from many physical ways of inflicting intolerable pain on the subject. Pain has been shown to be a relatively unreliable road to the truth because the victim will say anything to escape the pain, telling the interrogators anything they want to hear. In *24*, the injection of a truth serum is often coupled with some lie detection equipment for just this reason. (See *Lie Detection*.)

Lie Detection

Traditional lie detection involves various combinations of sensing skin conductivity, blood pressure, heartbeat, and breathing. In *24*, they add the parameter of sensing thermal changes in a subject's face. Yet another technique is voice stress analysis. All of these methods work to some degree, but too often can yield both false positives and false negatives. On the one hand, many people test as though they were lying because of the agitated state they are likely to be in as a result of any conflict-driven situation. On the other hand, cool, calculating liars can pass traditional lie detection tests by remaining calm.

Several famous spies have passed polygraph tests, including the most damaging double agent the United States has ever had, Aldrich Ames, who passed two polygraphs while spying for the Soviets. It might be supposed that Ames practiced special techniques to accomplish this feat, but, in fact, he was basically advised to "get a good night's sleep and go into the test rested and relaxed." Recently, with the publication of studies that hint that the brain scanning technique known as functional magnetic resonance imaging (MRI) might give some indication of truthfulness, there has been great interest in exploring this idea and even some early commercial applications of it. However, it has not been shown to be any more accurate than other lie detection methods. It is worth noting that, even though the polygraph has been around for nearly a hundred years in some form or other, polygraph results have never been deemed admissible in a court of law.

But of course the suspension of disbelief is so strong on *24* that even things that don't work in the real world can be used by Jack Bauer as superefficient adjuncts to his cause. On *24*, there's simply no time to quibble about caveats—and when you have Jack Bauer's instincts and track record, why quibble, anyway? ■

About the Contributors and the Cast

Dan Burstein, Editor, launched Squibnocket Partners LLC as an innovative content development company in 2003 with his business partner, Arne J. de Keijzer. The next year, they published *Secrets of the Code*, which went on to spend more than six months on the *New York Times* best-seller list and to become a global blockbuster, appearing in more than thirty languages and in multiple editions all over the world. *Secrets of 24* is the sixth title in the *Secrets* series. Altogether, there are over 4 million books in print in the *Secrets* series worldwide. Three Squibnocket titles—*Secrets of the Code, Secrets of Angels & Demons,* and *Secrets of Mary Magdalene*—have been turned into documentary films.

Maintaining an active full-time career as a venture capitalist (his "day job"), in addition to his involvement with the *Secrets* series, Burstein is founder and managing partner of Millennium Technology Ventures, a New York–based venture capital firm that invests in innovative companies. He has served on the boards of more than a dozen early-stage technology companies and is currently a director of Applied Minds, a leading-edge research lab, and Global Options, a publicly-traded international risk management company. From 1988 to 2000, he was senior advisor at the Blackstone Group, one of Wall Street's leading private merchant banks. He is also a prominent corporate strategy consultant and has served as an advisor to CEOs, senior management teams, and global corporations, including Sony, Toyota, Microsoft, Boardroom Inc., and Sun Microsystems.

Burstein is also an award-winning journalist and author of numerous books on global economics and technology. His most recent technology-related book is *BLOG! How the Newest Media Revolution is Changing Politics, Business, and Culture,* co-written with David Kline, and widely considered the most definitive book about the rise of the "blogosphere." Burstein's 1988 book *Yen!,* about the rise of Japanese financial power, was an international best-seller in more than twenty countries. In 1995, his book *Road Warriors* was one of the first to analyze the impact of the Internet and digital technology on business and society. His 1998 book *Big Dragon* (written with Arne J. de Keijzer), outlined a long-term view of China's role in the twenty-first century that has, so far, turned out to be prescient.

Working as a freelance journalist in the 1980s, Mr. Burstein published more than a thousand articles in over two hundred publications, including the *New York Times,* the *Wall Street Journal,* the *Los Angeles Times,* the *Boston Globe,* the *Chicago Tribune, New York* magazine, *Rolling Stone, Paris Match, le Nouvel Observateur, L'Expansion,* and many others in the United States, Europe, and Asia. Burstein has appeared on numerous TV documentaries and news specials, ranging from the programs broadcast on the History Channel, MSNBC, and CNN, and to *Charlie Rose* and *Oprah!*

Arne J. de Keijzer, Editor, is a writer, former China business consultant, and Dan Burstein's partner in Squibnocket Partners LLC. He is the author of an internationally best-selling travel guide to China, two books on doing business with China, and, with Dan Burstein, *Big Dragon: China's Future—What It Means for Business, the Economy, and the Global Order.* Also together with Dan Burstein, he created the "Secrets" series of books and was managing editor of *Secrets of the Code* and coeditor of *Secrets of Angels & Demons* and the *Secrets of Mary Magdalene.* He was also a contributing editor to *BLOG! How the Newest Media Revolution is Changing Politics, Business, and Culture.* de Keijzer's other work has appeared in publications ranging from *Powerboat Reports* to the *New York Times.*

Paul Berger, Contributing Editor, is a British freelance writer living in New York. His work has appeared in the *New York Times,* the *Washington Post, US News and World Report, Online Journalism Review,* and Denmark's *Weekendavisen.* He is the contributing editor of four books, including the *New York Times* and worldwide best-seller *Secrets of the Code,* and, most recently, *All the Money in The World: How the Forbes 400 Make—and Spend—Their Fortunes.* He writes the blog *Englishman in New York* at www.pdberger.com.

David Freeman, Contributing Editor, is a journalist and editor whose work has been published by in *Men's Health, Popular Mechanics, Consumer Reports, Reader's Digest, Businessweek,* and many other magazines, websites, and newsletters. He is the former editorial director of two publishing companies, Boardroom Inc. and New Hope Media, and is now is president of smartmandaily.com, an Internet startup.

Katherine Goldstein, Contributing Editor, is a Brooklyn-based freelance journalist who writes reviews, op-eds, and features. Her work has appeared in *AM New York, New York Press,* and *BUST* magazine, among others.

Shohreh Aghdashloo was born and raised in Tehran, Iran, but fled with her family in 1978 to escape the Islamic revolution. Along with starring as Dina Araz in Season 4 of *24,* she has had roles on TV's *Smith, Grey's Anatomy, ER,* and *Will & Grace.* Film credits include *The Nativity Story* and *House of Sand and Fog,* for which she was nominated for an Academy Award in 2004. She is also a cofounder, with her husband, Houshang Touzie, of a Farsi-language theater company, which tours all over the world. Upcoming projects include playing Saddam Hussein's wife in *Between Two Rivers,* an HBO/BBC miniseries about the dictator and his relationship with his family and advisers. She holds a BA in International Relations.

Stephen Applebaum is a UK-based freelance writer specializing in film, entertainment, social issues, and politics. His work appears regularly in newspapers and magazines worldwide, including *The Independent, The Guardian, The Scotsman, The Australian, Rolling Stone, BBC Online* and Filmfour.com.

Ginia Bellafante is a television, theater, and cultural critic for the *New York Times,* as well as a style reporter. She is also a former contributor to *Time* magazine.

Carlos Bernard joined the cast of *24* as CTU agent Tony Almeida in 2001. The recipient of an MFA degree from the American Conservatory Theater in San Francisco, he has acted in a variety of stage productions, including *As You Like It, Hamlet, The Cherry Orchard,* and *Scenes from an Execution.* Bernard has made guest appearances on *Walker, Texas Ranger* and *F/X: The Series,* among other TV shows, and he's been a regular on the daytime drama *The Young and the Restless.* Although not an experienced poker player, he once participated in a World Poker Tour tournament on behalf of a charity and won $10,000.

Mark Bowden, an *Atlantic Monthly* national correspondent, is an author, journalist, screenwriter, and teacher. His international best-seller, *Black Hawk Down: A Story of Modern War,* was a finalist for the National Book Award. Bowden is also the author of the best-seller *Killing Pablo: The Hunt for the World's Greatest Outlaw,* which tells the story of the hunt for Colombian cocaine billionaire Pablo Escobar. *Killing Pablo* won the Overseas Press Club's Cornelius Ryan Award as the best book of 2001. He has worked as a consultant and screenwriter on the film version of *Black Hawk Down,* and is currently adapting *Killing Pablo* for Jerry Bruckheimer Films. Mark Bowden teaches journalism and creative writing at his alma mater, Loyola College, and is a columnist for the *Philadelphia Inquirer.*

Rosa Brooks is a columnist for the *Los Angeles Times* and a professor at the Georgetown University Law Center. An expert on human rights and international law, she has been an advisoer to the U.S. Department of State, served as a consultant for Human Rights Watch, and served on the board of Amnesty International USA. She is a member of the Council on Foreign Relations and the co-author of *Can Might Make Rights? Building the Rule of Law After Military Interventions*, published in 2006.

James Jay Carafano is a leading expert in defense affairs, military operations and strategy, and homeland security at the Heritage Foundation. His academic posts have included the U.S. Military Academy in at West Point, the U.S. Naval War College, and the National Defense University. Carafano served 25 twenty-five years in the army, and is author of several military history books and studies, the latest being *GI Ingenuity: Improvisation, Technology and Winning World War II*. His editorials have appeared in the *Boston Globe, USA Today,* and the *Washington Times,* among others.

Brian Carney is an op-ed writer and member of the editorial board of the *Wall Street Journal*. Previously, for the *Wall Street Journal Europe,* he served as the editor of the editorial page and of the *Business Europe* column. In 2003, he received the Frederic Bastiat Prize for Journalism for writing that promotes free markets and free societes. Before joining the *Journal* in 2000, he was associated with the Innovations in American Government Program at Harvard University. He has also worked as a sternman on a lobster boat in Maine.

Michael Chertoff has been the secretary of Homeland Security since 2005. Prior to taking on this position, he was assistant attorney general for the Criminal Division at the Department of Justice, where he helped trace the 9/11 terrorist attacks to the al-Qaeda network, and also worked to increase information sharing within the FBI and with state and local officials. Before joining the Bush administration, Chertoff was a partner in the law firm of Latham & Watkins. He spent more than a decade as a federal prosecutor in New Jersey as well as assistant U.S. attorney for the Southern District of New York. As U.S. Attorney, Chertoff investigated and prosecuted several significant cases of political corruption, organized crime, and corporate fraud. Chertoff graduated magna cum laude from Harvard College in 1975 and magna cum laude from Harvard Law School in 1978. From 1979 to 1980 he served as a clerk to Supreme Court Justice William Brennan, Jr.

Tom Clancy is the author of a series of bestselling political thrillers, best known for their technically detailed espionage and military science storylines set during and in the aftermath of the Cold War. The most famous of these—*The Hunt for Red October* (his breakout best-seller), *Patriot Games, Clear and Present Danger,* and *The Sum of All Fears*— have been turned into commercially successful films. His 1989 novel *Clear and Present Danger* sold more than 1.5 million hardcover copies, making it the #1 number-one best-selling novel of the 1980s. Tom Clancy has also become a "brand." His name is on a series of similar action/adventure books written by ghostwriters, as well as a series of nonfiction books on military subjects and biographies of key leaders. In 1996, Clancy cofounded the computer game developer Red Storm Entertainment and has had his name on several of its most successful games. Clancy is also part-owner of the Baltimore Orioles, a major league baseball team.

Robert Cochran, co-creator of *24* with Joel Surnow, won an Emmy for Outstanding Writing for a Drama Series in 2002 for the show's pilot episode. Originally, he was doubtful that the concept of the show could be sustained for more than one season, but he has written many episodes since and has been an executive producer for all 144 hours of the show to date. Cochran's other television credits include serving as executive consultant for *La Femme Nikita*, co-executive producer of *The Commish*, supervising producer of *JAG*, and writer/producer on *Falcon Crest* and *Sons and Daughters*. A lawyer by training, he began his career by writing episodes for legal shows such as *L.A. Law* and *The Antagonists*. He also has also written two historical miniseries—*Atilla* and *Nothing Like It In the World*—and a feature film titled *1066*.

Jerome E. Copulsky is assistant professor of philosophy and religion at Goucher College. He was previously assistant professor and director of Judaic studies at Virginia Tech, and holds degrees from Wesleyan, Columbia, and the University of Chicago. His essays, stories and reviews have appeared in such places as the *New York Times*, the *Christian Science Monitor*, the *Journal of the American Academy of Religion*, the *Journal of Religion*, and *Azure*.

Manny Coto joined *24*'s creative team in 2005 as a co-executive producer and major writer for the show. A passionate "Trekkie" all his life, he was glued to the TV when the original series ran in after-school syndication, and even wrote his own *Trek* comic book. Eventually, he became co-executive producer and showrunner of *Star Trek: Enterprise*. After graduating from the American Film Institute, Coto specialized in the sci-fi and fantasy genres, writing and directing an episode of *Tales from the Crypt* and the children's film *Star Kid*, and writing and producing *The Outer Limits*. He also created the series *Odyssey 5*. He was a writer, cast member, and co-creator of *The Half Hour News Hour*, a short-lived, right-wing news satire show on the Fox News Channel in 2007.

David Danzig is the campaign manager, Public Programs Department, and Primetime Torture Project director for the New York City office of Human Rights First. The project addresses the negative fallout from the way that torture is presented on American TV programs like *24, Lost, The Wire, Sleeper Cell*, and others. He has worked at Human Rights First since 2002. Prior to joining the organization, he worked as an award-winning journalist for the *Jersey Journal* in Jersey City, New Jersey, and the *Hoboken (N.J.) Reporter*. He also spent three years working on Capitol Hill as a press secretary and legislative director.

Maureen Dowd, winner of the 1999 Pulitzer Prize for distinguished commentary for her coverage of the Clinton-Lewinsky affair, became a columnist on the *New York Times* op-ed page in 1995 after having served as a correspondent in the paper's Washington bureau since 1986. She has covered four presidential campaigns and served as White House correspondent. She also wrote a column, *"On Washington,"* for the *New York Times Magazine*. She is the author of two books, *Bushworld: Enter at Your Own Risk*, and *Are Men Necessary? When Sexes Collide*.

Colin Freeze is a reporter for Canada's national newspaper, the *Globe and Mail* of Toronto, specializing in national security issues.

Deirdre Good is a professor in the Department of New Testament, General Theological Seminary, New York City. A widely published author and prominent lecturer, she is also a program consultant to television on religious history. She is the author, most recently, of *Jesus' Family Values* and editor of *Mariam, the Magdalen, and the Mother*, a collection of essays exploring the religious and prophetic identity of Mary Magdalen(e) and Mary, Jesus' Mother, as Miriam figures. She is the editor of *Reconstructing the Tradition of Sophia in Gnostic Literature* and *Jesus the Meek King*, and contributed to *Secrets of the Code*. She was also a contributing editor to *Secrets of Mary Magdalene*.

Howard Gordon, screenwriter and producer, has been called *24*'s "mastermind." Gordon came to Hollywood fresh out of Princeton in 1984 and, with his fellow filmmaker and screenwriter Alex Gansa, broke into the industry with a few episodes of *Spencer: For Hire*. This project was followed by the Emmy-nominated series *Beauty and the Beast*, for which the pair were later named producers. From 1993 though 1997, Gordon and Gansa were writers and supervising producers for ninety-six episodes of *The X-Files*. After this series Gordon began to pursue projects independently. He cowrote one episode of *Buffy the Vampire Slayer* and then went on to work on Joss Whedon's *Angel*. Gordon joined *24* in 2001, where he wrote several episodes in Seasons 1 and 2 and crafted the entire story arcs for Seasons 3 and 4. Since 2006 Gordon has been *24*'s executive producer and showrunner.

Jing Guan, who is originally from Shanghai, received her Master of International Affairs degree from the Columbia School of International and Public Affairs in New York. She previously worked for CNN in New York and London as a production and editorial assistant, and for China's state media as a reporter and editor. She is also former senior editor for *Newsweek China*. Jing currently freelances on a wide range of media projects from her base in Shanghai.

Shane Harris writes feature and investigative stories about intelligence, homeland security, and counterterrorism. He is a staff correspondent for *National Journal*, and has written for publications such as *Slate*, the *Bulletin of the Atomic Scientists*, *Adbusters*, *Government Executive*, *Movieline*, and the U.S. Naval Institute's *Proceedings*. In 2007, he was named a finalist for the prestigious Livingston Awards for Young Journalists, which honor the best journalists in America under the age of thirty-five. He is also a fiction writer and a Sundance Film Festival screenwriting finalist.

Seymour Hersh is an investigative reporter for the *New Yorker*, specializing in national security and international affairs. He is the author of several books, including, most recently, *Chain of Command: The Road from 9/11 to Abu Ghraib*. During his long career he has won five George Polk awards in addition to winning the Pulitzer Prize for international reporting in 1970 for his coverage in the *New York Times* of the My Lai massacre during the Vietnam War.

Dennis Haysbert appeared in 5 five seasons of *24* as Senator and then President David Palmer, for which he received a Golden Globe nomination. He currently stars as Jonas "'Snake Doctor'" Blane in CBS's military drama, *The Unit*. His film credits include *Breach, Far from Heaven, Absolute Power, Random Hearts, Major League*, and playing Nelson Mandela in *Goodbye Bafana*, among many others.

David Heyman is director and senior fellow of the Homeland Security Program at the Center for Strategic and International Studies (CSIS). He is a leading expert on the global war on terrorism, bioterrorism, critical infrastructure protection, and risk-based security. Prior to joining CSIS, he served as in senior positions at the Department of Energy and the White House Office of Science and Technology Policy. Heyman's commentary and analysis has been seen on all major television networks and quoted in the *Washington Post*, the *New York Times,* and *USA Today*.

Laura Holgate is vice president for Russia/New Independent States Programs at the Nuclear Threat Initiative (NTI), an organization whose mission is to strengthen global security by reducing the risk of use and preventing the spread of nuclear, biological, and chemical weapons. Prior to joining NTI, Holgate led the Department of Energy's Office of Fissile Materials Disposition, and from 1995 through 1998 she directed the Cooperative Threat Reduction "Nunn-Lugar" program of U.S. assistance to Russia and other former Soviet states in eliminating the weapons-of-mass-destruction legacy of the cold war. Holgate has received numerous public service awards and is a member of the Council on Foreign Relations, the International Institute for Strategic Studies, and the Executive Board of Women in International Security. She recently joined advisory panels for the Pacific Northwest National Laboratory and Oak Ridge National Laboratory.

Laura Jackson is a best-selling rock and film biographer who has interviewed many of the world's leading celebrities and gained privileged access to their inner circles. Some of her subjects have included: Neil Diamond, Jon Bon Jovi, Paul Simon, Bono, Brian Jones, Daniel Day-Lewis, and Mick Jagger. *Kiefer Sutherland: The Biography,* is her latest book.

Evan Katz shared the 2006 Emmy Award for Outstanding Drama Series for his work as part of the creative team of *24*. He's been a TV producer and writer for other series as well, including *Special Unit 2, Seven Days,* and *JAG*.

Tony Lagouranis is a former U.S. Army specialist and interrogator who served in Iraq and worked at Abu Ghraib prison. He is the author of *Fear Up Harsh: An Army Interrogator's Dark Journey Through Iraq*. In addition to writing a much-discussed *New York Times* op-ed piece, titled "Tortured Logic," in 2006, he has appeared on *Democracy Now!, The Leonard Lopate Show, Frontline, Hardball with Chris Matthews,* and Human Rights First's *"Primetime Torture"* DVD.

John Leonard is a literary, television, film, and cultural critic who has written a weekly column on TV for *New York* magazine since 1984 and was the film and television critic for *"CBS Sunday Morning"* for sixteen years. He is currently a columnist for *Harper's,* and a frequent contributor to the *Nation,* the *New York Times Book Review,* and the *New York Review of Books*. He is the author of several novels as well as essay collections, among them *Lonesome Rangers: Homeless Minds, Promised Lands, Fugitive Cultures*.

Ben Liaw. Originally from Taiwan and educated in the United States, Ben received an engineering degree from Lehigh University and an MBA from Columbia Business School. He worked at Deloitte Consulting in Washington, D.C. as a management consultant, and Millennium Technology Ventures as a summer associate, before moving to Shanghai to pursue his own technology startup.

Rush Limbaugh has been a nationally syndicated radio political commentator since 1988. His strong conservative views are broadcast on 600 stations nationwide, and his fervent and loyal audience of some 15 million "dittoheads" have made him the number-one nationally syndicated radio talk show host in America—and the highest-paid radio personality in history. Limbaugh refers to himself as the "professor" of the fictional Limbaugh Institute for Advanced Conservative Studies, where he holds the (fictional) "Atilla the Hun Chair." His only reported brush with direct politics was when turned down an offer from Pat Buchanan to be his running mate during the 1992 presidential campaign. Limbaugh has raised a record $1.7 million–plus for the Leukemia and Lymphoma Society of America in his annual Cure-a-Thon, in addition to his personal donation of a quarter of a million dollars. Limbaugh was inducted into the Radio Hall of Fame in 1993. He is the author of *See, I Told You So* and *The Way Things Ought to Be*.

Jane Mayer is an investigative journalist who has been a staff writer for the *New Yorker* since 1995. She has also written for the *Wall Street Journal,* the *Washington Star,* the *Los Angeles Times,* and the *New York Review of Books*. She is the coauthor of two books, *Strange Justice,: the Selling of Clarence Thomas,* (with Jill Abramson) and *Landslide: The Unmaking of the President, 1984–1988* (with Doyle McManus).

Charles McGrath is the former editor of the *New York Times Book Review,* a fiction editor at the *New Yorker,* and he is currently a writer-at-large for the *New York Times.* He is a coauthor of *The Ultimate Golf Book: A History and a Celebration of the World's Greatest Game,* and the editor of *Books of the Century: A Hundred Years of Authors, Ideas and Literature.*

Rick Moran is a writer living in the exurbs of Chicago "on the banks of the beautiful Fox River." He is the associate editor of the online magazine *American Thinker.Com* (americanthinker.com), as well as a sports and political columnist for *Pajamas Media* (pajamasmedia.com). In addition, he is a contributing editor at *Family Security Matters* (familysecuritymatters.org), and the comment moderator for *Michelle Malkin* (michellemalkin.com). He is also proprietor of his own website, *RickMoran.Net.* Moran has appeared on several nationally syndicated radio shows as well as on C-SPAN and "The O'Reilly Factor." His own radio program, *The Rick Moran Show,* can be heard on *Blog Talk Radio* (blogtalkradio.com) every Tuesday afternoon. Moran graduated from Drake University in 1976 with a degree in fine arts.

James Morrison, the actor who played Bill Buchanan on the fourth, fifth, and sixth seasons of *24,* started his acting career as a clown and wire walker in the mid-1970s and then served his theatrical apprenticeship with the Alaska Repertory Theatre. Since then, he's performed in over a hundred plays at theaters ranging from the McCarter Theatre to the La Jolla Playhouse, the Mark Taper Forum, and the Old Globe. He's been in the films *Catch Me If You Can, American Gun, The One, Falling Down, Wilderness Survival for Girls,* and *Jarhead.* He was McQueen on the Fox network's *Space: Above and Beyond,* and he's handled dozens of episodic assignments for TV shows, including *Six Feet Under, The West Wing, Frasier, Millennium, The X-Files,* and *Cold Case.* Morrison is also a playwright, musician, and poet, and he has directed, written, and produced several award-winning short films. He is certified to teach hatha yoga by the White Lotus Foundation in Santa Barbara, where he still studies and teaches. He also conducts regular weekly classes at LA's oldest studio, *The Center for Yoga.*

Clarence Page is a syndicated op-ed columnist for the *Chicago Tribune.* He is a Vietnam veteran who has worked as an investigative reporter and foreign correspondent. He was awarded the Edward Scott Beck Award for overseas reporting on the changing politics of southern Africa in 1976. He won a Pulitzer Prize in 1972 for his participation in a *Chicago Tribune* task force series on voter fraud, and then went on to win another Pulitzer for commentary in 1989. Additionally, he is a contributor to the *NewsHour with Jim Lehrer,,* hosts documentaries on PBS, and is a regular panelist on BET's *Lead Story.* He is also the best-selling author of *Showing My Color: Impolite Essays on Race and Identity.*

Kal Penn attended the UCLA School of Theater, Television and Film. In addition to his television role as Ahmed Amar in *24,* his film acting credits include *Harold & Kumar Go to White Castle; Van Wilder 2: Rise of Taj; Superman Returns; A Lot Like Love;* and *The Namesake.* Penn also teaches courses in media images and teen movies in the Asian American Studies program at the University of Pennsylvania. Upcoming projects include *Harold & Kumar 2* and *Two Sisters,* a film directed by Margaret Cho.

Dorothy Rabinowitz has been a member of the editorial board of the *Wall Street Journal* since 1996. She writes the *Critic at Large* column for the *Journal*'s editorial page, which also appears on OpinionJournal.com as *Dorothy Rabinowitz's Media Log.* She won the 2001 Pulitzer Prize in commentary for her articles on American culture and society.

Mary Lynn Rajskub is an actor/comedienne and former performance artist, whose first national exposure came on the 1995 stream-of-consciousness comedy series *Mr. Show* on HBO. She subsequently was cast as a talent booker on *The Larry Sanders Show,* and has appeared in the films *Punch-Drunk Love, Sweet Home Alabama, Legally Blonde 2, Little Miss Sunshine,* and *Firewall.* Cast as Chloe on *24* for the 2003–2004 season, she has found a home on *24* ever since. In 2004 Rajskub also played Lynette "Squeaky" Fromme for the television version of *Helter Skelter.* She has twice been nominated for a Screen Actors Guild Award.

Frank Rich has been an op-ed columnist for the *New York Times* since 1994. He also serves as senior adviser to the *Times*'s culture editor on the paper's overall cultural news reporting. Before writing his column, he served as the paper's chief drama critic beginning in 1980, the year he joined the newspaper. Among other honors, Mr. Rich received the George Polk Award for commentary in 2005. In addition to his work at the *New York Times,* he has written about culture and politics for many other publications. His latest book is, *The Greatest Story Ever Sold: The Decline and Fall of Truth from 9/11 to Katrina.* Before joining the *New York Times,* Rich was a film and television critic at *Time* magazine. Earlier, he had been film critic for the *New York Post* and film critic and senior editor of *New Times* magazine.

John Robb, a former U.S. counterterrorism operation planner and commander, now advises corporations on the future of terrorism, infrastructure, and markets. While serving in the Department of Defense Counter-terrorism Unit, Robb participated in global operations as a mission commander, pilot, and mission planner. His training included advanced interrogation resistance training, terrorism survival, and clandestine mission operations. As a technology analyst, he led the move to cover Internet technologies at Forrester Research. Robb also ran a company that pioneered in weblogs and RSS technologies. He is a graduate of Yale University and the Air Force Academy, and his writings on war, terrorism, and technology have appeared the *New York Times* and *Fast Company.*

Tricia Rose is professor of Africana Studies at Brown University, whose teaching, research, and public lectures are focused on African-American culture, history, gender, and popular music. Her new latest book is *The Hip Hop Wars: The Top Ten Debates in Hip Hop, Why They Hurt Us and How to Fix Them.* is forthcoming from Basic Books in 2008. She is also the author of *Longing to Tell: Black Women Talk About Sexuality and Intimacy* and the award-winning book, *Black Noise: Rap Music and Black Culture in Contemporary America.* Her work has also appeared in publications such as *Essence, Vibe Magazine, Artforum, Bookforum, The Village Voice, Women's Review of Books,* and *Boston Book Review.*

Wiliam S. Sessions is best known to the public as the former director of the Federal Bureau of Investigation (1987–1993), but he has also had a long and distinguished career as a lawyer specializing in alternative dispute resolution. Before his appointment to the FBI, he served as the section chief of the Government Operations Section of the Department of Justice in Washington, D.C., the U.S. District judge for the Western District of Texas, and chief judge of that court. Judge Sessions currently serves as a member of the American Bar Association's Advisory Commission to the Standing Committee on the Law Library of Congress; the Innocence Project of the National Capital Region; and the International Center for Dispute Resolution, among other posts. Judge Sessions was named by his peers to the 2007 edition of *The Best Lawyers in America* for both alternative dispute resolution and corporate governance and compliance law. William Sessions joined the law firm of Holland & Knight LLP in 2000, where he remains a partner engaged primarily in alternative dispute resolution procedures.

David A. Shugarts is a journalist with more than thirty-five years' experience, having served on newspapers and magazines as a reporter, photographer, desk editor, and editor-in-chief. He obtained received a BA degree in English from Lehigh University, followed by service in Africa in the Peace Corps, then an MS degree in journalism from Boston University. His fields of expertise include aviation and marine writing. He was the founding editor of *Aviation Safety* magazine in 1981—for which he won five regional and national awards from the Aviation/Space Writers Association—and of *Powerboat Reports* magazine in 1988. As a writer, he has contributed to about a dozen books, including the best-seller, *Secrets of the Code: The Unauthorized Guide to The Da Vinci Code*, by Dan Burstein. He is the author of *Secrets of the Widow's Son*.

Joel Surnow is co-creator, with Robert Cochran, of *24*, which, in addition to its highly adrenalized plots, is the first television series to adopt a "real time" format. Surnow began writing for film soon after graduating from the UCLA School of Theater, Film and Television in 1975 and his breakthrough came when he began writing for *Miami Vice* in 1984. Surnow was also the creator and executive consultant of the television series *La Femme Nikita*, and supervising producer and writer for *The Equalizer*. Other credits include *Nowhere Man* and *Wiseguy*. In 2002 he shared the Emmy's Outstanding Writing for a Drama Series award with Robert Cochran, and, in 2006, he and his fellow producers of *24* won the Emmy for Outstanding Drama.

Kiefer Sutherland has engaged life as a musician, pool player, rodeo performer, rancher, father, *GQ* "man of the year," scotch drinker, cigar aficionado, tattoo-wearer, hockey player, and, oh, yes, a film and television actor who is the central character and heart of *24*. Born in London to the Canadian actors Donald Sutherland and Shirley Douglas, Kiefer left home in Toronto for New York at the age of seventeen to become an actor, and landed his first job as a character in the pilot of *Amazing Stories*, directed by Steven Spielberg. Sutherland has appeared in over fifty films, including *The Vanishing, At Close Range, Stand by Me, Twin Peaks: Fire Walk with Me, Young Guns, Lost Boys, Flatliners,* and *The Three Musketeers*. In 1992 he had a leading role, along with Jack Nicholson and Tom Cruise, in *A Few Good Men,* a movie with a plotline that would evolve and become adrenalized on *24*: the murder of a Marine on the grounds that it would ensure the safety of the whole unit. Sutherland has played Jack Bauer in commercials in Japan and Brazil, as well as twice in a speaking part on *The Simpsons*. In 2007, *Forbes* magazine listed him as the highest-paid dramatic actor on television (he reportedly earns $10 million a season).

Alvin Toffler, along with his wife, Heidi Toffler, are known around the world for their groundbreaking work on futurism, which has influenced presidents and prime ministers, top leaders in fields ranging from business to non-profit organizations, as well as educators, psychologists, and social scientists. Each of their books—which include such classics as *Future Shock, The Third Wave, Powershift,* and *War and Anti-War*—has been hailed for originality, clarity, and unusual insight into the challenges and opportunities racing toward us. Their newest book, *Revolutionary Wealth*, attacks key features of conventional economics as it paints the emerging global "wealth system" of the decades ahead.

Sarah Vowell is an astute social observer and best-selling author of four books, *Assassination Vacation, The Partly Cloudy Patriot, Take the Cannoli,* and *Radio On*. Her fifth book, *The Wordy Shipmates,* a history of American Puritans, will be published in 2008. She has been a contributing editor for public radio's *This American Life* since 1996, has twice been a guest op-ed columnist for the opinion page of the *New York Times,* and makes frequent television appearances. She is a former music columnist for *Salon.com* and *San Francisco Weekly*. Her criticism, interviews, and essays have also appeared in *Time, Esquire, GQ, Spin,* the *Los Angeles Times,* and the *New York Times*.

Judith Warner is the author of the *Domestic Disturbances* column for the *New York Times*'s electronic edition, *TimesSelect*. She is also a guest op-ed columnist for the paper. Her book, *Perfect Madness: Motherhood in the Age of Anxiety*, was a *New York Times* best-seller. She is currently the host of the *Judith Warner Show* on XM Satellite Radio.

R. James Woolsey is currently a vice president, of Booz Allen Hamilton, Inc. Before he joined Booz Allen as a partner in July 2002, Woolsey was an attorney with Shea & Gardner in Washington D.C., specializing in commercial litigation and alternative dispute resolution (arbitration and mediation). He served five times in the federal government for a total of twelve years, holding presidential appointments in two Democratic and two Republican administrations. He served as director of Central Intelligence (1993–1995), ambassador and chief negotiator for the Conventional Armed Forces in Europe (CFE) Treaty in Vienna (1989–1991), and delegate-at-large to the Strategic Arms Reductions Talks (START). Woolsey has served on numerous corporate and non-profit boards. From time to time he speaks publicly and contributes articles to newspapers and other periodicals on such issues as national security, energy, foreign affairs, and intelligence.

Amy Zegart, is an associate professor of public policy at the University of California at Los Angeles (UCLA) and one of the nation's leading experts on intelligence reform. She earned her doctorate from Stanford University, where she studied under Condoleezza Rice. Zegart worked on the Clinton administration's National Security Council staff and served as a foreign policy advisor to the Bush-Cheney 2000 presidential campaign. She is the author of two books on national security issues. The first, *Flawed by Design: The Evolution of the CIA, JCS, and NSC* has become a standard intelligence text. The second, *Spying Blind: The CIA, the FBI, and the Origins of 9/11,* examines why the CIA and FBI failed to adapt to the rise of terrorism after the Cold War.

Slavoj Žižek is a Slovenian sociologist, postmodern philosopher, and cultural critic who has a double doctorate in both philosophy and psychoanalysis. He is considered one of the world's leading contemporary cultural commentators. Žižek is the international director of the Birkbeck Institute for the Humanities at the University of London. His most recent publications books are *The Parallax View* and *How to Read Lacan*. He is the presenter in the film, *The Pervert's Guide to Cinema,* where he delves into the hidden language of film and explores what movies tell us about ourselves. The film had its debut at the Museum of Modern Art in New York in April 2007. In 1990 he was a candidate for president of the Republic of Slovenia, running under the banner of the Liberal Democracy of Slovenia party.

Acknowledgments

This is the sixth book in our Secrets series. Beginning with *Secrets of the Code* in 2004, and continuing through all the books and documentary films we have completed since then, the *Secrets* series has brought together the most relevant experts and the most thought-provoking commentators to think out loud with us and our readers about intriguing works of pop culture and important issues under broad public discussion in our society. *Secrets* books are collaborative efforts, and *Secrets of 24* is no exception. Many, many people have helped get us to the day (at the brink of the launch of *24*'s Season 7), when we can put this book in our readers' hands.

As always in our *Secrets* series, we are indebted to a talented group of contributing editors whose research, interviews, and writing are deeply embedded in this book, especially Paul Berger, David Freeman, and Katherine Goldstein. Paul Berger, in addition to writing an essay, interviewed Tom Clancy, Laura Holgate, and Frank Rich. David Freeman interviewed Mark Bowden, William Sessions, James Woolsey, and Amy Zegart. And Katherine Goldstein interviewed Shohreh Aghdashloo, Seymour Hersh, Tony Lagouranis, Kal Penn, and Alvin Toffler. Paul, David, Katherine: We thank you all; we could not have asked for a more helpful or astute editorial team.

At Sterling, our publishing company for this book, we thank Michael Fragnito for his ongoing faith in *Secrets of 24*, from the first time he heard about it through all the roller-coaster rides that any book like this entails. We also wish to thank the whole Sterling team, led by Charles Nurnberg, CEO & publisher. This includes Meredith Hale, Emily Seese, and Leonard Vigliarolo, who worked closely with us and shared much valuable advice. Diana Drew meticulously and cheerfully copyedited the complex manuscript, no mean feat in this jigsaw puzzle of a book.

A very special note of thanks is due to Miguel Sal, who took time out from his deadlines for his creative work for major global brands to develop the striking design concept for our cover.

Danny Baror of Baror International once again provided us with world-class agenting and support throughout this project.

We have been fortunate to have enjoyed the collaboration and to benefit from the work of some of the most talented actors, writers, journalists, critics, national security experts, and cultural observers on the contemporary scene. They include Shorheh Aghdashloo, Stephen Applebaum, Ginia Bellafante, Mark Bowden, Rosa Brooks, James Carafano, Brian Carney, Michael Chertoff, Tom Clancy, Jerome Copulsky, David Danzig, Maureen Dowd, Colin Freeze, Deirdre Good, Jin Guan, Shane Harris, Seymour Hersh, David Heyman, Laura Holgate, Laura Jackson, Tony Lagouranis, John Leonard, Ben Liaw, Rush Limbaugh, Jane Mayer, Charles McGrath, Rick Moran, James Morrison, Clarence Page, Kal Penn, Dorothy Rabinowitz, Frank Rich, John Robb, Tricia Rose, William Sessions, David Shugarts, Alvin Toffler, Sarah Vowell, Judith Warner, James Woolsey, Amy Zegart, and Slavoj Žižek.

We benefited greatly from the cooperation of numerous people at the Fox TV network and the producers and talented team at *24*. They welcomed us to the set and helped us get a deeper understanding of their process. In particular, we would like to thank the creative team behind *24* for their generosity in sharing with us the "secrets" behind their extraordinary success: Joel Surnow, Robert Cochran, Howard Gordon, Evan Katz, and Manny Coto. We also benefited from insights by the gifted actors Mary Lynn Rajskub (Chloe) and Carlos Bernard (Tony Almeida). Thanks are due as well to Chris Alexander, Fox senior vice president for corporate communications, who arranged our visit to the set of the show, as well as Mariana Galvez and Jenny Kay, who hosted us on the set.

We would also like to express our thanks to those who were helpful in arranging and scheduling interviews, tracking down contributors to the book, and providing answers to research queries: Rebecca Bartoli, Nancy Bonomo, Jennifer Goodwin, Alanna Kordell, and Nick Reavill. We also had help from Mary Mathis, Debbie Willie, and Antoinette Willis. Many thanks to numerous friends and supporters who pitched in wherever they could help: Judy Friedberg, Craig and Karina Buck, Sam Schwerin, Max Chee, Buck Goldstein, Bob and Carolyn Reiss, Clem and Ann Malin, and Brian and Joan Weiss.

As with all our books, the people to whom we owe the greatest debt are our families, especially Helen de Keijzer, Hannah de Keijzer, Julie O'Connor, and David Burstein. They watched *24* with us, asked probing questions, discovered intriguing details, and provided the day-in, day-out emotional and intellectual support network that is critical to success in running the marathon that all our books turn out to be— this one included.

Dan Burstein and Arne J. de Keijzer
October 2007
Visit us at www.SecretsOf24.com and www.SecretsOfTheCode.com

Index